DEGAS DANCERS

I. AU THEATRE. LE BALLET VU D'UNE LOGE
circa 1885, 24 × 18 *ins*.

CONTENTS

PLATES

after page 72

APPENDIXES

DEGAS AND HIS TIMES

The impact of the French Revolution upon the history of painting is so well known to students that it will not bear repetition in any detail. Watteau, whose tender and wistful art found its natural expression against the background of the Courts of Louis XV, beautifully opened the epoch of eighteenth century painting which, reflecting the growing depravity of French aristocracy, ended ingloriously with Greuze and the aged Boucher.

The dramatic events heralding the passing of the century demanded fresh pictorial formulae, and these, based on the antique, appeared as a reactionary answer to a revolutionary call. But time has proved how logical was this response; how European interest was aroused by Winckelmann's publications on the fundamentals of Greek art; how the cold purity of Classical art was needed as a corrective to eighteenth century indulgence; and how the regime of the People found it desirable to set up some ideal form of outward expression by which the world might recognise it.

The neo-Classical revival, admirably fitting in with Napoleon's *Imperator* concept, was faithfully carried out by artists and laymen down to the last detail of the domestic arts. But as its whole impetus was in the past it was doomed to die with the regime which fostered it, barren as the similarly pseudo pre-Raphaelite movement in England also proved itself to be.

The French artists who took their lead from David, like the English group around Hunt, Millais and Rossetti, became little more than competent, often brilliant, copyists. They failed to realise that, however sincere, superficial imitation is not enough; that an artist must absorb what he most admires in the Masters, using his own language for the expression of his particular personality, and all the while communicating the spirit of his time.

Any broad outline of an historical development inclines to be callous and sweeping, and therefore, while admitting that, in varying degrees, both the neo-Classical and pre-Raphaelite movements were dead ends in themselves, interesting mainly as historical freaks, it must not be supposed that each did not produce a few good artists.

On the one hand it is impossible to exclude Ingres from this category, as apart from the enormous value of the tradition he was instrumental in handing on to Degas, he cannot be said to have affected any future generation of artists—in other words to have opened new vistas by the freshness of his vision. On the other hand it is gross understatement to include him. For if the Classical revival had any final justification, it was embodied in this single figure, whose technical powers, especially in the field of draughtsmanship, were of surpassing quality.

It is interesting to remember that, coincident with the beginning of Napoleon's downfall, came the first public challenge to neo-Classical art with the exhibiting in 1812 of Géricault's picture, *The Officer of Light Horse*.[1] Ten years later a rebel in the very circle of David revealed himself, when Baron Gros expressed his ardent admiration for Delacroix' *Dante and Virgil in Hell*,[2] also exhibited in the Salon. Another page of art history was about to be turned.

The new movement, known as Romanticism, being contrary to all Classical dictums, found its ancestry in everything to which David and Ingres were opposed. The unemotional, plastic ideals of the antique were replaced by the passion and colour inspired by Titian, Veronese and Rubens; the general idea of Classical beauty, essentially objective in its outlook, giving way to a subjective individualism. The very term *Romanticism* implied that its adherents turned to the Romantic themes of writers such as Goethe, Scott and Byron, and that, even if they chose contemporary events as subject matter, these had to be of a nature to permit of dramatic emotional treatment. Draughtsmanship, the characteristic for which Ingres is famous, was, in the terms of the Classicists, so lacking in Delacroix, that despite—or perhaps because of—his admiration for the younger man, Gros tried to persuade him to join his studio in order to learn how to draw.

But the Romanticists were never to reign supreme as their predecessors had done. Ingres' belief, his complete oneness with the prescribed standards of the Empire, enabled him, after the first two decades of the century, to carry on the neo-Classical movement almost alone. In the early years of Romanticism his force constituted a lingering challenge; in its later years, the threat came from the Barbison school of landscape painters.

For more than two hundred years, since the time of Claude and Poussin, landscape painting had been neglected by French artists. Despite the love of nature professed by the aristocracy in the second half of the eighteenth century, and humoured by Fragonard and Hubert Robert in their theatrical *Fêtes Champêtres* and idyllic pastoral scenes, landscape had meant nothing but a background for playful fantasies.

But while attention was being focused on the struggles between the Classicists and Romanticists, a group of men, some of whom lived in the forest of Fontainbleau, were studying and painting nature with the fervent humility of the seventeenth century Dutch painters, and of Constable. Deriving their group-name from the village of Barbison on the edge of the forest, they lived in the greatest poverty, meeting with little or no worldly success until the end of their lives.

Corot, although his name is usually linked with those of Rousseau, Daubigny and others, stands somewhat apart. His formative years having been spent in Italy, his approach to landscape was more lyrical than that of his companions who, apart from actual technical similarities, were also closer in spirit to the paintings of Hobbema and Ruysdael they had seen in the Louvre.

Millet was another lone figure. His art found its fulfilment, not in pure landscape, but through a love and understanding of his fellow peasants. To him they represented the drama of life. He painted them with such sensitivity that while looking at his pictures the observer often feels an intruder at a family gathering, or a clumsy spectator of a poignantly tender scene.

[1] This picture, now in the Louvre, was shown at the Salon when Géricault was only twenty years old. He died at the age of thirty-three.

[2] In the Louvre.

DEGAS AND HIS TIMES

With the exception of the brothers Le Nain, and to a lesser degree Chardin, Millet and Daumier were the first French painters whose art was inspired by the life of the working man. But whereas Millet, the countryman, accepted his and the lot of his kind with quiet resignation, Daumier, of the city, protested vehemently against the social injustices suffered by the people. With incredible force of expression which less understanding would have turned into sheer brutality, he hurled his protests on to the pages of *La Caricature* and *Charivari*, suffering imprisonment for his ridicule of the king.

The third member of the trio—champions of democracy—was the vigorous Courbet. His rebellious acts, outside the field of painting, led him also to gaol.[1] It was he who used the title *Realism* for the show he held near the entrance gates to the Paris World's Fair in 1855, introducing thereby one of the most confusing terms in the designation of all art movements.

As the development of the arts is so closely linked with that of their social background, it might be as well to remember that the second half of the nineteenth century was characterised by the general tendency towards positive science as against religious belief, towards material rather than moral standards, and that although the age appeared to be one of awakening social conscience, it was prompted rather by political motives than by a sense of humanitarian responsibility.

By 1855, with the Second Empire in its third year, France was enjoying a period of material prosperity. The great encouragement given to industry and scientific development, the acknowledgment of long-needed social reforms and recognition of the claims of the poor, all seemed to augur a glorious and tolerant reign. The Emperor's magical name, together with the charm of his lovely Spanish wife, helped to make the Empire popular and his Court the most brilliant in Europe, and while Baron Haussman transformed the capital into the beautiful city she mercifully remains today, Paris, naturally and with authority became the leader of European culture.

In that hopeful year of 1855, the second great Industrial exhibition was held there.[2] Nothing was spared to make it an outstanding triumph and one in which great emphasis was laid upon the importance of the arts. For the occasion, Verdi wrote his opera *I Vespri Siciliani* to a libretto by Scribe, and Berlioz the *Imperial Cantata*, through which performance he achieved his long cherished ambition of conducting an orchestra of twelve hundred musicians. It was a period of lavish display. The operas of Rossini, Meyerbeer and Halévy, much in vogue, were staged with a grandeur now difficult to imagine; and the theatre acknowledging no limits to its potentialities, presented chorus, ballet and orchestra with every possible extravagance. But the great period of Romantic ballet was already over; Taglioni, Elssler, Grahn and Cerito had retired; Perrot and Marius Petipa had gone to Russia; and as no fresh inspiration grew with the new generation, ballet in France entered upon its steady decline.

Literature and painting were more fortunate. With the exception of Victor Hugo, who

[1] During the Commune, Courbet was elected to the chamber of Deputies and, wishing to eradicate all traces of the Empire, he ordered the destruction of the Column in the Place Vendôme. After the Commune was suppressed, he was sentenced to six months imprisonment and ordered to pay the cost of restoring the monument. He fled to Switzerland where he died in 1877.

[2] The first had taken place in England in 1851.

may be said to have carried Romanticism on beyond its allotted span in much the same way as Ingres did neo-Classicism, the Romantic movement in literature is generally regarded as having ended by the middle of the century. But while Hugo published his *Contemplations* in 1856, these were followed in the next year by Flaubert's *Madame Bovary* and Baudelaire's *Fleurs du Mal*, two masterpieces of French literature and in themselves sufficient justification for the whole of the movement known as *Naturalism*. But it was not to end there. France, in the second half of the nineteenth century, produced writers as great as her painters, for in 1855 the de Goncourts were young men, Zola and Daudet still in their 'teens, while de Maupassant was a mere child.

The neo-Classical, Romantic, Barbison and Realist painters were all contestants in the field of art and were given an excellent opportunity in *l'Exposition Universelle* to compete, not only with each other, but also with painters of twenty-eight other nations. Ingres, seventy-five years old, was honoured by a special gallery for his pictures; Delacroix, who after nine years' work had just finished his decorations for the libraries of the Chamber of Deputies, exhibited thirty-five; Corot, having begun his period of 'poetic effects' and at last attained worldly success, was represented by six; Millet, working on his *Gleaners*, had only one painting in the show; and Courbet, disgusted at the rejection of two of his most important canvases, showed fifty pictures in his own *Pavillon*.

This, then, was the Parisian background when, in that same year, a young man of twenty-one entered the Ecole des Beaux Arts as a student of Louis Lamothe's and, through him, a grand-pupil of Ingres. Pissarro had just chosen Corot as his teacher; and Manet had spent four restless years in the studio of Couture, who, as a pupil of the tragic Baron Gros,[1] was inclined towards Romanticism rather than Classicism. Thus these three men, destined to meet, and through their meetings to play so important a part in the history of painting, derived from beginnings so diverse.

    .   .   .   .   .

In appearance, Degas was smallish of stature. He had searching though melancholy eyes, a somewhat sensual mouth belying its possessor, and a large rounded forehead running into a nose retroussé at the tip which, even in extreme old age, gave a child-like quality to his face. The son of a wealthy bourgeois family,[2] in whose home culture and love of the arts were an accepted part of everyday life, he dressed correctly and conducted himself with an air of quiet dignity. He was born in Paris in the rue de Mondovi on the 19th July 1834, one of a family of five—three sons and two daughters[3]—and was educated at the Lycée Louis le Grand. He chose his companions then, as throughout his life, from among people of his own class, and it was while he was at the Lycée that he met Henri Rouart who became his oldest and dearest friend.

[1] Antoine Jean, Baron Gros (1771–1835), committed suicide because he found it impossible to reconcile his feeling for Rubens and Romanticism with the duty laid upon him by the exiled David—his former master and benefactor—to maintain the Classical tradition. Torn between his two loyalties, Gros drowned himself in a backwater of the Seine.

[2] His father, who wrote his name *de Gas*, came of an old French family; his mother had been Mlle Musson, a Créole from New Orleans. M. de Gas was a banker, and opened in Paris a branch of the family business originally established in Naples.

[3] Edgar was the eldest son; Achille, the second, was in the navy; René, the youngest, lived for some time in the United States, returning later to France. Of the two daughters, one married M. Fèvre, an architect; the other, her cousin, M. Morbilli of Naples.

DEGAS AND HIS TIMES

The story of his choice of profession is an old one. Like most fathers in a materialistic age, M. de Gas was averse to the uncertainty of an artistic career for his son. But when determination is so strong, the most resolute opposition can be no deterrent, and although Degas began by acceding to his father's wishes and became a student of the Law Schools, he was all the while formulating his own ideas for the future. He had come to know and to adore the Ingres drawings in the home of the Valpinçons, and it may have been these old family friends who helped persuade the father to let his son renounce a legal career and join the classes at the Beaux Arts where, short of the aged Ingres himself, tutelage under his pupil was the next best thing.

One of Degas' strongest characteristics was his loyalty to everything which touched him deeply. At times it was the sort of blind loyalty which might equally be called obstinacy or contrariness, occasionally it was so narrow as to exclude any deviation. But even as a young man he seemed to have a sense which directed him through attractive or repulsive superficialities right to the very core of things, so that for the most part his sympathies were not misguided. By the time he was twenty years old he was already a disciple of Ingres; and, notwithstanding his own stupendous achievements during the ensuing years, his admiration and respect were just as great when he died at the age of eighty-three. In the same way he was to remain constant to his life-long friends, his choice of subjects, his hatred of what is known as progress, and his mistrust of internationalism, of which his much stressed anti-semitism was a form.

The pupils of the Beaux Arts were expected to pay regular visits to the Louvre and Degas did this willingly, in fact with such zest that soon it was apparent he was becoming more and more a pupil of the Old Masters and less and less one of Lamothe.

In 1856, without any diplomas—for he was fortunate enough to be able to afford it—he went to Italy, first of all to Naples, then on to Rome, Florence and possibly to many smaller towns. Following Ingres' well-known injunction, 'il faut apprendre à peindre d'après les Maîtres, et n'aborder la nature qu'après,' probably taught him by his master, he continued his museum studies by making drawings after the Florentines, Bellini and Mantegna; perhaps at this impressionable age he also visited Arezzo and saw the frescoes of the great Piero della Francesca. Regardless of the landscape which had been the inspiration of Claude and Poussin, as later he was to be of the Parisian countryside so loved by Pissarro, Monet and Sisley, he nevertheless painted a few pictures of the Italian peasantry, besides doing some portrait drawings and etchings. By 1857 he was back again in Paris where, though he continued to live with his parents, he worked in his first studio which was in the rue Madame, on the left bank of the Seine.

Ingres had so persistently chosen to regard himself as an 'historical painter', that Degas, starting his career possibly in emulation of his hero, began with large compositions on historical themes and painted, between the years of his return to Paris and 1865, such pictures as *Jeunes Spartiates s'excerçant à la Lutte; Sémiramis construisant une Ville* (Pl. 1); *La Fille de Jephte* and *Les Malheurs de la Ville d'Orléans*.[1] But although these canvases were mainly Classical in conception, the two latter showed that Degas was well aware of Delacroix, and all bore evidence of

[1] *Jeunes Spartiates* is in the Tate Gallery, London; *La Fille de Jephte* is in the Smith College Museum of Art, Northampton, Mass.; and *Sémiramis* and *Les Malheurs de la Ville d'Orléans* are both in the Louvre.

the artist's observation of contemporary types. Moreover, *Sémiramis* was not an historical subject reconstructed by Degas, but an actual scene of the opera of that name. This picture therefore presages the vast achievement which is the subject of this book and will be discussed in detail further on.

Yet it is not impossible that Degas considered these compositions somewhat in the light of exercises, an attitude easily reconcilable with a man who could say, 'No art was ever less spontaneous than mine. What I do is the result of reflection and study of the great masters; of inspiration, spontaneity, temperament I know nothing.'[1] and who, though only vaguely visualising his ultimate goal, could name in detail and mostly adhere to, the studies he thought necessary for its realisation.[2] Side by side with these compositions, Degas was painting portraits—single figures and groups—which, while retaining the physical methods prescribed by Ingres, showed great imagination and independence of outlook. In such pictures as *The Belleli Family in Florence*; *Manet listening to his wife playing the piano*; and *La Femme aux Chrysanthèmes*,[3] the 'accidental' postures of the sitters are not only sufficiently unorthodox to have shocked the aged master, but absolutely comply with one of the demands made by Degas and jotted down in his notebooks—'Faire des portraits des gens dans des attitudes familières et typiques. . . .'[4]

Somewhere between the years 1860 and 1862—the exact date does not seem to be known—Degas met Manet in circumstances which will be told of later. It seems only natural that these two young men, with similar backgrounds, equal material advantages, and of a like intelligence and education, should have formed a friendship, their very difference of temperament being an added attraction in the early days of their association. But Degas never became really intimate with the circle of artists and writers who grouped themselves around Manet, first at the Café de Bade and, after 1866, at the quieter little Café Guerbois. Like Manet, his social position kept him apart; both of them were difficult to oppose in the lively arguments which so frequently arose, for their quick retorts, though brilliant and witty, too often disregarded the sensibilities of simpler minds. Degas' ideas, for the most part, were aloof and uncompromising, his reactions often unpredictable, so that although—when it was too dark for further work—he frequently joined the group, it was not on terms of easy comradeship but rather as a respected and formidable visitor. Apart from Manet, Duranty[5] alone was his equal and became his friend, and these three, together with Bazille, represented the wealthy bourgeois members of the group; Pissarro, Cézanne, Monet, Renoir, Sisley and Zola all being sons of humbler parents.

It is possible that Manet and Degas sometimes went to the races together, and although the latter painted *Aux Courses—le Départ* as early as 1860 (his first picture of a wholly contem-

[1] *Impressions and Opinions* by George Moore, edition 1913, p. 229.

[2] *Gazette des Beaux Arts*, Apl. 1921. 'Les Carnets de Degas au Cabinet des Estampes' by P. A. Lemoisne. '. . . Série sur les instruments et les instrumentistes, leurs formes; tortillement de la main, des bras et du cou du violiniste, par exemple gonflement et creusement des joues des bassons, hautbois, etc. . . . Beaucoup couper, d'une danseuse faire ou les bras ou les jambes, ou les reins; faire les souliers; faire les mains du coiffeur . . . pieds nus en action de danse. . . '.

[3] *The Belleli Family*, painted in 1859 during one of Degas' visits to Italy, is in the Louvre; *La Femme aux Chrysanthèmes*, painted in 1865, is in the Metropolitan Museum, New York.

[4] *Gazette des Beaux Arts*, Apl. 1921. 'Les Carnets de Degas,' *op. cit.*

[5] Louis-Emile-Edmond Duranty (1833–1880), critic and novelist, was a disciple of Champfleury. In 1870 he published a brochure, *La nouvelle Peinture, à propos du groupe d'artistes qui expose dans les galeries Durand-Ruel*, in which he showed great understanding of the new movement in painting. Degas did several portraits of him.

porary theme), and *Course de Gentlemen avant le Départ* two years later, the stylisation of the one and the careful execution of the other, stand in marked contrast to Manet's daring treatment of a similar subject, *Les Courses, Longchamps*, done in 1864.[1]

But Degas was not to be hurried. About 1866 he painted his second theatrical subject, *Mlle Fiocre in the ballet 'La Source'* (Pl. 3), but still in a fairly tight and conventional manner; as late as 1869, rigidly keeping to his self-imposed task of working from the old masters, he copied Holbein, Poussin and Lawrence—a choice which revealed his awareness of the necessity of perfecting every technical aspect of picture-making—while gradually he allowed himself a little more licence, again in portraits, such as the one of James Tissot[2] and that of Désiré Dihau in the picture called *L'Orchestre de l'Opéra* (Pl. 4). It was during these years that he was exhibiting at the Salon.[3]

In the summer of 1868 Manet went to London for four days and invited Degas to go with him. Once there it appears that Degas realised he could not see all he wanted to in so short a time, and that Manet returned alone leaving him to follow later.[4] As far as is known, and with the exception of his passing through Liverpool on his way to and from the States in 1872, this is the only visit paid by Degas to England. But he evidently retained lively impressions of its customs and particular form of humour, for in later years he took delight in teasing Sickert about them.

In 1870 the upheaval of the Franco-Prussian War and the tragedy of the Commune dispersed the men of the Café Guerbois group, interrupting their work, their struggles with the Salon, and even—in some cases—their fight against poverty. Monet and Pissarro went to England; Cézanne retired to the South of France; Manet joined the National Guard in which he found himself serving under Meissonier; Renoir joined the cuirassiers; and Bazille, a Zouave regiment in which he was killed.

Looking back now upon Degas' life and attitude, it is not altogether surprising that, on this occasion, he allowed the staunch Parisian in him to take precedence over the artist. Although far from being a supporter of the Republic which succeeded the surrender of Napoleon III, he enlisted in the infantry from which, on account of the defection in his right eye, he was transferred to an Artillery regiment which happened to be under the command of his school friend, Henri Rouart.

Survivors of the Paris siege have, according to M. Hertz,[5] told how Degas used daily to visit a field hospital near the Etoile to cheer the inmates and bring them news from his part of the town; and how his kindness helped to lessen the sufferings of the patients. Yet this was the beginning of his own suffering, the growing anguish of which was to be his daily companion for

[1] *Aux Courses—le Départ* is in the Fogg Art Museum, Harvard University; *Course de Gentlemen avant le Départ*, in the Louvre, was partly repainted about 1880; *Les Courses, Longchamps* is in the Art Institute, Chicago.

[2] The portrait of James Tissot is in the Metropolitan Museum of Art, New York.

[3] He exhibited each year from 1865–1870.

[4] Manet's invitation to Degas was written from Boulogne on the 29th July 1868 to Degas' home in the Rue de Mondovi. In London Degas stayed at the Hotel Conte in Golden Square, from where he wrote to Tissot telling him of his arrival and of his efforts to find Tissot at Victoria Grove, Bayswater. The latter happened to be in Paris at the time from where he answered Degas advising him to call on Legros, Prevost and Whistler; to visit Richmond and Windsor, Greenwich by boat, and above all not to miss seeing the Docks. For all this he said Degas would need at least a month. (These letters, which have never been published, are in the possession of M. Jean Nepveu Degas.)

[5] *Degas* by Henri Hertz, pub. Paris, 1920, p. 74.

the next fifty years. He endured it with quiet courage, perhaps grumbling to his friends and appearing more formidable to acquaintances during the periods when his eyes were so trouble-some as to prevent his working. But who does not know what it is like to be threatened by some real or imaginary doom, one so awful that, even in thought, it cannot be faced; what infinite relief when, the fears proving groundless, the suffocating load is lifted, releasing the spirit to flights of ridiculous happiness. Degas never knew this relief. On the contrary, the passing of years confirmed his direst fears. For a painter, the cruellest of fates awaited him. Blindness became a certainty. The freezing nights of that winter when he was out on duty or sleeping in the cold guard-room are said to have made his disease chronic. At first it was merely a nuisance, but slowly becoming more and more pronounced, the sight grew in defec-tiveness until finally the eyes refused service altogether.

After the wars the friends returned to Paris, if possible strengthened in purpose, as were the citizens in their determination to rise above the humiliations imposed upon them by the Prussians. A new spirit of resolve permeated the city and the succeeding years showed how splendidly it was justified.

While also taking refuge in London, Durand Ruel had opened a gallery there and had shown, together with those of the Barbison painters, works by the Batignolles group.[1] Back in Paris he decided to continue his support, not only morally but materially, and, although he had not yet sold their pictures with any degree of success, he determined to back his judgment by risking his money. The future seemed bright.

Degas resumed his work where he had left off. *L'Orchestre de l'Opéra*, which had been exhibited at Lille during the war years,[2] must be considered a picture of the utmost importance. Artistically it is a masterpiece of collective portraiture whose truth and originality would have delighted the painter of the *Night Watch*; historically it marks the beginning of all the magnifi-cent *Danseuses sur la Scène* which were to come. Degas followed it up in 1872 with the first version of *Robert le Diable* (Pl. 8) and the *Musiciens de l'Orchestre* (Pl. 5); and as he still found portraiture the most satisfactory outlet for his growing powers, his finest canvases of this period include such works as *Degas' Father listening to Pagans*; *Mlle Dihau at the Piano*; and *Portrait of Mlle Valpinçon*.[3] It is not mere coincidence that, with one exception, all the pictures just mentioned suggest that Degas was interested in music. Daniel Halévy says that he was passionately fond of Gluck,[4] and indeed Degas' own letters confirm the pleasure and refreshment which this form of art continually gave him.

Late in the October of 1872, Degas, with his younger brother René, embarked at Liver-pool for New York on the 'fast and sure' English ship *The Scotia*. The sea voyage took ten days, and after another four in a train whose modern luxury greatly impressed him, they reached René and Achille's home in New Orleans.

---

[1] The friends of the Café Guerbois circle were known as the Batignolles group. Their common aim being their fight against official art, this neutral title did not imply any false idea as to similarity of conception.

[2] See note on Pl. 4.

[3] *Degas' father listening to Pagans* belongs to John T. Spaulding, Esq., Boston; *Mlle Dihau at the Piano* to the Louvre; and *Mlle Valpinçon* to the Wildenstein Gallery, New York.

[4] Introduction to 'Degas Exhibition' Catalogue, Galerie Georges Petit, Paris, Apl.–May 1924.

Shortly after his arrival, Degas wrote to the Danish artist, Frölich, 'Que de choses nouvelles j'ai vues, que de projets cela m'a mis en tête . . . j'y renonce déjà, je ne veux plus voir que mon coin et le creuser pieusement. L'art ne s'élargit pas, il se résume.'[1]

Degas was not seeking fresh material in the New World, for he believed that only long familiarity could lead to understanding—'L'instanté, c'est la photographie et rien de plus,'[2] and although he was much attracted by the negress nursemaids whose dark skins contrasted so pictorially with their little white charges; by the steamboats with their funnels tall as factory chimneys, and by the fruit-shops overflowing with their colourful wares, he painted but few pictures as a result of his trip. Among these there is the well-known *Le comptoir de Coton à la Nouvelle Orléans*,[3] *Enfants assis sur le perron d'une maison de campagne*,[4] as well as several portraits of members of his family who, he complained, did not take him seriously and whose taste had to be regarded to a certain extent. Never again was he to make such a compromise.

Degas' biographers have offered various reasons for the journey. M. Hertz[5] suggests that having been upset by the tragic events of 1870, and worried as to the future of his country since it had fallen into the hands of the Republican Bourgeoisie, Degas, in an effort to regain his inner calm, paid this visit to his brothers.

M. Rivière[6] offers an entirely different explanation. He says that the journey was unpremeditated. That after René's stay in Paris, Degas went to the station to see him off but could not resist jumping on the train at the last moment and, having got as far as Le Havre, decided to go all the way. This theory not only sounds unlikely for obvious reasons, but is actually refuted by Degas in a letter to Désiré Dihau,[7] in which he tells how the carefully laid plan to keep his arrival a surprise to the family was thwarted at the last minute by a yellow-fever scare in New Orleans, on account of which the brothers sent a telegram asking whether Degas' visit was considered safe.

Degas himself implies that he went on family business, the exact nature of which is not known because of his persistent reticence over private affairs. But as throughout his life he took his family responsibilities with the utmost seriousness, and had a deep affection for his brothers of whose success he spoke with almost fatherly pride, it is evident that they were the primary reason for his American trip.

The need to rest his eyes was, according to his correspondence, the secondary factor. In 1872 Degas was already worrying about their condition, and although at this stage part of the trouble may have been a neurosis (some unsympathetic writers declare it was entirely imaginary and a convenient affectation), this very anxiety over his sight can only have aggravated the trouble which undoubtedly existed, and which was to hang over him like a threatening cloud for the rest of his life.

---

[1] and [2] *Lettres de Degas* recueillies et annotées par Marcel Guerin, preface de Daniel Halévy. Edition Paris, 1945, pp. 22–3.
[3] In the Musée de Pau.
[4] Catalogue, 1st Sale, Atelier Degas, No. 45.
[5] M. Henri Hertz, *op. cit.*, p. 76.
[6] *Mr Degas (Bourgeois de Paris)* by Georges Rivière, pub. Paris, 1935, p. 179.
[7] *Lettres de Degas*, 1945, *op. cit.*, p. 19. Désiré Dihau, an intimate friend of Degas, was a bassoonist in the Opera orchestra.

Early in the following year Degas returned to Paris, about the same time as Duret[1] who had been on a visit to Japan. But in these few months things had changed. Most of their friends had gone to settle in the country, only Renoir and Monet remained, and, for Degas, Paris without the Opéra was not the same in any case. A few months later, the disastrous slump which, with monotonous regularity follows inevitably upon the heels of every post-war boom, set in. Durand Ruel, finding himself in financial straits, had to curtail his activities and temporarily to withdraw his support. The question of exhibiting became acute. Only Manet and Eva Gonzales continued sending to the Salon, the others, either because of their contempt for its false standards or because they were certain to meet with refusal, did not even submit. For ten years, since the *Salon des Refusés*,[2] the *peintres indépendants* had not asserted themselves *en masse*, but now some form of concerted action was again a necessity; some effort to appeal to a wider public had to be made.

Against Duret's advice, the group organised an exhibition which opened in April 1874 in Nadar's[3] old studio, just off the Boulevard des Capucines. Of the friends, Manet alone refused to exhibit, determined after the fiasco of the *Salon des Refusés* to show only at the official Salon. He frankly admitted his desire for public acclamation and official recognition, but he also nourished the hope that he might finally break down academic prejudice and win a battle for the modern cause. According to a letter discussing arrangements with Bracquemond it appears that Degas, right up to the last moment, imagined that it might be possible to persuade Manet to participate, 'Manet, excité par Fantin et affolé par lui-même, se réfuse encore, mais rien ne semble décisif de ce côté.'[4]

All the members set about getting recruits to swell their number and in this, as well as in practical details, Degas played a leading part. Thinking that it would help financially and perhaps soften the vituperations of the press, Degas invited the collaboration of less provocative and generally accepted painters such as Lepine, Boudin, Cals, Manet's friend de Nittis, as well as his own friends Bracquemond, Rouart and Lepic.[5] In this first 'Impressionist Exhibition'[6]

[1] Théodore Duret. Political writer and art critic, went on a tour of the East with Cernuschi 1871–72, when they formed the collection which is housed in the Musée Cernuschi, Paris. Duret published *Les Peintres Français in 1867*; *Voyage en Asie* in *1874*; and *Les Peintres Impressionistes*. In 1893 he wrote his most important work, *Historie de France de 1870 à 1873*. Whistler painted a well-known portrait of him.

[2] In 1863 the jury of the Salon rejected more than four thousand works, even including those of such painters as Jongkind and Manet who had been more or less regularly accepted up to that year. The jury's attitude was so bigoted and its acceptance meant so much to buyers, that bitter complaints reached the Emperor's ears. He inspected the rejected pictures and ordered that they should be exhibited in another part of the *Palais de l'Industrie*; any painter who did not wish to participate could withdraw. The exhibition was a sensation and the public flocked to see it, but only to ridicule, as it could not understand. Degas did not start sending to the Salon until 1865, so he did not figure in this *Salon des Refusés*.

[3] Nadar, the photographer, whose real name was Gaspard Félix Tournachon (1820–1910), described himself as 'Artiste en daguerrotypie'. It was he who first attempted aerial photography from a balloon and became the butt of one of Daumier's caricatures on this subject.

[4] *Lettres de Degas*, 1945, *op. cit.*, p. 34. Bracquemond, the engraver and friend of Fantin. He is said to have discovered Hokusai prints packed around some china in 1856, and being so impressed showed them to his friends, of whom Degas became one of the most intimate.

[5] Ludovic Napoléon Lepic, Vicomte (1839–89), painter, sculptor and engraver, had been a pupil at Gleyre's studio at the same time as Bazille and Monet.

[6] The exhibitions became known as 'Impressionist' because of an article written by Leroy in the *Charivari* in which he spoke of the pictures as being 'Impressions'. Of the group only Pissarro, Monet, Renoir and Sisley can really be called Impressionists, the inclusion of the others is a common mistake.

there were thirty participants, the most important being Pissarro, Degas, Monet, Renoir, Cézanne, Sisley and Berthe Morisot. Courbet was an exile, Fantin preferred the Salon, and Corot disapproved.

The exhibition caused nothing but trouble for Degas who showed ten pictures. He was accused by some of his 'group' friends of having smothered their work by including that of so many outsiders; and these in their turn reproached him with hanging their pictures in bad positions, in poor light, and in certain cases with not even showing them until the exhibition had been open for several days. The latter appears to have been a concession that Degas was forced to make to his *Indépendant* friends, but obviously it was unjust and certain to cause friction. The press devoted itself to attacking the *Indépendants* and passed the others by; the public showed little interest; and so the compromise, for which Degas in all good faith had been responsible, ended disastrously.

But it is hardly possible to organise such an exhibition without hurting individual susceptibilities, and it is greatly to Degas' credit that he did not then and there give up the whole affair, especially as any financial gain would have meant less to him than to the other members of the group who, being poor, could not have shouldered any of the losses. But it is unworthy to speak of him in these terms. He loved a fight and, in spite of all the petty worries and difficulties which the first exhibition caused him, he was patient enough to see the thing through. In the eight Impressionist exhibitions which were to follow, he refused to send on only one occasion.

In 1876 the second exhibition took place in Durand Ruel's gallery in the rue Le Peletier, and this time Degas showed over twenty-four pictures. The general press was as hostile as ever and the powerful Albert Wolff wrote in the *Figaro*, 'After the opera fire here is a new disaster overwhelming the district. . . . Try indeed to make M. Degas see reason; tell him that in art there are certain qualities called drawing, colour, execution, control, and he will laugh in your face and treat you as a reactionary. . . .'[1] M. Wolff was right; Degas must certainly have laughed, as have succeeding generations, but not in the way the critic envisaged. Small wonder that Degas later said, 'Art criticism, is that a profession? When I think of it, we painters are so stupid to bother ourselves about the compliments of people like that and to put ourselves into their hands. It's a disgrace. We should not even permit them to discuss our work.[2]

But though the exhibition of 1876 was materially richer through the acquisition of a wealthy new member, Gustave Cailebotte, it suffered artistically because of the loss of Cézanne who did not participate on account of Durand Ruel's hostility to his work. It is curious now to reflect upon the lack of sympathy which also existed between Cézanne and Degas, for distance shows so clearly the bonds which unite these two great figures, setting them apart from the other *Indépendants*. Although from the outset Degas mapped his programme with care and precision, allowing himself freedom within his own broad channels, while Cézanne's development by way of Courbet and Pissarro was far more haphazard, they finally arrived at the same conclusion. The Impressionist ideal, though nicely balanced between emotion and science, did

[1] *History of Impressionism*, by John Rewald, pub. New York, 1946, pp. 298–9.
[2] *Edgar Degas: Nach Eigenen und Fremden Zeugnissen*, by Hans Graber, pub. Basel, 1942, p. 187.

not satisfy either; they could not find fulfilment in the concentration upon accidental effects of light. This predilection sacrificed form and ultimately it is form which endures. To call either an Impressionist is to misunderstand the very essence of his art—Degas' sculptural grandeur through the medium of line and Cézanne's architectural nobility through the medium of paint.

The third, and in many ways the most important exhibition, took place in 1877. This time there were only eighteen exhibitors—Cézanne again being of their number, but most of them showed more pictures than ever before, pictures which are now acknowledged to be among their finest work. Degas had a small gallery more or less to himself and showed twenty-five paintings, pastels and drawings. The press was as derisive as ever and, although the attendance was good, the general public, still believing that 'a good picture like a good fiddle should be brown', was indignant against these pictures in which even the shadows were composed of pure colour. But the *Indépendants* could no longer be ignored. They had achieved notoriety, the first step towards acceptance, and had become the butt of caricaturists and the subject of stage jokes. Meilhac and Halévy wrote their comedy *La Cigale* around the figure of an Impressionist painter, Marignan, whose pictures could be shown normally or upside down with an equally telling effect. Degas designed the studio scene[1] in the same humorous spirit as later he posed for the *Apothéose de Degas*,[2] and in a letter to Ludovic Halévy wrote, '. . . Vous savez du reste, que je suis à votre disposition pour l'atelier de Dupuis. J'ai beau mal y voir, la chose me plait beaucoup à faire et je la ferai.'[3] *La Cigale* was produced at the Théatre des Variétés in October 1877. M. Georges Rivière[4] says that he and Renoir were at the opening performance and found the show very amusing and that, as the authors poked only good-humoured fun at the Impressionists, Degas' friends at the Nouvelle-Athènes[5] did not resent his participation in it.

In 1878 no Impressionist exhibition was held, the fourth taking place in the following year. Renoir exhibited at the Salon, and so another original member was lost to the group. Degas' entries in the catalogue numbered twenty-five but he is said not to have sent this number. Monet, prompted by Renoir's success and in despair at the hardships he had had to endure for years, did not participate in the show of 1880 but also submitted to the Salon. Degas was furious. He was utterly incapable of understanding any weakness, whatever its provocation, in matters relating to art. Monet had violated the rules; like Renoir and Sisley he had allowed himself to be forced into a compromise, and from that time on Degas would have nothing more to do with him.

After that there were three more exhibitions.[6] Degas, though he continued to pay his subscription, did not exhibit in the seventh because some of his followers were excluded; but to the last, held in 1886, he sent a large number of pastels, including a fine series of nudes—women bathing, dressing and in dancing positions.

[1] Reproduced on the cover of *La Scène*, No. 5, December 1877. José Dupuis played the part of the artist; Mlle Baumaine a model, Catherine, who posed as a laundress beating her washing in the tub. See Vignette, p. 422.
[2] See p. 39.
[3] *Lettres de Degas*, 1945, *op. cit.*, pp. 41–2.
[4] Georges Rivière, *op. cit.*, p. 91.
[5] The remaining friends of the Café Guerbois circle followed Marcel Desboutin to the Café de la Nouvelle Athènes, Place Pigalle.
[6] The sixth in 1881; the seventh in 1882, the eighth and the last in 1886.

DEGAS AND HIS TIMES

Some writers declare that, having sacrificed the name he had made in official circles by joining and adhering to the Impressionists, Degas was finally deserted by them, and that they left him to fight alone while they gradually broke away. This accusation is in any case untrue of Pissarro, who, poor as Renoir, Monet and Sisley, emerges in his constancy as the hero of the chapter. In the natural order of things the original members of the group must have drifted apart sooner or later, and Degas, despite all his fine qualities, is known to have been difficult and autocratic. Although after about 1876 he was more or less dependent upon the sale of his pictures[1]—letters written to Faure[2] and later to Durand-Ruel[3] bear evidence to this fact—like both Manet and Cézanne he never knew dire necessity and in all fairness it must be admitted that it was comparatively easy for him to maintain his attitude of aloofness towards the Salon. It seems therefore that M. Hertz exaggerates when he writes, 'Lui reste seul, sur la brèche qu'il a ouverte pour eux contre lui-même.'[4]

. . . . .

The year 1886, which saw the last of these historic exhibitions, roughly marks the close of the first half of Degas' working life. It is therefore convenient to pause for a brief survey of the subjects which already he had made his own, for although the chronological placing of pictures must largely be based on stylistic evidence, and is therefore a matter of personal opinion, it would not be misleading to say that, from about this time on, the aesthetic consideration grew to be of such primary importance that the individual subject either disappeared or was completely subordinated.

From the middle of the 'fifties and thenceforth for more than thirty years, Degas had painted portraits of himself, his family and his friends. All were seen with utter truthfulness and with a sympathetic understanding amounting at times to tenderness, a quality not usually associated with Degas. Apart from the insistence upon the 'accidental', in portraits already mentioned, he also aimed at giving 'à leur figure le même choix d'expression qu'on donne à leur corps',[5] and achieved it with brilliant success in such pictures as *Carlo Pellegrini*, *Femme adjustant ses Gants* and *Bouderie*.[6] But one of the most remarkable qualities in Degas' portraits is the complete unity between the sitter and his background. In the earliest canvases the relationship is established through tonal values alone, while later it is achieved through compositional means. In these portraits—of which *Duranty*[7] is one of the most famous, so strikingly original in conception, so daring in arrangement and, though deeply considered, so apparently casual, the sitter is allowed to grow out of his particular environment; his surroundings, being part of his everyday life, are absolutely inevitable.

---

[1] Degas is said to have sacrificed the greater part of his fortune to help one of his brothers out of a serious financial difficulty.

[2] *Lettres de Degas*, op. cit., 1945, pp. 38–40.

[3] *Les Archives de l'Impressionisme*, Lionello Venturi, pub. Paris.

[4] Henri Hertz, op. cit., p. 79.

[5] P. A. Lemoisne ; *Les Carnets de Degas*, op. cit.

[6] *Carlo Pellegrini*, in the Tate Gallery, London; *Femme adjustant ses Gants*, Wildenstein Gallery, N. Y.; *Bouderie*, in Metropolitan Museum, N. Y.

[7] *Duranty*, in Burrell Collection, Glasgow Art Gallery; and others in National Gallery, Stockholm; and Adolphe Lewisohn Collection.

DEGAS AND HIS TIMES

Degas made collective portraiture the excuse for many of his subject pictures as may be seen in *Le Bureau de Coton à la Nouvelle Orléans*; *La Répétition de Chant* (a double portrait of Mlle Fèvre); *Le Vicomte Lepic avec ses deux Fillettes*, which might easily be called 'The Morning Walk'; and the well-known *L'Absinthe* (portraits of Desboutin and Ellen André).[1] All were painted between the years 1873 and 1876, and the two latter are excellent examples of the audacity of his composition. *Le Vicomte Lepic* also shows his fondness for the cutting of figures in an unexpected manner, one of the lessons which Degas learnt from the Japanese draughtsmen, and which was to become one of his most marked compositional characteristics.

But the portraits have other than their own intrinsic value, for beginning with *Mlle Fiocre* and continuing with *L'Orchestre de l'Opéra* and *Robert le Diable*, they gradually introduce the *danseuses sur la scène*. *L'Orchestre* is frankly a portrait group in which the dancers assume the same unimportance as Degas allotted to landscape—simply that of the background; *Robert le Diable* is only less so; but a third picture *Musiciens de l'Orchestre* has its interest reversed. The three heads of the musicians, dark against the light and occupying more than half the canvas, lead the eye to the dancer on the stage, upon whom all attention is focused as, in the full glare of the footlights, she acknowledges her audience.

The dancers had come into their own. Degas had discovered another art through the exploration of which his own was to find fulfilment. No other field allowed such unlimited possibilities of form in movement, a fact which he himself admitted by his relatively small series of Horses, Blanchisseuses and Modistes. The story of his researches into the Dance is reserved for another chapter of this book, but here it must be emphasised how inevitable was his choice, for dancing is the fundamental expression of the human body, and the human body the fundamental form in European art.

.   .   .   .   .   .

During the reign of Napoleon III, the horse 'reigned gloriously' in France. In both the elegance of daily life and the dandyism of the 'Jockey Club', its position was supreme. Although much of the glitter went from high society with the fall of the Empire, racing continued to be its acknowledged sport, and regular meetings were held at Longchamps, Chantilly and Vincennes, besides several other courses. Thoroughbreds and jockeys were imported from England; gentlemen riders still took the field; and, as the American, Tod Sloan,[2] had not yet arrived to revolutionise the technique of race-riding, long stirrups were still in vogue.

Degas—like Lautrec—was a natural lover of horses. There is no evidence to show that he ever rode himself, neither could he be called a 'racing man'. His frequent visits to meetings were made simply as an artist seeking information. They started in the early 'sixties with his first pictures of the subject, and continued at any rate until after 1890, the time when Sickert,

---

[1] *Le Bureau de Coton*, in the Musée de Pau; *La Répétition de Chant*, in the M. Robert Wood Bliss Collection, Washington; *Le Vicomte Lepic*, in a private collection; and *L'Absinthe*, in the Louvre.

[2] Tod Sloan, the American jockey, came to England in the season of 1897 and won a good proportion of races by tactics diametrically opposed to the English riders. His successes led to an influx of American jockeys who all rode with the saddle forward on the withers and very short stirrups, a practice which was then adopted by English and French riders.

making calls at the Rue Victor Massé, was greeted by Zoë with 'Monsieur Degas est en courses; il ne va pas tarder de rentrer'.[1]

Most of Degas' racing pictures are of horses at the starting point, for it was there—while waiting for the fall of the starter's flag—that he found the greatest variety of positions. There these beautiful animals danced restlessly about, their shiny coats damp with nervous sweat, their nostrils dilated, their whole beings keyed up to an almost unbearable pitch of excitement as, tossing their heads, they strained to be away.

Degas is the first artist who perceived and realised all these nervous characteristics especially peculiar to the racehorse. In comparison with his pictures, those of the English racing painters, though lovable in their naïveté and appealing because demonstrative of a certain phase of English life, cannot be taken seriously, either as works of art or as showing profound knowledge of the horse. Perhaps Degas' own eyesight was not entirely responsible for his astonishing observations, and that for this purpose he made use of instantaneous photography.[2] For those who have spent hours watching the training of these highly-strung animals will recognise in his work the multitude of apparently impossible contortionist feats which, for the flash of a second, horses attain.

Constantin Guys alone has approached Degas, not only in his understanding of the moving horse but also of the exact relationship between it and its rider. His enchanting drawings obtain just the same degree of truth, but rather through suggestion than, like Degas', by actual statement of fact.

In the racecourse scenes there are lovely suggestions of landscape, dreamy translucent backgrounds blending perfectly with the main theme. But Degas was not a painter of landscape and, unlike the Impressionists, was violently opposed to the *plein air* theory. Vollard quotes his opinion on the subject which, though stated in amusingly exaggerated terms, nevertheless shows his characteristic strength of feeling: 'Vous savez ce que je pense des peintres qui travaillent sur les grands chemins, c'est à dire que si j'étais le gouvernement, j'aurais une brigade de gendarmerie pour surveiller les gens qui font du paysage sur Nature. . . . Oh! je ne veux la mort de personne, j'accepterais bien encore qu'on met du petit plomb pour commencer.'[3] But naturally there were exceptions, 'Renoir, ce n'est pas la même chose; il peut faire tout ce qu'il veut.'

It has been suggested that Degas' weak eyes would not allow of his painting in the open and that, for this reason, he sought his lighting effects in the comfort of the theatre; almost as great a fallacy as the theory of increasing blindness having been responsible for the ultimate development of his art. To begin with, even drawing in a theatre, unless it be on a minute scale, is extraordinarily uncomfortable, as an empty seat on the side of the working arm is necessary for freedom of movement, and one on the other desirable for placing material. And secondly, in the days when Degas first started on his theatre scenes, his eye trouble was practi-

---

[1] *The Life and Opinions of Walter Richard Sickert by Robert Emmons*, pub. London, 1939, p. 62.

[2] In 1872, Muybridge's photographs, taken in California, of racehorses in motion, furnished proof of the drawings made from Marey's serial chronographs done some time previously. (*History of Photography*, by J. M. Eder, translation, New York, 1945.)

[3] *Degas*, by Ambroise Vollard, pub. Paris, 1924, p. 58.

cally negligible and would have been no deterrent to his working out of doors had he wished to do so. But finally, and it seems conclusively, Degas' attitude to painting before nature was only what might have been expected, absolutely consistent with his deepest convictions. The sudden and exciting impact of a scene upon the artist's imagination was a splendid reason for a sketch, for the seizing of a mood—and it was in this light that he regarded his own landscapes in pastel. But when it came to the painting of a more enduring work, something more profound than an impression, then quiet contemplation and, with the lapse of time, slow digestion of the idea, were needed. Only in this way could the seductive and redundant be separated from the essential.

. . . . . .

In 1874 Degas exhibited two *Blanchisseuses* in the Impressionist exhibition. It seems that it was Daumier—not de Goncourt[1]—who, through his painting *The Washerwoman*,[2] called Degas' attention to the possibilities of this theme. Although he does not seem to have singled Daumier out for any especial praise, there is much in the latter's painting which should have appealed to Degas—his weight of form, bigness of movement and force of purpose. One of Degas' earlier 'Washerwomen' pictures, *Blanchisseuses portant du Linge*,[3] though most suggestive of Daumier's in its rhythmic movement, has nothing of the same purport of human tragedy behind it; it is charming and tender, and suggests the rise of a gentle wave just before it breaks on to the beach.

Most of the other pictures pertaining to this subject are of *Repasseuses*, and again the artistic problems, rather than the human, are of primary importance. Degas was far from oblivious to the fascinating atmosphere of the hand-laundry; to the clouds of steam which give a certain mystery to the atmosphere, to the pungent smell holding an almost repellent attraction, to the dull thump of irons heavily pressed upon the garments and to the incessant chatter which rises above the noise. Yet beyond all this his pleasure lay in the large physical movements which the job entailed, in the ponderous bend of a figure over the ironing table, or the swinging turn of the hips as with extended arms, in measured interplay, the women fold sheets, handing one corner to the other. This was indeed the skilled worker at her task, and whether that task was high or lowly, respect was due according to its fulfilment.

. . . . . .

The few pictures of the *Femmes se peignant* group link up with the *Blanchisseuses* in their juxtaposition of figures, flowing gesture and boldness of pattern. The *Modistes* are also closely attached, but on the whole they are more intimate and feminine, and often have the added appeal of portraiture.

Being intensely interested in every feature of a woman's toilette, Degas visited milliners

---

[1] Edmond de Goncourt wrote in his *Journals* of 1874, concerning Degas' preference for dancers and laundresses: 'Je ne puis trouver son choix mauvais, moi qui, dans *Manette Salomon* ai chanté ces deux professions comme fournissant les plus pictoraux modèles de femmes de ce temps pour un artiste moderne.' M. de Goncourt seems to have allowed himself some artistic licence, as it has not been possible to find any reference to laundresses in his novel.

[2] *The Washerwoman*, by Daumier, in the Louvre, *circa* 1863.

[3] *Blanchisseuses portant du Linge*, in the possession of Mr and Mrs Howard J. Sachs, New York. Exhibited in fourth Impressionist Exhibition, 1879.

and dressmakers with his friend Mme Straus, the daughter of Fromenthal Halévy. Concerning one of these appointments Degas wrote to Manzi, 'Après vous avoir quitté hier, j'ai rencontré Mme Strauss (sic) et j'ai dû vous abandonner pour demain. C'est presque le seul jour que cette personne dévorée par le monde a de libre et de simple, et je l'avais tellement abandonnée que j'ai dû céder. On m'a entraîné chez une grande couturière ou j'ai assisté, comme un Béraud, à l'essayage d'une toilette à grand effet. . . .[1] When Degas was challenged he would make teasingly disparaging remarks about women, but his letters show that he was just as much attached to their wives as to his friends themselves, and when he thought they warranted it— as in his opinion did Mary Cassatt and Suzanne Valadon—he could even take their art seriously.

During the years between his painting of *Jeunes Spartiates* and his so-called retirement from public life, Degas had studied, experimented and achieved so much that, by the time he was fifty-two, he was an acknowledged master among painters who themselves were of considerable stature. As is only normal, but like most normalities for that very reason overlooked, it is always the artists who discover greatness in their midst, and the judgment of Degas by his contemporaries was no exception to this rule. Pissarro, whose letters to his son proclaim him a critic of outstanding worth and judgment, though he found Degas difficult and 'peppery' at times, wrote in 1883: 'You will be pleased to find in reading the book (Huysman's *L'Art Moderne*) that you are not alone in your enthusiasm for Degas, who is without a doubt the greatest artist of the period;' and again: 'You must follow Degas' advice to the letter and with an iron will, it is much more important than you imagine.'[2]

Having early in his career selected the path along which his aesthetic impulse was to travel, and found the aspects in the contemporary field best suited for its expression, Degas set about discovering the medium through which to achieve their complete integration. His studies of the Old Masters had made him marvel at their methods, especially their respect for material, thanks to which so many wonderful pictures had remained unchanged through the centuries; and he was worried because the artists of his time did not show the same desire to perfect the practice of their *métier*. The painter Jeanniot says that he, Degas and Chialiva often discussed this question and that Degas once said, 'Nous vivons à une drôle d'époque, il faut avouer. Cette peinture à l'huile que nous faisons, ce métier très difficile que nous pratiquons sans le connaître! pareille incohérence ne s'est sans doute jamais vue. Il y a des méthodes très sures que pratiquaient les artistes des XVIIe et XVIIIe siècles; ces méthodes que connaissait encore David, élève de Vien, qui fut doyen de l'Académie des Beaux-Arts, mais que ne connaissaient plus les peintres du commencement du XIXe siècle.'[3] And the preservation of material was naturally only part of Degas' researches; the possibilities of varying mediums, the combinations of one with another, the different ways in which they could be handled, all

[1] *Lettres de Degas*, 1945, *op. cit.*, p. 147. Manzi (1849–1915) was of Neapolitan origin. He had a great flair for, and knowledge of the different methods of reproduction. In 1881 he joined the Goupil Gallery; and in 1893, with Maurice Joyant, became associated with the firm of Boussod Valadon. About this period he published the album of reproductions of Degas' pastels and drawings. As a hobby he drew lively portraits of his friends. (See p. 44.)

[2] *Camille Pissarro, Letters to his Son*, ed. John Rewald, pub. New York, 1943, pp. 31 and 39.

[3] *Degas: A la Recherche de sa Technique*, by Denis Rouart, pub. Paris, 1945, p. 9. Luigi Chialiva (1824–1914), of Italian origin, was a chemist, architect and painter, whom Degas met in Rome about 1865. He had studied the chemistry of colours and it was according to his recipe that Degas was able so successfully to fix his pastels.

fascinated him and prompted endless experiments. He worked with colours from which an excess of oil had been drained in such a picture as *Jules Perrot Debout* (Pl. 24),[1] with distemper as in *Danseuses à la Barre* (Pl. 46) and with gouache in his fans and sometimes for the heightening of pastels.

In his early years, as Ingres had instructed, he handled oil paint smoothly and thinly *comme une porte*, and later with more freedom but still little impasto. Although he continued using it until about 1890, oil paint had actually, some ten years earlier, given way to his favourite colour medium of pastel. He said, 'Dans la peinture à l'huile il faut procéder comme avec le pastel,'[2] and in their more daring colours laid on with a 'hatching' method, the later oil paintings show the effect of his then chosen material.

Before 1870, Degas had used pastel only for small studies of landscapes, sea and skies, little portrait heads, and for studies for larger portraits afterwards carried out in oil paint. For several years he forsook the medium altogether, returning to it in his maturity of the 'eighties with eyes wide open to its allure and with the satisfying knowledge that, having mastered the more difficult medium of oil paint, he was at liberty to make use of the easier. He found it exactly suited to his requirements. No delays between workings risked the loss of original excitement, and his passion for drawing could be fulfilled in colour without the sacrifice of any force of line. Moreover his failing eyesight began to make demands, and on this subject Sickert wrote, 'It may safely be said that the curious and unique development of the art of pastel that this obstacle (his sight) compelled him to evolve, would not have come into being but for his affliction. A larger scale became a necessity. For the shiny medium of oil paint was substituted the flat one of pastel. Minute delicacies of delicate execution had to be abandoned. A very natural dread that the affliction might grow made, of the necessary delays that oil painting exacts, an intolerable anxiety. A pastel is always ready to be got on with.'[3] Despite its painter-like truths, this statement is a little too sweeping. The development of Degas' art was so logical and consistent that its final consummation could hardly have been achieved except through the means he eventually chose.

Up to Degas' time, pastel had been regarded as a medium through which to obtain delicate effects, almost exclusively in the field of portraiture. It was used essentially in eighteenth century France and by such exponents as Quentin de la Tour and Chardin. Degas' audacious handling, and his application of it to such different subjects and problems, revolutionised its meaning. It is to him that the contemporary revival of interest in a material formerly regarded as *démodé* is due. He has handed down this new art through Lautrec and Vuillard, but he has not passed on the secret of insuring the pastel's permanence without the loss of sparkle. This recipe, known only to Chialiva, died with the latter.

As Degas believed any means justified, providing the desired effect was obtained, and often mixed so many mediums in one picture as to mystify the most discerning scholar, so he used the new invention of snapshot photography—a custom which was followed, in his later

[1] This method is known as 'Peinture à l'Essence sur Papier'.

[2] Robert Emmons, *op. cit.*, p. 64.

[3] 'The Way of a Painter', from the preface to a catalogue of an *Exhibition of 20th Century Art*, Leicester Galleries, London, Jan. 1930.

years, by Sickert. The assistance given by photographs to the making of a picture has been severely criticised, and despite their brilliance of execution it must be admitted that the camera is responsible for a certain false note struck in many of Sickert's canvases of the 'thirties. In none of Degas' pictures is there any hint of such mechanical aid, and were it not for his own confirmation and the testimony of friends, this device could never have been suspected. No further proof is needed of its legitimacy. In 1876, Degas wrote to M. Faure,[1] 'N'oubliez pas de rappeler à Mérante les photographies qu'il m'a offertes hier. Je suis pressé de les voir et de combiner ce que je ferai du don de ce danseur.'[2] Degas himself owned a Kodak and among the mass of material found in the studio after his death were enlarged photographs of the country-side around Saint Valery-sur-Somme where his friend Braquaval[3] lived. M. Guérin says that these are closely related to a series of pastel landscapes which Degas did at this time.[4] Another very interesting photograph is the one of M. Poujaud, Mme Fontaine and Degas in the Salon Chausson.[5] Degas posed his friends and then joined the group, the arrangement emphasising his fondness of rhythm through posture, and his unerring sense of boundary cutting.

.   .   .   .   .   .

From 1855 until 1884—with a few more attempts about 1890—Degas included engraving among all his other activities. Two of his first plates were the *Self Portrait* of his student days, and a portrait of the engraver Tourny[6] done in Rome, where the latter probably helped him in his early stages. But he also turned to Rembrandt and etched, *contre partie*, the *Jeune Homme Assis et Réfléchissant*, and it was while etching Velasquez' *L'Infante Isabelle* in the Louvre that he met Manet. With the courage of youth, Degas worked before the picture directly on to his plate, and Manet, who happened to be in the gallery at the time was so impressed that he could not help addressing the stranger, 'Vous avez de l'audace de graver ainsi, sans aucun dessin préalable, je n'oserais en faire autant.'[7]

For the next ten years Degas confined his etching to finely executed portraits, and in 1875, after a considerable break during which no prints were produced, his engraved subjects fell into line with his work in other mediums. With his insatiable curiosity he tried his hand at dry-point, aquatint, *vernis-mou* and lithograph. He learnt much from his engraver friends Burty, Lepic and Desboutin,[8] and above all from Bracquemond whom he refers to with affectionate

[1] Jean Baptiste Faure (1830–1914). The famous baritone who made his début at the Opéra-Comique in 1852 where he remained until 1860. He sang at the Opéra from 1861–76 and retired from the operatic stage in 1878, singing afterwards only in concert. He appeared in the premières of *L'Africaine, Don Carlos, Faust*, etc.

[2] *Lettres de Degas*, 1945, *op. cit.*, p. 39. For Mérante, see pp. 53–4. Unfortunately it has not been possible to trace the photographs of which Degas speaks.

[3] Braquaval, a painter, to whom Degas offered advice with the words, 'Voulez-vous de mon poison.' See *Revue de France*, 15th March, 1931. 'Souvenirs anecdotiques sur Degas,' by Mme Jeanne Raunay, for further details of their relationship.

[4] *Lettres de Degas*, 1945, *op. cit.*, p. 224, note.

[5] Reproduced *Lettres de Degas*, 1945, *op. cit.*, Pl. XXII.

[6] Joseph Gabriel Tourny (1817–80) was a pupil of Martinet. In 1846 he won the Grand Prix de Gravure, went to Rome, and there devoted himself to painting in watercolour.

[7] *Le Peintre Graveur Illustré*, Vol. 9—Degas, by Loys Delteil, pub. Paris, 1919, note Pl. 12.

[8] Phillipe Burty (1830–90), draughtsman and later engraver, was one of the first to appreciate the prints of his contemporaries. He was deeply impressed by Japanese art, of which he formed a large collection. Sometime art critic for the *Gazette des Beaux Arts*, he published various books. Marcelin Desboutin (1823–1902), writer, painter and engraver. Chiefly remembered on account of his association with the Indépendants (Manet and Degas both painted portraits of him and it was he who posed for *l'Absinthe*) and also for his own gay spirit and somewhat romantic life.

deference as 'Maître' and to whom the eternal student Degas wrote about 1880, '. . . Les 'grains' marchent, même sans vous (qui devriez nous apprendre au lieu de nous laisser aller d'un côté et de l'autre).'[1]

As with everything he did, Degas was hardly ever satisfied with his prints and re-worked his plates so often that some of them reached the twentieth state. Such a one is the well-known etching and aquatint, *Mary Cassatt au Louvre*, first worked on about 1876. When Degas later bought his own press, he printed plates for Pissarro. These impressions which are very rare are inscribed by the artist, 'imprimé par Degas.'[2]

In a letter to Pissarro dated by M. Guerin as 1880, Degas goes into technical details over a plate of the former's, telling him where he thinks it fails and asking how Pissarro obtained certain admirable effects.[3] The problems of colour engraving were interesting them chiefly, and although neither Degas nor Pissarro seems to have achieved much in this direction, some of Mary Cassatt's loveliest work is the series of coloured dry-points and aquatints—much influenced by the Japanese—which she produced about 1891. Degas thought highly of this American woman's talent and gave her a splendid *Nude* in exchange for one of her own pictures. He refers to her prints as 'des essais délicieux de gravure'.

About 1875 also, Degas started lithography, and owing to the less exacting demands this method made upon his eyes, was able to continue it for several years after being compelled to abandon the finer and more meticulous one of engraving. His lithographs number twenty-two and, although interesting, are not as impressive as might be expected of a medium whose richness and strength seemed especially suited to him, and of which he could say, 'Si Rembrandt avait connu la lithographie, Dieu sait ce qu'il en aurait fait.'[4]

He worked on his stones and plates, again by means known and unknown, as a relaxation, an amusement. He retouched his prints with ink, heightened them with chalks and coloured them with pastel as he did his monotypes, until the originals were little more than a foundation. His series of monotypes done in black and colour were intended as illustrations for Ludovic Halévy's charming book, *La Famille Cardinal*[5] (Pls. 132a, 167a and 179a), but Halévy not liking them, another artist was commissioned, and it was not until 1918 that Degas' were published with the work for which they were intended.

This was the only book which Degas actually illustrated, although his *Scènes des Maisons Closes*—his little *plats du jour* as he called them—were used by Vollard for beautifully produced volumes of de Maupassant's *Maison Tellier* and Piérre Louys' *Mimes des Courtisanes de Lucien*. They were engraved with much truth and spirit by Maurice Potin as were the drawings with which Vollard also illustrated Paul Valéry's book, *Degas—Danse—Dessin*. These *plats du jour* are the only hint of eroticism in Degas' work, and such was his reputation for celibacy that Georges

---

[1] *Lettres de Degas*, 1945, *op. cit.*, p. 48.
[2] *Camille Pissarro, Letters to his Son*, op. cit., p. 28, note, 1883.
[3] *Lettres de Degas*, 1945, *op cit.*, pp. 52–4.
[4] *Degas, Danse, Dessin*, by Paul Valéry, pub. Paris, 1938.
[5] In 1872, Ludovic Halévy published (Michel Lévy) *M. et Mme Cardinal* with vignettes by Ed. Morin; in 1880, he published (Calmann-Lévy) *Les Petits Cardinal* (which title also included various short stories), with vignettes by Henri Maigrot. In 1883 these two volumes appeared under the collective title of *La Famille Cardinal*.

Rivière even goes so far as to say that they were inspired by le Musée Secret de Naples rather than by Degas' personal experiences![1]

* * * * * *

It is not perhaps an exaggeration to place Degas' sculpture as the most revealing and intimate part of his *œuvre*. Intimate, because—with the exception of three done in plaster—Degas had none of his models cast,[2] and must therefore have regarded their making as for his pleasure and information alone; and revealing, because practically everything he stood for is summed up in the seventy-three bronzes which were allowed out into the world shortly after his death.

He began in the middle 'sixties doubtless influenced by his friend M. Cuvelier,[3] who specialised in delicate wax studies of horses, both mounted and unmounted, which he sent to the Salon during the same years as Degas exhibited there. Having already shown his awareness of the pictorial possibilities of these animals, not only by his copies of Gozzoli's frescoes,[4] by their inclusion in three of his early compositions, as well as by the two racing pictures already painted, it is not difficult to understand how Degas came to make models of them in the manner of his friend. For up till then, although not always in static positions, his use of horses had been confined to the profile, and such limited knowledge could never satisfy Degas. The logical way to study, when it was impossible to have the living model before him, was—for a man obsessed by form—to make his own. So he started sculpture, not as an end in itself but as a means of acquiring information.

Immediately upon his return from race-meetings and using the memory he had so assiduously trained, he modelled horses from remembered observations, only attempting to make recordings in retrospect back in the quietness of his studio. One of his earliest sculptures was for the horse in *Mlle Fiocre* of 1866, and twenty-two years later he wrote that he had not yet finished with these animals.

In the Impressionist Exhibition of 1881 Degas showed *La Petite Danseuse de Quatorze Ans* (Pls. 96 and 97). From stylistic evidence this appears to be the earliest of his figure models and his first piece of sculpture in its own right. The dancer was made in wax, and Degas dressed her in satin shoes, white tarlatan ballet-skirt, white material bodice over which was run a layer of wax, and tied her hair with a blue satin bow. The effect must certainly have been startling. It brought from Huysmans, '. . . Le fait est que, du premier coup, M. Degas a culbuté les traditions de la sculpture comme il a depuis longtemps secoué les conventions de la peinture . . . cette statuette est la seule tentative vraiment moderne que je connaisse dans la sculpture.[5] Like Degas' earlier oil paintings, this statuette is smoothly handled and carefully considered in all its details; for it he did various drawings of the young girl with and without clothes (Pls. 91–4), besides modelling a preparatory sketch, *Etude de Nu* (Pl. 95). Although not as beautiful as many

---

[1] Georges Rivière, *op. cit.*, p. 163. Le Musée Secret de Naples houses the collection of erotic antiquities from Pompeii and elsewhere.

[2] Degas told Vollard that it was too much responsibility to leave behind him something in bronze . . . it lasted for eternity. (*Degas*, by Ambroise Vollard, pub. Paris, 1924, p. 111.)

[3] Joseph Cuvelier was killed in the siege of Paris in 1871.

[4] *Lorenzo dei Medici and his Attendants*, in the Riccardi Chapel, Florence.

[5] *L'Art Moderne*, J. K. Huysmans, pub. Paris, 1883, pp. 226–7.

of the later figures, its mood as well as its notoriety has made it the most famous of all his sculptures. As the years progressed, Degas, becoming increasingly absorbed in the abstract problems of his art, grew correspondingly remote from its human aspect, and it is in its human appeal that *La Petite Danseuse* stands unique.

．　　．　　．　　．　　．

In the second half of his working life Degas was to narrow the field of his activity more and more, and by so doing to provoke the criticism of the worldly Zola: 'I cannot accept a man who shuts himself up all his life to draw a ballet-girl as ranking co-equal in dignity and power with Flaubert, Daudet and Goncourt.'[1] But so material a mind could never reach the loftiness of an ideal which Degas, prompted by an Ingres drawing of a woman's hand he had just bought, epitomised, 'That's my idea of a genius, a man who finds a hand so lovely, so wonderful, so difficult to render, that he will shut himself up all his life, content to do nothing else but indicate fingernails.'[2]

After 1886, Degas did more or less shut himself up. He no longer exhibited in 'the brothels that picture shows are', although he showed the landscapes done at Saint Valery-sur-Somme in his one and only one-man exhibition held at Durand Ruel's in 1893, and allowed a retrospective group of pictures to be included in the 'Centennale' of 1900. His passion, next to his own work, was to surround himself by that of others, and even though his wants were small, money had to be found to buy the pictures he so frequently coveted.

He was living in the Place Pigalle where Sabine[3] had died two years previously and where Zoë, who was faithfully to tend her master through his sad last years, came to look after him. But soon his collection began to outgrow his apartment, and in 1890 he moved to the Rue Victor Massé, where he devoted a whole floor to its housing. Here, in the centre of Paris, he lived like a hermit, 'like an alchemist of old times surrounded by sketches, canvases, drawing boards, copper plates, lithographic stones, mixing bowls to try out new methods, all the materials of his art.'[4] His collection, which on his death comprised two hundred and thirty-seven items, included pictures by Cuyp, Corot, Delacroix, Pissarro, Cézanne, Forain, Gauguin, and naturally an impressive number by Ingres.

Degas never missed a sale in which a work by Ingres was offered, and when the contents of Courbet's studio were dispersed, became so excited that he insisted on having this or that lot at any price. Durand Ruel frequently financed his purchases, and although there were always collectors anxious to buy, Degas hated parting with anything and only sold or made an exchange when the need was really great. He was once told of an American who would pay 'almost anything' for one of his *Atelier des Modistes*. 'C'est bien tentant,' he replied, 'je pourrais avec cet argent me payer un Delacroix que je guigne depuis longtemps; mais il y a décidément dans cette toile quelque chose qui ne me va pas.' Then taking out a knife he eliminated one of the figures from his picture.[5] The Delacroix had been renounced.

---

[1] and [2] George Moore, *op. cit.*, p. 219.

[3] Degas' housekeepers were Sabine Neyt who died in 1884; Clotilde —— who is said to have gone mad; and Zoë Closier who was with him for over twenty years.

[4] Daniel Halévy, *op. cit.*　　　　　　　　　[5] Ambrose Vollard, *op. cit.*, p. 112.

His own letters continually refer to new acquisitions: 'Mercredi matin, je laissais tout pour regarder bien au jour, avec la loupe, et longtemps, les magnifiques Gavarni que vous m'avez donnés,'[1] or 'Ne me privez pas de la petite copie d'Ingres, ne me faites pas cet affront et ce chagrin. J'en ai vraiment *besoin*. . . . J'y ai pensé toute la nuit.'[2]

There is some mystery as to why Degas left no instructions for the disposal of the collection after his death. It seems that he always intended bequeathing it to the nation, but in the absence of any such proviso it was dispersed by auction in 1918, two months before the contents of his studio. The only light thrown on the subject is by M. Etienne Moreau-Nelaton, who presented his own collection to the Musée des Arts Decoratifs in 1906, and who was chided by Degas for having done so without consultation with him. Degas' mistrust of state-run concerns explains why he did not make a bequest to a museum, and indeed his attitude must have been reinforced—if it was not actually prompted by—the Government's reception of the magnificent Caillebotte legacy.[3]

Apparently Degas had hoped that it might be possible to establish a small, privately financed museum, to which Moreau-Nelaton would also give his collection, and however impracticable his plan may have been, was upset that his friend had made his own arrangements unbeknown to him. Moreau-Nelaton tried to persuade him that, in the Musée des Arts Decoratifs, his pictures would be properly cared for and that he would be given a free hand in their supervision. But Degas was not to be convinced. 'First of all your (Nelaton's) pictures are not well hung. Opposite the window there are reflections, one cannot see a thing, one wouldn't hang a picture like that. If a canvas hangs opposite the light, shutters should be used so that the light is concentrated only on the picture.'[4] And so he preferred that the collection which had given him such joy to accumulate during his life-time should be dispersed far and wide after his death. Fortunately many of the pictures have found their way into museums where they can be enjoyed by painters, for no amateur can hope to understand or treasure them in just the way that he did.

. . . .

The dislike that Degas had for selling his own pictures was because he always hoped to arrive at something better; and although dissatisfaction with work not seen for some time is in itself quite usual and understandable, with him it mounted almost to an obsession. When his friends admired anything he liked, he insisted on giving it to them, delighted that they should find pleasure in his work and perhaps subconsciously realising that, as long as it was in their possession, he would always be able to lay his hands upon it. But he had to be resisted with firmness. Once Degas got hold of a picture the owner never saw it again, his efforts to improve it usually ended in its ruin, and although he must have known that this would happen, he simply could not help himself.

Ernest Rouart[5] tells of his father's experience in such an instance. He owned a beautiful

---

[1] To Alexis Rouart. *Lettres de Degas*, 1945, *op. cit.*, p. 204.

[2] To Durand Ruel. *Lettres de Degas*, 1945, *op. cit.*, p. 220.

[3] Caillebotte left his collection of sixty-five paintings, chiefly by Impressionists, to the State. Despite his will, which stipulated that the collection should go undivided to the Luxembourg, the authorities would not accept such 'filth' and selected from it certain less 'evil' works. (See Paul Cézanne by Gerstle Mack.)

[4] Hans Graber, *op. cit.*, p. 185.   [5] Hans Graber, *op. cit.*, p. 179.

pastel which Degas persuaded him needed minor alterations, and as the artist was so pressing, Rouart felt that he had no alternative but to allow him to have the picture back. Months went by until Degas finally confessed that he had completely spoilt it. The owner never forgave himself but learnt his lesson. In its place, Degas gave him *Deux Danseuses à la Barre*, and after some time, finding the watering-can 'idiotic', wished to be allowed to take it out. This time he did not get his way, M. Rouart was adamant and was even said to have chained the picture to the wall—an amusing legend, as his son points out.

M. Faure had a similar experience. Through Durand Ruel he had bought six pictures, about which, as soon as they had left his possession, Degas grew unbearably worried. At any cost he had to get them back. It was arranged, therefore, that all should be returned to Degas who, in exchange, and with the additional payment of eight thousand francs, would paint four large pictures upon subjects agreed. The first two, of which *Robert le Diable* was one, were handed to Faure in 1876. The other two were not finished until 1887 and not before the latter had been forced to bring an action against Degas for their delivery.

. . . . . .

Whether justified or not, Degas, in his middle fifties, already considered himself an old man. His passion for his work intensified, the advancing years, declining health and sight all stressed the urgency to accomplish as much as possible during the time left to him. Behind locked doors he worked with more frantic energy than ever, visiting his few chosen friends, occasionally allowing them into his sanctuary, and only pausing in order to give his eyes a rest. 'Si je n'étais pas comme je suis avec les gens, je n'aurais plus une minute à moi pour travailler.'[1] For Degas was famous, else his barricade would have been unnecessary. And so it was that the legend of his misanthropy grew. For instead of appreciating the reason for his solitude and accepting with thankfulness the fruits of his laborious work, it was still demanded of Degas that he should be a social animal.

Although difficult, as are often those with strong convictions, and exacting because his own ideals were high, Degas was not as *méchant* as he liked the world to suppose. His reputation suited him as a safeguard against the fools he could not suffer, and his caustic wit frightened those whose insincerity he quickly penetrated. Outside the field of art they did not matter, but inside all were his concern. Whistler especially could not be spared the severity of his tongue— he is said to have been the only person of whom the American was afraid—for with such talent there was no need for futile posing, and Whistler behaved as if he had no talent. 'Le rôle de papillon doit être bien fatiguant. J'aime mieux moi être le bœuf, quoi? . . .'[2]

But his real friends, excusing his weaknesses and adoring his greatness, were allowed to see the human being behind his coat of armour. They knew of his loneliness, his sympathy, his humour and his kindness, as well as his ill-humour, his obstinacy and his prejudices. They knew how dependent he was on them both for the discussion of work and for the warmth of human contact. They knew also that they could depend upon him, for Degas—as men who for one reason or other renounce domesticity are apt to—made a cult of friendship.

[1] Vollard, *op. cit.*, p. 33. [2] Robert Emmons, *op. cit.*, p. 62.

However, much as Degas prized his friends, there was a gap they could not fill. In his letters creep little notes of wistfulness as he compares their happy married lives with his own solitary existence and promise of a lonely death; and even he could not have visualised just how heavily those last years of blindness were to weigh upon him, nor how the Great War would disperse his surviving friends, leaving hardly any in Paris to follow him to his grave. He told Vollard, '. . . il faut se marier. Vous ne savez pas ce que c'est la solitude quand on vieillit,'[1] and wrote to Rouart, 'Je fais dans mon rhume, des réflexions sur le célibat, et il-y-a les trois quarts de triste dans ce que je me dis.'[2] But, apart from a certain feeling he is said to have had for Mlle Dihau in his youth,[3] there is no evidence that he ever felt passionately towards a woman, and indeed his art stresses this lack of sensuality.

William Rothenstein relates the 'amusing' story that Degas, having been twitted by his friends over his indifference to the opposite sex, felt that he must make some show of gallantry. Finding that one of the little dancers who sat for him was going to America, he thought this an opportunity for the appropriate gesture. He booked a passage on the boat following hers, stayed quietly on board when it got to New York, then returned on the same boat to France. 'Impossible to do more,' he said, than show himself capable of pursuing a lady all the way from Paris to New York.[4] Hardly a story to be taken seriously, but the implication behind it, far from being amusing, seems full of pathos.

Degas was a man with a keen sense of humour and appreciative of jokes against himself, so that he must have been amused by Manzi's fanciful portrait of him wearing tights and toe-shoes and standing in fourth position in front of a long mirror.[5] Neither did he take himself so seriously as to let his reverence for Ingres forbid the harmless piece of fun poked at both of them in Barnes' photograph, *Tableau vivant—Apothéose de Degas*.[6] Perhaps it was even he who suggested this amusing parody in which he is seated on the steps of a villa as if on a throne, with the sisters of John Lemoinne standing behind as Muses about to crown him, and the two young sons of Ludovic Halévy in attitudes of adoration at his feet. Degas' expression is one of great solemnity, but the young people obviously found it difficult to conceal their mirth.

According to M. Blanche,[7] Sickert proposed that the group of friends gathered in Dieppe in the summer of 1885 should have some photographs taken. They had met a photographer named Barnes who was in a desperate situation, and had decided to do all they could to give and to find him work. Degas' own concern for Barnes, who was a comparative stranger, is shown in a letter he wrote to Ludovic Halévy, 'Surveillez Barnes, tout en protégeant, de façon qu'il devienne tout simplement heureux.'[8] And there are numerous other proofs of his kindness and generosity in times of trouble; his gifts of pictures, among others, to sales in aid of John Lewis Brown's widow and the destitute musician, Cabaner; and his buying of a painting from Gauguin's sale when the latter was in difficulties and despite the fact that the two were on bad

---

[1] Vollard, *op. cit.*, p. 70. [2] *Lettres de Degas, op. cit.*, 1945, p. 209.
[3] *Lettres de Degas*, 1945, *op. cit.*, note 2, p. 17.
[4] *Men and Memories*, by Sir William Rothenstein, pub. London, 1934, p. 105.
[5] and [6] *Lettres de Degas*, recueillés et annotées par Marcel Guerin, ed. pub. Paris, 1931, Pls. 3 and 6 respectively.
[7] *Portraits of a Lifetime*, by J. Emile Blanche, pub. London, 1937, Vol. 1, p. 56.
[8] *Lettres de Degas, op. cit.*, 1945, p. 107.

terms at the time. Of this Pissarro wrote, '. . . although afraid to go and face Degas, Gauguin nevertheless wrote to him to ask for his support. Degas who, after all, is very fine and sympathetic to people who are in trouble, put himself at Gauguin's service and bought a canvas at the sale.'[1]

Vollard also tells how Degas, when the wife of a well-known Jewish man died, put some finishing touches to a portrait he had painted of her and sent it to the husband hoping to soften his loss.[2] The date of this episode is not given, but it is certain to have taken place prior to 1899, the year which marked the beginning of the Dreyfus scandal. Up to that time Degas probably had anti-semitic tendencies, but that they were only latent in him is proved by his great affection for the Halévy family, his respect for Pissarro, and even by the fact of his having painted a portrait of the Chief-Rabbi Astruc.[3]

The violence which the 'Affaire' aroused, far beyond the borders of France, is an old story. In the bitter struggles attendant upon it, the Frenchman in Degas—as had happened in 1870—once again took precedence. He would have nothing more to do with Pissarro, completely broke his ties with the Halévy family, and let slip no opportunity of raging against the people of their faith. Although he keenly felt the loss of his old friends, he remained implacable, perhaps even taking pride in his firmness. But, while Degas' ferocious anti-semitism during the last twenty years of his life cannot be denied, to accept it as his life-long attitude is as misleading as to hold a man to an opinion formed with all sincerity in his early 'teens.

.   .   .   .   .   .

And yet Degas did form one opinion in his 'teens which he was never to retract, the certainty that for him Ingres was the master the most to be revered and followed. With the instinct of an animal knowing what food to eat and what to reject, he went direct to Ingres for nourishment at a time when, in the eyes of the young progressives, the master's reputation was on the wane.

His personal meeting with the great man came about in a happy way. Ingres wanted to include one of his *Turkish Bathers* in the 'Exposition Universelle' of 1855, but its owner, M. Valpinçon, being nervous of the risks involved, refused to lend it. Degas was horrified that anybody should deny Ingres, and persuaded the family friend to change his decision. Together they went to tell the master the good news and thus it was that Ingres met his unknown disciple. M. Moreau-Nelaton says that it was during this visit that Ingres had a stroke and that Degas rushed to the rue de Lille to fetch Mme Ingres.[4]

After that, Degas met Ingres on several occasions before the latter's death in 1867, but he never met Delacroix. He said that he once saw him crossing the street and that every sub-

[1] *Camille Pissarro Letters, op. cit.*, p. 170.

[2] Vollard, *op. cit.*, p. 1.

[3] Degas painted, about 1870-1, a double portrait of the Chief-Rabbi Astruc and General Mellinet. Elie-Aristide Astruc (1831-1905) was appointed assistant to the chief Rabbi of Paris in 1857 and became chaplain of the Paris lyceums of Louis le Grand, etc. During the war of 1870 he distinguished himself both as Jewish minister and French patriot (*Jewish Encyclopedia*).

[4] Hans Graber, *op. cit.*, p. 184. There are other accounts as to how Degas met Ingres, but both M. Moreau-Nelaton and Sickert quote the above as having been told them by Degas himself; Sickert however says that Ingres' attack took place years later and proved fatal (*Burlington Magazine*, December 1917).

sequent time he passed the spot which, being on the way to his frame-maker's, was very often, he thought of this 'wizard' and of how much work he had accomplished.

Apart from the general influence that Degas exercised on the younger generation, he himself had three devoted disciples, each a native of a different country. The first—Mary Cassat, a rich young American woman whose work he had noticed in the Salon of 1874, and who began exhibiting in the Impressionist Exhibitions in 1879. The second—the English painter Sickert—charged by Whistler to take the *Portrait of My Mother*[1] to Paris in 1883, was also given a letter of introduction to Degas. The latter, immediately attracted by the young man, allowed him to become a frequent visitor at the rue Victor Massé, the 'lighthouse of my existence' as Sickert called it. It was the consequences of this meeting that caused the breach between Whistler and his pupil, for Sickert naturally fell under the spell of the great French painter, and though he continued to acknowledge himself a 'pupil of Whistler', the latter could not tolerate divided admiration. Sickert's telling pen has described Degas as having 'the good nature and high spirits that attend a sense of power exercised in the proper channels, and therefore profoundly satisfied'.[2]

But the most famous of the three, the one who openly declared himself a worshipper, was Toulouse Lautrec. The childlike adoration which this cynical and worldly man had for the artist, whom he considered the supreme master of contemporary painting, is more than touching, and is expressively described in M. Joyant's eye-witness account of Degas' visit to an exhibition of Lautrec's work held at the Goupil Gallery in 1893. A special invitation had been sent to Degas, and Lautrec anxiously awaited his arrival. 'Un soir, vers six heures, ce dernier arrive, enveloppé de son mac-farlane, examine tout attentivement, en chantonnant, fait le tour sans dire un mot et s'en fut descendre. Se retournant, le buste émergeant à moitié de l'étroit escalier en colimaçon, M. Degas dit à Lautrec, timide et anxieux, "Ça, Lautrec, on voit que vous êtes du bâtiment." Je vois encore Lautrec, épanoui dans tout un contentement intime, de cette approbation jetée négligemment.'[3]

When Lautrec took up his first independent home he chose, out of the whole of Paris, an apartment at 19 bis rue Fontaine Saint Georges, the building in which Degas had his studio before his move to the rue Victor Massé. But nothing came of this proximity, for Degas and Lautrec never really knew each other; in any case the wide divergence between their characters and the way in which each conducted his private life would have forbidden any possible intimacy. Lautrec was content to worship from afar and to get news of his hero through their mutual friends the Dihau family. Degas had known them for years, Désiré, Henri and their sister—all musicians; Lautrec made their acquaintance in 1890. He painted their portraits— 'timidly and humbly' asking whether they would bear comparison with those by 'Monsieur Degas'—and did many lithographs for the covers of Désiré's published compositions. Vuillard tells the charming story of how he was once a guest at one of Lautrec's elaborate luncheon parties given in honour of Thadée Natanson. Lautrec, a true gourmet, knew the specialities of

---

1 The *Portrait of My Mother*, by Whistler, formerly in the Luxembourg.
2 'Personal Account of Degas,' by Sickert, *Burlington Magazine*, December 1917.
3 *Henri de Toulouse Lautrec, Peintre*, by Maurice Joyant, pub. Paris, 1926, p. 122.

every restaurant in Paris and took his friends to eat this dish here and that one there; the wines he brought from his family cellars. Finally, just as his guests were wondering how this ceremonious banquet could end without an anti-climax, Lautrec rose 'and started to lead us God knows where, without saying a word. A little suspicious of whatever extravagant notion might be sprouting in his unruly brain, we followed him up three flights of stairs leading to the apartment of the Dihau family in the rue Frochot. Scarcely taking time to greet his hosts, Lautrec led us before the portrait of Dihau playing the bassoon in the orchestra of the Opéra, by Degas, and announced with a flourish, ''There's my dessert.''[1]

Lautrec quite openly and unashamedly took what he wanted from Degas, and were it not out of place here to go into such detail, individual pictures by Lautrec could be quoted as having been directly suggested by Degas' Café Scenes—*L'Absinthe* and *Femmes à la Terrasse d'un Café*; his Café Concerts—*La Chanson du Chien* and *Chanteuse Verte*;[2] his Circuses, such as the lithograph *Au Cirque Medrano*; his Brothels used as illustrations; and even his *Blanchisseuses*. Moreover, Lautrec learned much from Degas' strikingly original powers of composition, and through him absorbed the teachings of the Japanese; he also used the medium of pastel, handling it in similar ways and within a like range of colour. Replying to Degas' question as to what she thought of Lautrec, Suzanne Valadon answered, 'I think that he dresses rather in your clothes'—'remodelling them to suit himself', Degas interjected quickly.[3] And so it was—only the material remained.

For despite these affinities, and despite the fact that both men were essentially draughtsmen, they were really poles apart. First of all, Lautrec was primarily an illustrator, in the best sense of the word; and secondly, sensuality—the trait so singularly lacking in Degas—was the force which overwhelmed Lautrec with an abnormality distorted as his own poor body. (A striking example of its insistence pictorially was his twisting into a phallic symbol the scroll of a double-bass, which motif he had borrowed from Degas.[4]) Lautrec, with that sense of urgency shared by Van Gogh and all who know their time to be short, imparted a feeling of brilliant impatience whose meteoric character was diametrically opposed to Degas' steady labour and detached consideration. And while the latter's instinctive sympathy with classical ideals carried him into the weighty realms of plastic form, Lautrec, crying against his own physical deformity, denied all nobility to the human body.

. . . . . .

Drawing being the structure upon which a picture is built, and the study of the Nude the most searching means through which fine draughtsmanship may be attained, it is evident that the keystone of painting is figure drawing. Whether the artist's emphasis be on colour or on line, this study is one which he dare not relinquish without achieving less than otherwise he might have done.

[1] *Toulouse Lautrec*, by Gerstle Mack, pub. London, 1938, p. 59.
[2] *L'Absinthe, Femmes à la Terrasse d'un Café*, in the Louvre; *La Chanson du Chien*, in the Horace Havemeyer Collection, New York; *Chanteuse Verte* in a private collection.
[3] *Degas*, by Gustav Coquiot, pub. Paris, 1924, p. 127.
[4] Compare Pls. 52 and 53 with Lautrec's poster, *Jane Avril*, 1893 (*XIX Century French Posters*, pub. London, 1944, Frontispiece).

At the beginning of his career Degas, like other students, drew in this manner—as an exercise, a step towards the achievement of an aim. His early studies of figures with and without clothes were in preparation for his Classical compositions—a means of acquiring knowledge. Despite his admiration for Delacroix and the normal desire of youth to move with the times, he found that his natural inclination was towards Ingres and what he stood for. So, having the courage to follow his intuition, he turned to the master with whom he felt himself in sympathy.

It is possible that, at this early stage, Degas' predilection for the linear approach was still a subconscious factor, and that for some years, until he had experimented himself, and through the Impressionists been brought face to face with the stress which could be laid on colour, he did not realise the strength of his convictions. But the more he used oil-paint, the more he resented the effacement of line in which the application of this medium inevitably results, and this could only imply that the beautiful texture of paint meant less to him than the purity of line unconcealed.

Although he urged his colleagues to seek for new combinations along the path of draughtsmanship which he considered a more fruitful field than that of colour,[1] Degas was not yet willing completely to renounce the latter. Had he been born in any previous generation he might have solved his difficulty in the manner of the Florentines, Poussin or Ingres; but the Impressionist tenets had naturally left their mark upon him and other means for the resolution of his problem had, of necessity, to be evolved.

He came upon it when, at the second attempt, he turned to the medium of pastel and found that instead of painting he could draw with it. 'Je suis coloriste avec la ligne,'[2] he announced triumphantly, having discovered his ability to unite two separate paths which had hitherto appeared to run parallel to each other, while at the same time maintaining the freshness and spontaneity demanded by his associates. But though his rich and sometimes startling colour shows his evident enjoyment at the time, its primarily emotional appeal meant very little to the least emotional of artists, and as time went on his disregard for it increased.

. . . . . .

As a painter, a maker of pictures, Degas reached his height in the late 'eighties. The attention he paid to drawing-studies was the same as in his early youth. With the humility which partners great achievement, Degas always considered himself a student, and it is revealing to note how faithfully he adhered to his drawings (see Pls. 20 and 21; 42 and 43; and 116 and 117, to quote a few examples), not scorning to use a plumb line whenever he felt it necessary. By this time he had become a superb draughtsman, a composer of great originality, a designer with a strong feeling for rhythmic movements, and a colourist of daring. He had explored his particular subjects in so personal a way as to forbid their approach by any subsequent painter of lesser stature, and while retaining his link with the classical tradition, was essentially an artist of his own time.

Then, coincident with his retirement, his art passed into a higher and more esoteric plane. As he shut himself away from the world, solitary and independent of all but his own

[1] Robert Emmons, *op. cit.*, p. 62.   [2] Henri Hertz, *op. cit.*, p. 55.

little circle, so he refused to make even the slightest artistic concession. Indeed it seemed as if he deliberately went to the other extreme. Drawing, in its own right, and upon the most exalted plane, became synonymous with modelling in the great series of figure studies, enormous in scale and content, upon which he concentrated absolutely. Mystery of atmosphere, effects of light, feeling for texture and allure of colour, all were subordinated as, summing up, he stated with the greatest possible economy the synthesis of plasticity and movement. His interest did not lie in arrested movement—the frozen gesture of a film suddenly stopped— but in the continuous progression of a form passing from one attitude to another, so that no explanation is needed as to what has gone before, nor suggestion as to what will follow.

The idiom he employed was the feminine body in its most agile and natural of states; his dancers cut the air with the spread of their limbs, the tension held from finger-tip to finger-tip, from chin to *pointe* of toe; his women rise out of their tubs lifting all the weight of their bodies, with a drive of the inevitable, the relentless force of life. And as the Nudes became more and more abstract, relating to the human body but magnificently soaring above it, a lofty splendour, aloof and detached as the artist, manifested itself. This was the natural evolution of Degas' art, continuing its rise up to its grandest peak.

· · · · · ·

In 1889 Degas went to Spain and Tangier with the painter Boldini, and in the following year toured Bourgogne in a tilbury driven by Bartholomé. The holiday had been suggested by Degas ostensibly with the idea of visiting his friends M. and Mme Jeanniot,[1] who lived at Diénay, and whom they reached after a fortnight's travelling during which Bartholomé had to drive for many days with only his left hand, the right one having been badly stung. Degas wrote, 'Si j'ai été le fou qui a pensé ce voyage, Bartholomé est le sage qui va finir par l'exécuter.'[2] But in his own way he enjoyed the tour and wrote daily reports to the Halévys which are full of amusing comments and lively observations; they even reveal Degas as a *bon viveur*, for when he had a meal which particularly delighted him, he sent full details of the menu to his friends. As the two approached Melun, Manzi—who has done an amusing pastel of the pair seated side by side in the tilbury[3]—drove in a coupé to meet them; a little further along the road they were welcomed by Forain . . . on his tricycle!

Most of Degas' holidays were spent with his friends the Valpinçons at the Chateau de Menil Hubert in the valley of the Orne; with de Valernes at Carpentras, and with Braquaval at Saint Valery-sur-Somme. From time to time he went to Naples on family affairs; to Switzerland in the 'nineties for his health; and in 1897 to Montauban in order to visit the Ingres museum and arrange about taking some photographs of the drawings. But he was restless and unhappy, and found it 'impossible de vivre loin de mon atelier et de ne pas travailler', and even there he could not find fulfilment, for now work was almost an impossibility.

In 1912 came a bitter blow. The building in which he had lived and worked for twenty-

[1] Either the painter Pierre Alexandre Jeanniot (1826–92) or his son and pupil, Pierre Georges born 1848.
[2] *Lettres de Degas*, 1945, *op. cit.*, p. 165. Albert Bartholomé, born 1848. Sculptor and painter especially known for memorial sculpture and portrait busts.
[3] *Lettres de Degas*, 1931, *op. cit.*, rep., Pl. IX.

two years was about to be demolished to make way for a modern block. The wrench was almost more than this old man could bear. He had planned to pass the rest of his days in his own familiar surroundings and now he had to uproot himself at the age of seventy-eight so that a 'monstrous' new building could be erected.

Suzanne Valadon—whose drawing he admired so greatly—helped him find and move into his last home in the Boulevard Clichy. But now his work was over. Unable to see enough to model or to draw, he spent his last years wandering about the streets of Paris. The kidney disease from which he suffered magnified his fondness for walking and turned it into a necessity. The city he so dearly loved was again to be menaced by German guns, but Degas was scarcely aware of the tragedy. For him, time had toned the picture of life, so that all things, significant and insignificant, possessed an equal value.

·   ·   ·   ·   ·

Daniel Halévy has given a description, full of dignity and pathos, of this great artist at the end of his life. 'Quel Parisien n'a rencontré, regardé, quel d'entre eux, l'ayant vue, a oublié cette figure singulière, ce veillard à barbe blanche, couvert d'un lourd MacFarlane, qui recevait la pluie avec indifférence, avançant d'un pas rapide, un peu penché en avant et tâtant du bout de sa canne l'angle de la chaussée? Ses marches duraient des heures, il les continuait jusque dans la nuit. Homère aux yeux vides, Lear hagard au bord de la falaise, n'eurent pas plus de grandeur tragique que le vieux Degas errant dans nos rues parisiennes. La dernière exposition où nous le vîmes fut celle qui précéda la vente de la collection de son grand ami Henri Rouart; Degas se penchait sur les chers tableaux, compagnons de sa vie, les Daumier, les Prudhon, les Delacroix et les Corot, il les touchait comme pour reconnaître, saisir avec ses mains ces colorations, ces lignes, cette beauté picturale dont il restait avide. Il revenait chaque jour; un groupe d'amateurs, d'amis, de jeunes gens, l'entourait, l'accompagnait, se relayait à ses côtés pour ne pas le laisser seul dans son deuil.'[1]

·   ·   ·   ·   ·

Degas died in a deserted Paris on the 26th September, 1917. Few friends were left to attend his funeral, the devoted Forain being one of them. Degas had told him that he wanted no funeral oration, but 'Si, Forain, vous en ferez un, vous direz donc, ''Il aimait beaucoup le dessin, moi aussi,'' et vous rentrez chez vous.'[2]

[1] Daniel Halévy, *op. cit.* (The Rouart sale took place in 1912.)   [2] *La Revue de France, op. cit.*

DEGAS AND THE BALLET

Had he been born in the fourteenth century, Degas would probably have gone down to history as the *Master of the Ballet Dancer*, and indeed that is how he is thought of in the twentieth century, only instead of his patronymic having been lost his two appelations have become synonymous.

The layman's most immediate way of recognising an artist's work is through the subject matter, and as his knowledge gradually increases, so in proportion does his response to subject diminish, and he becomes aware of the more reliable evidence of personality and period. With the newly awakened interest in ballet as a complete and living form of art, it is only natural that the majority of people think of Degas in terms of his connection with it; but as they probe beneath the surface they will realise that instead of Degas being the interpreter of ballet he has, on the contrary, used that art for the exploration of his own.

Today it seems as if Degas has said the last word on ballet and it is difficult to conceive how any succeeding painter may get a fresh angle upon it. Not only this, he has also accomplished the rare feat of delighting equally the devotees of the pictorial as well as of the Terpsichorean arts. Professionals of both are wholly satisfied because he has thoroughly understood the one while expressing it in terms of the other. He has shown his respect for the Classical ballet by his absolute faithfulness to its laws and conventions, and by so doing has refuted the theory of incompatability between factual accuracy and artistic expression. His effects have been obtained without his feeling the need for distortion—or artistic licence, as it may be called— and it is necessary to stress this point in an age all too ready to tolerate a laxity which, in its aesthetic culmination, finally proves to be unjustified.

Curiously and rather ironically, Degas lived through the period in which French ballet for the first time in its history lost its inspiration and became sterile. The great Romantic epoch had been at its height in 1834, the year in which he was born; by the time he reached his majority all but one of its stars had retired[1]; and although alive in 1909 when Diaghilev's company showed Paris the highest creative achievements of which the integrated ballet is capable, he was then an old man, practically blind, who for more than twenty years had renounced his intimate connection with the art as a separate entity.

It is unwise to lay too much importance on a subject which, after all, should remain part of the whole and not be overstressed; it is useless to admit that Degas' work would not have been enhanced had he been a contemporary of either Taglioni or Pavlova. The fidelity of all dancers is firstly to their art and they cannot help regretting the twist of fate which caused their greatest pictorial protagonist to know it at its lowest ebb. Their imaginations persist in wandering back across the years and playing with what they know to be irrelevant ideas. They lament

[1] Taglioni in 1847; Elssler in 1851; Grahn and Cerito in 1854; only Grisi retired two years after in 1857.

46

that Degas saw Mauri leap where Taglioni would have floated, and Sangalli move where Elssler would have flashed. Did he too have these regrets? Perhaps the wings of the *Sylphide*[1] brushed his cheeks as he lay in his cradle, and her spirit hovered about his nursery bidding him embrace her art in his own future greatness. Years later perhaps she guided his footsteps towards the Opera House where her *Ballet of Nuns*[2] was being performed, he, unsuspecting, thinking it was Meyerbeer who had drawn him there.

· · · · · ·

It would be quite logical to assume that, after the Revolution, the neo-Classical movement would have led the dance away from the gradually developed and highly stylised tradition of Louis XIV, from the theories and laws laid down for it by Noverre in his *Lettres sur la Danse* of 1760, towards the normal 'natural' gestures as seen through Greek eyes. This would imply that artists in the persons of Myron, Polycleitus and Pheidias would have become teachers of the dance which, through the medium of Isadora Duncan, actually happened a century later. As it was the influence took just the opposite form and was generally brought about by the adoption of the Classical fashion in dress.

So slender a reason for such a development might on first thoughts appear surprising, but costume plays much the same part in a dancer's performance as material does in the painter's. In other words it limits or enhances her freedom of expression; she can move only as far and as freely as her trappings will allow, and this is why the costume designer bears so much heavier a responsibility in ballet production than he does in opera or other dramatic performances.

Instead of the choreographers having borrowed the soft flowing movements suggested by Greek vases and sculpture, they took advantage of the freedom allowed to the limbs by the classical tunic and loose floating gowns. Sallé and Noverre[3] had fought for such liberty in the past, but public taste had proved too strong for them, and they had been unable sufficiently to modify their conventional costumes so restricting to choreographic development. But now turns and leaps came within the bounds of possibility; large floor-covering steps were no longer forbidden by weight of costume or tightness of skirt; heel-less sandals allowed of more complicated *batterie* and paved the way for the dancers' *pointe* work;[4] and for the first time the beauty of the dancer's strong and slender leg, the curves of the body moving with grace and flexibility, were—through the gauze-like dresses—poetically displayed.

And not only was the liberation confined to the individual possibilities of the dancers, for

[1] Taglioni created the title role in *La Sylphide* first produced at the Théâtre de l'Académie Royal de Musique in March 1832, with choreography by Filippo Taglioni, book by Nourrit, music by Schneitzhoeffer and costumes by Lami. This ballet should not be confused with Fokine's *Les Sylphides* of 1909. Taglioni endured great poverty after her retirement; some of her last years were spent in London, teaching dancing and deportment at a girls' school. She died in Marseilles in 1884.

[2] Taglioni created the role of Helena in the *Ballet of Nuns* in Meyerbeer's opera *Robert le Diable*, first produced at Paris in 1831.

[3] Marie Sallé (1707–56), being unable to carry out her reforms in dress, went to London where she produced her own ballet at Covent Garden and wore a much simplified costume. Two pictures of her were painted by Lancret (see *l'Art Français—Nicholas Lancret*, by Georges Wildenstein, Nos. 144 and 206). Jean Georges Noverre (1727–1810) also included costume among his desired reforms for the dance. Like Sallé he had to go abroad to win recognition.

[4] Danseuses took up poises *sur la pointe* early in the nineteenth century in order to give an illusion of extreme lightness. But *pointe work*, as it is known today, could not have been developed until the advent of the stiff-backed shoe, for contrary to general statements, the darning of the toe—a habit practised by all dancers—gives no support whatsoever to the foot.

pas, however brilliant, do not of their own accord mean fine choreography. The Revolution had inevitably introduced a new theatre-going public, one which, being far removed from the fastidious and aristocratic conventions of court circles, allowed the choreographer to express his own personality without having to pander to the tastes of his audience. And although the years of the First Republic and the Empire were barren ones for ballet, since like painting it had suffered from attempts to turn it into a means of political propaganda, whilst the 'Reign of Terror' had driven its stars into hiding, the path was all the while being prepared for the glorious era which was to come.

One of the most teasing questions in the history of the interpretative arts is the exact status, in contemporary terms, of the Italian born Marie Taglioni. Her name is still pronounced in a hushed voice, a mixture of reverence and wonder, and her legend is such that any but complete acceptance of it suggests something akin to heresy. As already admitted, one of the weaknesses of this time is the desire to find in history the exact niche into which each great figure may be fitted. But Taglioni and her colleagues defy such classification, their reputations rest unmolested by modern values and, for want of other evidence, must be accepted according to the writings of their contemporaries.

Marie Taglioni, the final liberator of the dance from the stylisation of the eighteenth century, was the embodiment of lyricism in ballet. Although she had appeared in Paris in 1827, it was not until five years later, with her appearance in *La Sylphide*, that her glory spread throughout Europe. Since that time, and despite the magnificent dancers who have succeeded her into this century, only the name of Pavlova approaches hers in conjuring visions of an ethereal being, a spirit from another planet. While belonging to her time it seems as if she stood apart in it, for in her art was mystery imponderable, an almost supernatural power of obtaining wondrous effects through apparently effortless means.[1] Her *Sylphide* was as elusive in the Romantic setting as Elssler's[2] creations—an expression in a different medium of the voluptuous and richly coloured Romanticism of Delacroix—were intelligible. Chorley says of Taglioni and Elssler, 'The one floated on to the stage like a nymph; the other showered every sparkling fascination round her like a sorceress, with that abundance which finds enjoyment in its own exercise.'[3] With two such stars in opposite firmaments it is not surprising that their admirers were divided into separate camps, as the followers of Camargo[4] and Sallé had been a century before, and those of Ulanova and Lepeschinskaya[5] are in Russia today.

[1] Ballet historians compare Taglioni's amazing elevation and power of remaining in the air with that of Auguste Vestris and Nijinsky. It was concerning Vestris that his father made the well-known boast, 'If "le diou de la Danse" touches the ground from time to time, he does so in order not to humiliate his comrades.' Such elevation as Taglioni is said to have had is all the more remarkable in a woman.

[2] Fanny Elssler (1810–84), the Viennese dancer and Taglioni's serious rival.

[3] A *Short History of Ballet*, by Cyril W. Beaumont. New edition pub. London, 1944, p. 2.

[4] Marie Camargo (1710–70) is generally said to have been the first danseuse to 'cut' an *entrechat-quatre*, but Mlle Bernay writes, '. . . bien qu'on ait dit merveille des *entrechats-quatre* battus par la Camargo en 1730, c'est à dire 30 ans après que Mlle Lamy avait déjà battu des *entrechats-six*' (*op. cit.*, p. 21). Lancret painted many pictures of Camargo; they are in the Wallace Collection, London; Musée Municipal de Nantes; Musée de l'Ermitage; Nouveau Palais Potsdam (in 1923); besides which there are several others whose whereabouts are unknown. (Wildenstein, *op. cit.*, Nos. 140–1943.)

[5] Galina Ulanova (born circa 1913–14). Soviet ballerina of the Leningrad ballet and a dancer of great lyrical quality. Olga Lepeschinskaya (born 1916), the first pupil in more than a century to graduate from the Moscow schools with the title of *prima ballerina*, is remarkable for her virtuosity.

DEGAS AND THE BALLET

Although the age of the *Danseur* had been superseded by that of the *Danseuse*, Taglioni's one time partner, and later Carlotta Grisi's lover, Jules Perrot, could still be classed among the finest of male dancers. He is said to have been possessed also of an extraordinary elevation so that Gautier, who generally seems to have abhorred men dancers—as incidentally did Ingres—called him the 'male Taglioni'. Besides this, Perrot was an excellent choreographer, and has to his credit an impressive list of ballets which were produced in London, Paris and Milan, and after 1848 in St Petersburg. It was he who arranged the *pas de deux* for Cerito and Elssler at the command of Queen Victoria for her State Visit to Her Majesty's Theatre in 1843, and was bold enough to follow it up two years later by assembling the four great stars, Taglioni, Cerito, Grahn and Grisi[1] in the celebrated *pas de quatre*. It does not require a great deal of imagination to realise that Perrot, on top of all his other qualifications, must have been a diplomat of the highest order; yet if discord was the keynote behind the scenes, an arrangement of perfect harmony and brilliance was presented to the audience. Like the *pas de deux* it was produced at Her Majesty's Theatre, and has been perpetuated by Chalon in a much sought-after lithograph.

Romanticism in both the pictorial arts and the dance flourished predominantly in France. In painting it was perpetuated by only two figures of note, and although the actual movement was of but short duration, its virility was such as to impress itself upon the powerful artists who succeeded generation by generation right through into the twentieth century. In ballet, Romanticism was represented by a galaxy of stars whose collective brilliance has only once been rivalled in the whole history of dancing. It achieved its full glory within the also short space of their working years, then choked as it were by its own riches, and lacking in vigour and imagination, it steadily sank into a hopeless sterility.

The reasons for its decline seem obvious, but the placing of the responsibility is not so simple, as, being an expression of vast collaborate performance, ballet is greatly dependent upon economic factors. It would be easy to say that the fault lay with the inability of the librettists and choreographers to keep in line with contemporary thought. This of course is the underlying truth, but events suggest that it was the fickleness and misplaced understanding of the public which was really to blame. Instead of having appreciated in ballet a complete and complex form of art, it blindly idolised the ballerinas, and when it was time for them to retire, it retired also. In the circumstances there was little incentive, perhaps even no possibility, for choreographic experiment, and so ballet continued on its downhill path, dragged by outworn traditions.

The great dancers who had lifted their art to such a height were thus the indirect cause of its downfall, and in more ways than one. The *ballet d'action* became sterile not only through its failure to develop, but because it had been seduced by its own famous stars; their brilliance had so overwhelmed the producers that the latter neglected the ballet as an artistic whole and directed their attention to displaying each individual talent in its most favourable light. But generally the choreography of the Romantic period does not seem to have been worthy of the *danseuses*, and the cult of the supernatural was one full of danger. In *La Sylphide* its problem was

---

[1] Fanny Cerito (born Naples, 1821); Lucile Grahn (1821–1907); Carlotta Grisi (1821–99).

properly solved, for the human and the phantom, being two separate roles, were performed by dancers of different psyche. But despite all the charms of the famous *Giselle*,[1] it seems that Gautier's ardour made him ask the impossible, and lose sight of the ballet in his concentration upon Grisi. For the bucolic 'girl' in the first Act is the *Wili* in the second, and although the part is usually regarded as a test of the ballerina's dramatic powers, it actually resolves itself into a contradiction, much like expecting Le Nain to have followed up one of his *Peasant Families* with a vaporous landscape in the mood of Corot.

The *ballet d'action* might have been superseded by a splendid era of *Divertissement*—the chamber music of ballet, but the younger *danseuses*, either because they had been pushed into the background, or because their gifts were insufficient, fell far behind the standards which had been set so high; while the men, relegated to the status of *porteurs*, lost all individuality and became demoralised. One by one the latter left the country. In 1847 Marius Petipa[2] went to Russia, where a theatre for drama, opera and dancing had been organised in 1672; a state school founded under the direction of a Frenchman in 1735 and where the famous French *maître de ballet*, Didelot, had begun the real development of ballet in Russia at the beginning of the nineteenth century. Petipa was followed by Jules Perrot a year later; and just before the latter retired in 1859, Saint-Léon also arrived in St Petersburgh and produced a number of new ballets. Italy, where most of the great dancers of the Romantic era had been trained, now retained her pupils who appeared in spectacular productions at the Scala; but the Italian tendency being to sacrifice artistry to virtuosity, St Petersburg assumed the former Parisian role and became the centre of international ballet.

· · · · · ·

Cyril W. Beaumont[3] singles out only two *danseuses* of any note who were born in France after 1840. The one, Emma Livry, brilliant protegée of Taglioni, died a tragic death at the early age of twenty-one;[4] the other, Léontine Beaugrand, is of particular interest in this book, because it was in the *Ballet des Niniviennes*, in the première of the opera *Semiramis*,[5] that she began to claim the attention of the public. The opera was originally produced on the 9th July, 1860, and is the subject of Degas' first theatre picture (Pl. 1). He chose a moment in the second act, immediately preceding the ballet, with the scene set in the Hanging Gardens of Babylon; the Queen is surrounded by her woman attendants, and as the ballet begins she moves into the shade of a pavilion and seats herself upon a golden throne.[6] In the August of 1861, the ballet alone was presented at a special benefit performance given for Mme Petipa, and on this occasion

[1] *Giselle ou Les Wilis*, book by Vernoy de Saint-Georges and Théophile Gautier suggested by a passage from Heine's *De l'Allemagne*; choreography by Jean Coralli and Jules Perrot; music by Adolphe Adam. First produced Théâtre de l'Académie Royal de Musique, Paris, 28th June, 1841. Carlotta Grisi, with whom Gautier was in love, danced the title role.

[2] Marius Petipa (1822–1910); Charles Didelot (1767–1836).

[3] Cyril W. Beaumont, *op. cit.*, p. 26.   [4] See p. 66.

[5] Over twenty different operas entitled *Semiramide* were written, mostly by Italian composers, between 1671 and 1802. In 1825, Rossini wrote an opera of that name to words by Rossi; in 1860 it became *Semiramis*, was turned into a four-act opera by Mery, and a ballet with music by Carafa inserted; the *décor* was by Thierry and Cambon. Gaston Vuillier in *History of Dancing*, pub. 1898, says that Beaugrand first became famous when she made her début in the third Act of *William Tell* (Rossini) in 1860.

[6] *La Presse*, 15th July, 1860; and 12th August, 1861.

the critic of *La Presse* wrote, '. . . on applaudit toujours le brio pétillant de Mlle Beaugrand, une petite danseuse à la tête et aux pieds d'oiseau.'[1] But Mlle Beaugrand never attained international fame. Although greatly praised by Gautier and other critics, she was without the necessary influential backing and was always forced to stand aside for those with foreign names and lesser talents.

In 1866 Saint-Léon's ballet *La Source*[2] was produced, and it was this which inspired the second of Degas' theatrical subjects (Pl. 3). In it Beaugrand was given merely a minor part, the chief role of *Naila* being danced by Mme Salvioni, the second by Mlle Eugenie Fiocre as *Nouredda*. Two men, who later appeared in Degas' pictures, were also in the cast; M. Mérante as *premier danseur* in the part of *Djémil*, and M. Pluque as *Ismail*.

Paul de St Victoire wrote of Mlle Fiocre, 'Coiffée d'un bonnet en forme de Mitre, étroitement serrée dans son justaucorps d'icoglan, les jambes flottantes dans des pantalons de gaze piqué d'or, elle danse en tenant entre ses bras une haute guitare au manche élancé. C'est la réproduction à peu près exacte d'une peinture qu'on voit souvent sur les boîtes persanes. . . .'[3] This scene,[4] either before or after Nouredda's dance with the guitar, has been perpetuated, not by the Persians, but by Degas. He apparently shared Vizentini's opinion that Fiocre, tall and well formed and always appearing to pose as a model, was a fitting subject for a sculptor,[5] or—as in his case—for a painter.

In Degas' picture, Nouredda, with two attendants, is seated beside a stream from which a horse is drinking.[6] All is quiet and still and entirely devoid of the movement which later was to absorb Degas so intently. The composition is in a simple diagonal with the ballet shoes naïvely serving as a high-light between the darkness of the horse's legs. The painting in no way suggests that it was prompted by an interest in the ballet, it is just a scene upon a stage, carefully observed and faithful to fact.

In 1871 the Opéra reopened and continued the interrupted run of Saint-Léon's Coppelia.[7] Nuitter,[8] who devised the ballet from Hoffman's *Der Sandmann*, had always intended Léontine Beaugrand for the title-role, but Perrin[9] considered that a dancer with a foreign name would

[1] *La Presse*, 15th July, 1860; and 12th August, 1861.

[2] *La Source*, ballet in three acts and four scenes. Book by Nuitter and Saint-Léon; music by Minkus and Delibes; décor and costumes by Desplechin and Lavastre, and Rubé and Chaperon. First produced at Théâtre Impérial de l'Opéra, Paris, 12th November, 1866.

[3] *La Presse*, 18th November, 1866.   [4] In the first act of the ballet.

[5] *A Miscellany of Dancers*, Cyril W. Beaumont, pub. London, 1934, p. 68.

[6] The spectacle of *La Source*, according to contemporary reviews, was of more importance than the actual ballet. Real horses and water were used, and the *Figaro* of the 29th October, 1872, wrote, 'Hier soir à l'opéra, pendant la représentation du ballet, un cavalier qui figure dans le cortège n'a pu empêcher le cheval qu'il montait de se désaltérer à la source.' The same paper wrote on the 19th November, 1872, 'Tout se passe à merveille. Les chevaux eux mêmes ordinairement si inconvenants pendant le 3e Acte, se comportent ce soir le mieux du monde.' These reviews refer to a revival of the ballet in 1872. Mlle Fiocre was still dancing her permanent role of Nouredda, but Mme Salvioni's part of Naila was danced by Rita Sangalli who made her brilliant début in the ballet. Of the two leading *danseuses*, the *Figaro* wrote (6th October, 1872), 'Cette distribution indique que la Source selon le ballet est représentée par Mlle Sangalli; la Source d'après Ingres et la correction plastique le sera par Mlle Eugénie Fiocre.'

[7] *Coppelia*, ballet in 2 Acts and 3 Scenes. Book by Nuitter and Saint-Léon; music by Delibes; scenery by Cambon, Desplechin and Lavastre; costumes by Lormier; choreography by Saint-Léon. First produced Théâtre Imperial de l'Opéra, Paris, 25th May, 1870.

[8] Charles Nuitter, *archivist* of the Opéra.

[9] Emile Perrin, *Administrateur* at the Opéra in 1862, and *Directeur-entrepreneur*, April, 1866–September, 1870, see p. 46.

be a greater attraction. For once fate was kind to Beaugrand, though at the expense of a young dancer's life. Mlle Grantsova, the Russian who was originally engaged, found the rehearsals too prolonged and departed before the production was ready; while her Italian successor, the fifteen year old Bozacchi, died of the fever which raged through Paris during the siege. The management fell back on Beaugrand who made a brilliant success of the role devised for her. Mlle Fiocre danced the leading 'male' part of Franz; her figure being strong and tall, she was well-known for such travesty roles, indicative of the degeneracy into which ballet had fallen.

It is interesting to note that men dancers never appear in Degas' pictures excepting as *Maîtres de ballet*. He apparently shared the prevalent feeling of contempt for them; and his sense of propriety must have been offended by woman's assumption of a masculine role, a fact which he has stressed by the ridiculous figure of a woman in male attire and wearing a moustache in *Scène de Ballet* (Pl. 52).

Towards the end of 1871, Meyerbeer's opera *Robert le Diable*,[1] constantly played since its original presentation in 1831, was performed. The *Ballet of the Nuns*, led by Mlle Laure Fonta,[2] a dancer of little renown, gives the third title of a definite production known to have been painted by Degas. He did two versions of it (Pls. 8 and 9); the first, an 'upright', is dated 1872; the second, a few inches off the square and introducing more portraits in the foreground, is the one commissioned by M. Faure and finished in 1876. These two pictures must be studied together with *L'Orchestre de l'Opéra* (Pl. 4), which precedes them both, and *Musiciens de l'Orchestre* (Pl. 5) of the same date as the original *Robert le Diable*. All are an extraordinary advance on *Sémiramis* and *La Source* in their nice mixture of reality and illusion, the interest of their composition, and in their feeling for movement. As already pointed out, the earliest of this group is a study in collective portraiture in which the stage is merely used as a background; in the *Robert le Diable* canvases, the emphasis is more evenly divided; while in *Musiciens de l'Orchestre* it is actually reversed.

Ballet, as such, had begun to fascinate Degas. The lively and enquiring mind of the artist wanted to know more about it. If there was so much splendid material to be gathered from the front of the house, how much more must there be behind the scenes. There the dancers work, unadorned, away from public gaze, oblivious to any but the master's eye upon them. Intent upon their own strenuous efforts, they have no time to worry about an artist who might be making studies in their particular domain. And for the painter who desired to 'peep through a keyhole', who loved the 'accidental', it was all ideal.

Apart from his inherent love of music which, in any case, would have taken him to the Opéra, Degas had friends whose professions tied them to its daily life—the Halévy family of composers and dramatists, and Désiré Dihau, a bassoonist in the orchestra. They could have arranged for him to go into the classes, and they probably did, for soon he became a frequent visitor at the opera schools.

[1] *Robert le Diable*; book by Scribe, and ballet by Filippo Taglioni (1778–1871), the father of the famous Marie and also of Paul.

[2] In 1860, Mlle Zina Richards (afterwards Mme Mérante) danced the role of Helena, originally created by Taglioni. From 1865 it became Mlle Fonta's permanent part.

There he found that as much toil goes to the making of a dancer as a painter, and a good deal more sweat. He discovered that, just as he has to draw each day, repeating and correcting scores of times, observing ceaselessly, remembering gestures, tones, masses and changes of light, so the dancer must discipline herself and, like him, without becoming mechanical. Daily, in the heat or cold, whether physically inclined or not, she must work for hours at the *barre*, and then in the centre at *adage* and *allégro*—*élévation*, *batterie*, *pirouettes* and *pointes*; every part of her body needing separate attention until all can be co-ordinated; until technique, becoming so perfected, no longer requires conscious thought and all can then be given to artistry. There he realised that one vocation can be just as exciting as another, and that each in its different way calls for the same degree of application.

· · · · · ·

The year 1872 marks the beginning of the countless drawings of dancers which Degas did from life both in class and in his studio. They were used as studies for pictures subsequently painted away from the scene, a practice which he never failed to follow. Among the earliest of these drawings, small in scale, finely executed, frequently on pink paper, is that of Josephine Gaugelin (Pl. 12), one of the few to be inscribed with a name and date by Degas. The drawings of this time (Pls. 10–16a, and 18–20) lead up to the two lovely and carefully detailed little pictures of practice-classes in the rue le Peletier[1] (Pls. 16 and 17), and to the two slightly later ones (Pls. 22 and 23). Apart from their own intrinsic value, they show what use Degas made of his studies, and how in many cases he was faithful to their smallest detail.

The two earlier *Classe de Danse* paintings are quiet in feeling, subdued in colour, and—especially the one without the *maître*—minute in size. Their compositions are similar and of obvious deliberation, hence the chair in the foreground of one and the violin case in that of the other. In neither has Degas risked showing the dancer in the middle of her *pas*, instead he had modestly placed her in the preparatory position of *quatrième derrière*, while her fellow pupils stand by watching or stretching at the *barre*. In only one of the pictures is the *maître de danse* visible, and although the age of the violinist-teacher was not quite over,[2] it should not be supposed that the old man, seated with his back against the piano (Pl. 17) was acting in this dual capacity.

The *maître* who is seen taking the class in the other picture (Pl. 16) is, however, not 'M. Moraine'[3]—as some writers and even the Louvre catalogue state—but the well-known dancer and choreographer, Louis François Mérante. Born in 1828, Mérante made his *début* at the age of six, became *premier danseur* at Marseille in 1846, and two years later joined the Opéra as understudy to Lucien Petipa. From then onwards he was intimately connected with the Opéra until the time of his death in 1887. As *jeune premier* he created many roles; as choreographer he was responsible for a number of successful ballets, the two last of which were produced as late as 1886; and, at the same time as his wife was *professeur de la danse*, he succeeded Arthur Saint-

[1] Rue le Peletier, see p. 46. [2] See p. 70.
[3] There is no trace of any M. Moraine either as a dancer or as being connected with the Opéra, so it seems that the name has got muddled with the correct one of 'Mérante'.

Léon as *maître de ballet de l'Opéra*, after the latter had served for a short time in that office on his return from Russia. Degas is known to have been in touch with Mérante—if he was not actually intimate with him—according to the letter already mentioned.[1]

In these two *Classe de Danse* pictures of 1872, as in the others which were to follow, the dancers are dressed in the correct practice costume of the day; flesh tights, longish *tutus*,[2] and knickers which, tightly fitting below the knees, are much in evidence every time the leg is raised. Apparently the brightly coloured sashes around the trim little waists, as well as the inevitable black-velvet ribbon around the throat, were an artistic licence which Degas allowed himself. Mlle Suzanne Mante, despite the suggestion in the pictures *La Famille Mante* (Pls. 72 and 73), does not remember that either of these adornments were worn in class, a statement corroborated by M. Jacques Rouché.[3]

In any case it is amusing to compare this charming precision of the past with the almost deliberate carelessness of the practice costume of today. Admittedly conditions now demand practicability instead of ceremony, but it is impossible to avoid a certain nostalgia for a tradition which desired that, even in the class-room, the disciples of Terpsichore should pay her the compliment of ceremonious attire.

The two later class-room pictures (Pls. 22 and 23), which were closely followed by the well-known one in the Burrell Collection (Pl. 34), and the three dancers at their *adage* doing a *developpé à la seconde* (Pls. 35–7), are also painted in oil-colour. They are much larger both in scale and size than the earlier pair; in handling they are freer and in feeling less tender, with more individual characterisation in the figures. Also they are lighter in key and the colour seems calculated rather than felt. Both compositions are boldly diagonal, but the dancer who is working is, in the earlier of the two (Pl. 22), still in a static position (for which the drawing Pl. 10 is the identical study), while the later (Pl. 23) shows her in the middle of an *enchaînement* in the position of *attitude*.

It is generally said, but again erroneously, that the *maître* in these two pictures is Père Pluque. Actually it is the famous Jules Perrot whom Degas has painted taking a class. The latter did a drawing of him, seated and holding a stick, which he inscribed '*le danseur Perrot*'. It is reproduced in the Degas Sale catalogue[4] on the same page as another drawing entitled *Le danseur Perrot debout*; this second one is identical with the *peinture à l'essence* (Pl. 24), and as this is dated '1875' it appears to have been done from the oil-painting of 1872–4. Perrot would have been about sixty-three when Degas did his drawings of him (he was born in 1810); he returned from Russia in 1859 and lived the life of a gentleman-of-leisure in Paris. But he kept in touch with his old friends at the Opéra, and sometimes gave classes himself. It is nice to think that Degas perpetuated on canvas one of these lessons which must have been rare and highly prized experiences in the lives of those students fortunate enough to have received them.

From the very few identified photographs of Ernest Pluque, it seems probable—though

---

[1] See p. 33.

[2] *Tutu*—a ballet skirt, derives from the French slang word meaning 'bottom'.

[3] Mlle Mante (see also p. 60) and M. Jacques Rouché, former director of the Opéra, gave personal interviews to the author at their Paris homes in the summer of 1947.

[4] Third Sale, No. 157, 3.

by no means certain—that the *maître* seen in the distance in the *Classe de Danse* (Pl. 34), is this stalwart of the Opéra ballet. Père Pluque, as he is commonly known, figures in the Opéra lists as early as 1874 and as late as 1895 in the office of *Régisseur de la Danse*, in which appointment he succeeded Eugène Coralli. He occasionally danced small character parts, his first appearance at the Opéra having been in *La Source* (1866) and his last in *Deux Pigeons*[1] (1886). Evidently a stern disciplinarian, he earned another and less benign nickname, 'César' Pluque— 'Il inspire une grande terreur aux danseuses et la physique de cet homme est fait pour cela. . . . Cette physionomie respire la pédanterie, la lâcheté et la sécheresse du cœur—valet avec ses supérieurs et arrogant avec les faibles. Grossier et impoli, cet homme ne répond jamais à un bonjour ni à une salutation. . . .'[2] The *mère* in a bonnet, on the extreme right of the picture, is Degas' housekeeper, Sabine Neyt (see also Pl. 60).

But only part of the dancers' practice takes place in the class-room, and Degas followed to watch rehearsals on the Opéra stage. Between the years 1873 and 1877 he did three pictures in different mediums of this subject (Pls. 28, 30 and 31). They closely resemble the *Classe de Danse* paintings of the same time, the view, instead of being down the length of the class-room is, in their case, the breadth across the stage. With the chronological progression of these *Répétitions sur la Scene*, again came greater freedom of handling, as well as more solidity in the figures and a striking advance in the daring of the poses. Degas' fondness for using the edge of a canvas as a cut for his figures was given additional scope on stage-sets. The flats, behind which the dancers stood while waiting for their entrances, half-revealed them in unexpected ways, and when these flats represented trees or foliage, the shapes they made were particularly exciting.

Into the foreground of the two later *Répétitions* Degas has introduced the scroll of the double-bass as a pronounced feature of the composition. The origin of this interesting motif can be traced back to 1868 to the naturalistic *l'Orchestre* (Pl. 4); and Degas subsequently used it in other pictures such as *Scène de Ballet* and *Danseuse sur la Scène* (Pls. 52 and 53), in much the same way as he later used the motif of the 'Woman with a Fan' (Pls. 106, 107 and 109).

The *maître* who is taking the rehearsal in these two pictures bears a strong resemblance to Eugéne Coralli, the son and pupil of Jean Coralli. His name first appears in the Opéra casts in 1840, a year after which he danced the role of Wilfred, the Duke's Squire, in the première of *Giselle*. He became noted as a mime and, as already mentioned, was appointed to the position of *Regisseur de la Danse de l'Opéra*. It is probably M. Coralli, wearing a skull-cap, who is seen again on the extreme left of the canvas *Ecole de Danse* painted about 1876 (Pl. 36), although by then he was no longer attached to the Opéra; and who also appears, this time given white hair by Degas in the *Leçon* with dancers on the piano (Pl. 82). It has not been possible to identify either of the two figures seated in the corner of the stage in the two later versions of the *Répétitions*. The man in the top-hat is, anyhow, unrecognisable; while the one sprawling in a chair differs greatly in the two pictures and can hardly be reconciled with the model from

[1] Ballet in 3 Acts. Book by Regnier and Mérante; music by Messager; décor by Rubé, Chaperon and Lavastre; costumes by Bianchi; choreography by Mérante. First produced at the Théâtre de l'Opéra, Paris, 18th October 1886.
[2] *Mystères des Coulisses de l'Opéra* by Gabrielle Randon, pub. Paris, 1885. Pluque died in 1897.

whom the drawing was done (Pl. 31a). It might readily be assumed that he was the director of the Opéra—up to 1870 M. Emile Perrin and for the next eight years Mm. Halanzier and Dufrenoy; that he was the *Maître de Ballet*, M. Saint-Léon before 1870 and afterwards M. Mérante; or that he was one of the other of the many officials who might have been watching a rehearsal. But available photographs and engravings have failed to give information, and in the absence of inscribed drawings by Degas himself, it seems that these figures must remain anonymous.

Through the *Répétitions sur la Scène* Degas has shown himself a forerunner of a method of modern cinema direction. After the 'shot' of the *pas de deux* rehearsal from the distance of the box, he approached to take a 'close-up' of the dancers appearing in all their finery before the footlights in an almost identical position (Pl. 50); then, and this time moving still nearer, he took another 'close-up' as the dance progressed (Pl. 51). Both of these pictures were painted within a year or so of the famous *L'Étoile* (Pl. 55) and the *Danseuse sur la Pointe* (Pl. 54).

Then followed the series of *Danseuses sur la Scène* which were painted within the next ten years; the many variations on *L'Étoile* theme (Pls. 141–5 and 178); the charming *Danseuse saluant* pictures (Pls. 56–9); and the group of *Danseuses aux Cheveux Longs* (Pls. 160–5). In them the dancer no longer shares honours with audience or orchestra, but is given the whole of the canvas for her own display. She is on the stage and this is her moment, the *raison d'être* for the countless hours of patient, laborious training. If all sorts of doubts and fears assailed her while waiting in the wings for her entrance—fears particular to a dancer—the tearing of a shoe ribbon, the finding of a greasy patch on the boards, the stickiness of too much resin on the shoes, besides a natural nervousness which may discount the most perfect balance and mar the cleanest execution, once before the footlights these anxieties are hidden; she has only one canvas upon which to work and her realisation must be decisive and sure. Yet in the course of time her performance will be only legendary, while Degas' will remain to testify for or against him. And so the muses meet, the dancer's transient moment being translated by the painter into terms of an eternity.

Unfortunately it seems impossible to name the ballet being rehearsed in the *Répétitions*; the choreographic clues are far too slender, while the costumes and *décor* of the actual performance shed no further light upon the subject. Apart from the three already mentioned, and with the exception of the study from *Faust* (Pl. 124) which Degas himself has inscribed with a title, and which in any case is of lesser interest from the dancer's point of view, only three other ballets, one in 1884, a second in 1886 and a third in 1909 are identifiable in the whole of Degas' work. The picture in the Louvre (Pl. 56) is usually referred to as the *Ballet de l'Africaine*,[1] but it is puzzling to know how this title originated because, according to his custom, Degas, preferring the *tutu*, has ignored the designer's costumes; while the backcloth and 'props' bear

[1] *L'Africaine*, opéra by Meyerbeer, text by Scribe (original title *Vasco da Gama*), was produced in Paris in 1865, a year after the composer's death. It was continually presented at the Opéra and by 1892 had reached its 468th performance there. It should not be supposed that, irrespective of their themes, the ballets of the time were performed in *tutus*. All the more important ones had their appropriate costumes, the designs of which may be seen in the Musée de l'Opéra, together with the *décors*. With the exception of Faust (Pl. 124) and the pastels of *Danseuses Russes* (Pls. 242 and 243) Degas has chosen to dress his dancers in ballet skirts.

no resemblance whatsoever to those used in *L'Africaine*, in fact they could rather be reconciled with Cheret's décor for *Le Roi de Lahore*.[1] But even this possibility must be discounted, for the original production took place in April 1877, the very month in which Degas' pastel was exhibited in the third Impressionist exhibition, and as this contemporary catalogue lists the picture simply *Ballet*, there seems to be no other means of ascertaining the title of its original inspiration.

.   .   .   .   .   .

Between the burning of the rue le Peletier opéra house in the autumn of 1873 and the opening of Garnier's building in January 1875, both the performances and classes were held at the Salle Ventadour. But for the first eight months the Opéra had to share the premises with the Théâtre-Italian and therefore being limited to only three days a week, it was unable to stage its more ambitious productions until the second company had ended its season. Sangalli[2] had gone away from Paris, so the management once again fell back on Léontine Beaugrand, and for the second time she became *première danseuse*, appearing in *Coppélia*[3] and in the new production of *l'Esclave*.[4] But her fortune was short-lived. Garnier's Opéra opened with a gala performance which included acts from *La Juive*,[5] *Huguenots*[6] and *La Source*, and for this last named ballet, Sangalli was recalled. Beaugrand, disheartened by such treatment and even worse which was to follow, prematurely retired in 1880, leaving her rival and a new-comer, Rosita Mauri, to dance the roles she should have filled.

In 1876 Mérante's ballet *Sylvia* was produced with Sangalli, Marquet and Sanlaville dancing in it; in 1878 Rosita Mauri made her *début* in Gounod's opera-ballet *Polyeucte*; in 1879 Mérante's Japanese flavoured *Yedda* had its première; and in the following year Mauri created the 'star' role in *La Korrigane*. 1881 saw the *début* of Subra in the *Hamlet divertissement*; and in 1882 Lucien Petipa's *Namouna* and also *François da Rimini* were produced. In 1883 there were *Henry VIII* and Mérante's *La Farandole*; in 1885 *Sigurd* and *Le Cid*, and in 1886 *Les Deux Pigeons* with Mauri, Sanlaville and Hirsch.[7]

[1] *Le Roi de Lahore*. Opéra in 5 Acts and 6 Scenes. Libretto by Louis Gallet; music by Massenet. Produced Théâtre de l'Opéra, April 1877. Ballet in 3rd Act, choreography by Mérante.

[2] Rita Sangalli, the Italian dancer (born Milan 1849).

[3] *Coppélia ou la Fille aux yeux d'Email*. Ballet in 2 Acts and 3 Scenes. Book by Nuitter and Saint-Léon; music by Delibes; choreography by Mérante. First produced Théâtre Imperial de l'Opéra, Paris, May 1870.

[4] *L'Esclave*. Opera in 4 Acts and 5 Scenes; libretto by Foussier and Got; music by Membrée. Produced Théâtre National de l'Opéra, July 1874. Ballet in 3rd Act, choreography by Mérante.

[5] *La Juive*. Opera in 5 Acts; libretto by Scribe; music by Halévy. Produced l'Académie Royale de Musique, February 1835. Ballet in 3rd Act; choreography by Filippo Taglioni.

[6] *Les Huguenots*. Opera in 5 Acts; libretto by Scribe and Deschamps; music by Meyerbeer. Produced l'Académie Royale de Musique, February 1836. Ballet in 5th Act; choreography by Filippo Taglioni.

[7] *Sylvia ou la Nymphe de Diane*. Ballet in 3 Acts and 4 Scenes; book by Barbier and Baron de Reinach; music by Delibes; décor by Cheret, Rubé and Chaperon; costumes by Lacoste.

Polyeucte. Opera-ballet in 5 Acts; adapted from tragedy by Corneille; music by Gounod. Ballet in 3rd Act; choreography by Mérante.

Yedda. Ballet in 3 Acts; book by Gille, Mortier and Mérante; music by Métra; décor by Lavastre senior and junior and Carpezat.

La Korrigane. Ballet in 2 Acts; book by Coppé and Mérante; music by Widor; décor by Lavastre, Rubé and Chaperon; costumes by Lacoste.

Hamlet. First produced in 1868. Opera in 5 Acts; music by Ambroise Thomas. Ballet in 4th Act, choreography by Petipa.

[*continued* on p. 58

DEGAS AND THE BALLET

On the occasion of *Les Fêtes de l'Industrie et du Commerce Parisien* a special gala performance *L'Histoire du Théâtre* was given at the Opéra on the 26th January 1886. *Les Jumeaux de Bergame—Théâtre Italien* after Florian, was presented with a prologue written by Théodore de Banville and spoken by Coquelin l'Aîné. Mérante was responsible for the choreography and it was the Harlequinade in the first act of this ballet which prompted another series of pastels by Degas. In these Mme Subra is easily recognisable as *Coraline* (Pl. 171); while it is probably *Harlequin junior*—Alice Biot—who is flirting with 'his' mask (Pl. 169) and *Harlequin senior*—Sanlaville[1]—who is seen with 'his' threatening sword (Pls. 170 and 171).

. . . . . .

Sometime between 1879 and 1884, the period of M. Vaucorbeil's directorship of the Opéra, Degas wrote to his and Manet's friend, Albert Hecht, 'Avez-vous le *pouvoir* de me faire donner par l'Opéra une entrée pour le jour de *l'examen de danse*, qui doit être jeudi, à ce que l'on me dit? J'en ai tant fait de ces examens de danse, sans les avoir vu (sic) que j'en suis un peu honteux;' and a few days later, '. . . Je pensais me glisser dans l'Opéra, au milieu des mères, avec un petit papier, et vous voulez me conduire vous-même aux pieds de Mr Vaucorbeil.'[2]

According to the dancer's contract on entry into the Opéra, it is stated: 'Il y aura chaque année un ou deux examens, tant pour se rendre compte de la situation des classes, que pour donner de l'avancement aux élèves et combler les vides qui auraient pu se produire. Le directeur en fixera le jour.'[3] But it is evident that when Degas wrote his letters he had never seen an examination, and that after he had done so—presuming that he did—he never painted the subject. For despite the fact that this title has been given to some of his pictures (it appears in both the first and second Impressionist exhibitions) there does not seem to be one which conforms with the actual facts.

Mlle Mante says that this examination day was the most terrifying of the whole year for the dancer. In front of a large examining board which included the director, the *maître de ballet*, the *régisseur de la danse*, the *professeurs* of various classes, and other favoured personages, all of whom sat in the front rows of the stalls; besides the mothers and kindly *concièrges des artistes* allowed into the darkness of the boxes; the dancer, all alone on the enormous empty stage, and

Namouna. Ballet in 2 Acts and 3 Scenes; book by Nuitter and L. Petipa; music by Lalo; décor by Rubé, Chaperon and Lavastre; costumes by Lacoste.

Françoise da Rimini. Opera in 4 Acts; music by Ambroise Thomas; Ballet in 3rd Act: choreography by Mérante.

Henry VIII. Opera in 4 Acts and 5 Scenes; music by Saint Saëns. Ballet in 2nd Act, choreography by Mérante.

La Farandole. Ballet in 2 Acts and 3 Scenes; book by Gille, Mortier and Mérante; music by Dubois; décor by Rubé, Chaperon and Lavastre.

Sigurd. Opera in 4 Acts and 9 Scenes; libretto by du Lode and Blau; music by Reyer. Ballet in 2nd and 3rd Acts; choreography by Mérante.

Le Cid. Opera in 4 Acts and 10 Scenes; libretto by Ennery, Gallet and Blau; music by Massenet. Ballet in 2nd Act; choreography by Mérante.

Les Deux Pigeons. Ballet in 3 Acts; book by Regnier and Mérante; music by Messager; décor by Rubé, Chaperon and Lavastre; costumes by Bianchini; choreography by Mérante.

[1] Mlle Sanlaville was the danseuse to whom Degas dedicated one of his sonnets. Another was dedicated to Mme Caron, the Brunehilde in *Sigurd*. See p. 71 note 2.

[2] *Lettres de Degas*, 1945, *op. cit.*, pp. 63–64.

[3] *Engagement de l'élève*, consulted in the Archives Nationales, Paris.

to the thin accompaniment of a single piano, had to undergo her test. 'C'était vraiment froid' was Mlle Mante's summing up of these dreaded days which, even more than the public performances, were nerve-racking alike both to *sujet* and *rat*.

.   .   .   .   .   .

Apart from the fact that there could have been little of pictorial value in the spectacle of a small lone figure on a vast, barren stage, without even the help of any lighting effects, Degas must have infinitely preferred the dancers off their guard in the class-rooms. And although he painted numerous pictures *sur la Scène*, they were easily outnumbered by those behind stage such as the *Danseuse dans sa Loge* (Pls. 60, 61 and 62); *Dans les Coulisses* (Pls. 63, 64, 132, 136, 138, 139, 174, 175, 179–81, 208, 210–3, 224–31 and 244); those of the dancers in relaxation between their work; as well as the pictures and hundreds of studies at practice.

Perhaps it is only a professional who can fully appreciate the depth of Degas' understanding of the fundamental characteristics which mark the classical ballet dancer. There is a particular air, a way of carriage, a certain kind of seriousness which stamps her all over and makes her recognisable even in out-door clothes. It is precisely this that he has realised, whereas other painters of the ballet, like Carriere-Belleuse, Henri Meyer, Paul Destez and Renouard, apart from artistic considerations, have hopelessly failed. Besides this, Degas' technical knowledge obviously went beyond the bounds of superficiality; every single attitude, whether hesitant or assured, is the attitude of a dancer according to her experience; and that he went to some pains to enlarge his knowledge is apparent in the remarks which he has written on some of his drawings, a reminder to him of the different names of the movements, as well as their errors in execution. On one of the drawings of a small girl who is making a pathetic attempt at an exercise which requires control far beyond her years, he has written its technical name of *battements sur les pointes à la barre* (Pl. 76); on another, *battements à la seconde à la barre* (Pl. 77), he has written the justifiable criticism 'bien arrondir l'os du coude'; but he has not failed to notice how beautifully the legs are 'turned' from the thighs and how the little girl, instead of keeping her eyes in front, could not resist the temptation of looking round to see whether all was well with her leg and her arm. A third drawing of the same young dancer[1] is inscribed '*ronds de jambe à terre*' (Pl. 78), and there are other numerous drawings (Pls. 105, 122, 127 and 146–151) which bear the names of the movements or pertinent remarks as to their execution; they only relate to the practice of the dance and therefore in the later drawings when this form of art has become subjected to Degas' own, they do not appear at all.

A dancer forms the habit of taking advantage of every minute once she is dressed in the attire of her profession, so that even in moments of repose she cannot allow herself to relax, but will, almost subconsciously, find herself 'turning out' her thighs, stretching her instep, forcing her *pointes* or pulling back her shoulders. These characteristics are especially noticeable in the two seated dancers (Pls. 99, 206 and 207); *Danseuse Rose* (Pl. 200) and *La Jupe Verte* (Pl. 202); in *Sept Danseuses dans la Salle de Danse* (Pl. 177); in *Trois Danseuses se preparant à la Classe* (Pl. 185); and in *La Danseuse de Quatorze Ans*, as well as in its studies; but they are also apparent

---

[1] Mlle Mante says her name was Dugés, and it is confirmed by Degas in his inscription on Pl. 78.

in other pictures too numerous to mention. Degas' trained observation has seized upon all these intimacies, nothing has remained unnoticed, and that is why his pictures are as true in fact as they are in spirit to the art he has chosen to depict.

. . . . . .

It would be of enormous interest if it were possible to identify more of the dancers who appear in Degas' pictures, but as this has not been done by writers of his own or even of the next generation, it is difficult to see how it can be accomplished at this stage, especially as Degas himself has left such scanty information. As far as is known he has inscribed the names of only four different dancers on his drawings, and in three cases they are dancers of no importance who would probably never have been heard of but through their connection with him. One is a Josephine Gaugelin, 'autrefois danseuse à l'Opéra puis actrice au Gymnase'; Degas has drawn her full-length in a ballet skirt (Pl. 12) and also done a bust of her wearing outdoor clothes (Pl. 17a). It seems very possible that it is she who figures in both the early *Classe de Danse* pictures (Pls. 16 and 17) as there is certainly a facial resemblance between the pupil about to perform and the small study of Mme Gaugelin's head.[1] But it is easy to romance on such a theme and to be persuaded that there are far more interesting likenesses than those of this unknown dancer, it is therefore important merely to state the possibilities in the absence of more definite proof. Another, who is known only through the drawings Degas did of her in 1878, is a Melina Darde (15 ans, d'aujourdhui à la Gaiété, Pl. 68); it is obviously she who appears in various other drawings (Pls. 66, 67 and 69); while the third is the little Dugés already mentioned. There is also a Mlle Malo of whom Degas did several portraits (Pl. 56a).[2] Two dancers of this name appear in the Opéra lists but neither was of any importance and it is therefore not known which sat for Degas.

But now come names of some standing in the Opéra ballet of the last quarter of the nineteenth century. *La Famille Mante* of 1880 (Pl. 72) is one of the most endearing of Degas' earlier pastels, and may have been suggested to him by Halévy's *Les Petits Cardinal* published in the same year, for both the picture and the book relate to a family whose two daughters were dancers in that theatre.[3] But the Mante family was actually more involved than this, for its whole life circulated round the Opéra where *le père* Mante was a bassoonist in the orchestra, and where all the three daughters of the family, Louise, Blanche and Suzanne, entered the classes as young children. *La Famille Mante* and its rather 'ugly sister' (Pl. 73) show Mme Mante dressing Suzanne in preparation for her class, while Blanche stands by, a quaint little figure in her now curiously old-fashioned clothes. Suzanne was seven years old at the time—her sister a little older, but now she only remembers Degas in later years as a quiet, kind old man who wore blue spectacles to protect his eyes, and who used to stand at the top or bottom of the many staircases in the building, drawing the dancers as they rushed up and down. She says that he used to ask them to pause for a moment, just as they stood, in order that he could make some quick sketches of them (Pls. 38a and 45a). Degas was fascinated by the effect of figures on the stairs (Pls. 34 and 45), and together with the rest of the paraphernalia found in the studio after his death, there was, besides his tub, a small model of a spiral staircase.

[1] See note to Pl. 20.   [2] See note to Pl. 56a.   [3] See pp. 34 and 69.

DEGAS AND THE BALLET

La Famille Mante was painted about 1880, and five years later, at the age of twelve, Suzanne made her *début* in *Le Cid*. By 1897 she had become a *premier sujet*, and both she and Blanche remained at the Opéra to become *professeurs des classes de danse des jeunes élèves*. On the 26th September 1931, *Comoedia* wrote of Mlle Blanche Mante, '. . . le nouveau professeur des classes enfantines reste toujours l'une des deux petites filles de *La Famille Mante*. . . . Le Bon Théo (Gautier) disparu, c'est Degas qui viendra assurer la liaison entre deux phrases de la danse théâtrale; dans un tableau à Londres, le peintre fixa sur la toile le blafard vertige du sépulcral ballet des Nonnes dans *Robert le Diable*, ce prototype du romantisme chorégraphique. . . .'

Besides the Mantes, there is Mlle Sangalli whom Degas mentions in a letter written from New Orleans in November 1872 to Désiré Dihau, '. . . Mlle Sangalli restera l'hiver sans doute. Je pourrai donc en jouir à mon retour,'[1] and of whom he drew a portrait in outdoor clothes (Pl. 39*a*). He also writes about other dancers in his correspondence. Of Mlle Salle he also did some portrait studies; one in 1886 of three different views of her head (this is the fourth dancer whose name is inscribed, Pl. 184*a*); and a bust, apparently done a little later, of her in ballet costume (Pl. 173*a*). The Opéra records show that Mlle Salle was dancing there between the years 1888 and 1919, but this former date simply implies that by this time she had already served her several years apprenticeship, first as a *jeune fille élève externe*, then in the second or first *quadrille*. In 1895 her name is included in a list of *seconds sujets* and she is mentioned as having danced in *L'Etoile* (1897), *La Burgonde* (1898) and *La Ronde des Saisons* (1905).[2] A contemporary writer describes her in terms of doubtful flattery: 'Elle se consacre volontiers aux travestis. Le costume masculin convient, d'ailleurs, à son tempérament quelque peu fougueux; la danse ne lui suffit pas et elle pratique avec entrain la bicyclette, l'escrime et autres sports.'[3]

In 1883 Degas wrote a letter to Ludovic Halévy in which he mentions that both Mlle Salle and Mlle Sacré have had their contracts renewed. This letter, together with a previous one, concerns the future of a young dancer, Mlle Chabot, who at this time was nineteen years old and had been at the Opéra since the age of eight. She had asked Degas to help in her promotion, and he wrote with amused understanding: 'Vous devez savoir ce que c'est qu'une danseuse qui veut qu'on parle pour elle. Elle revient deux fois par jour savoir si on a vu, si on a écrit. Êtes vous mieux? Si vous en avez le courage ou la force écrivez un mot à Vaucorbeil, à Mérante non sur ses appointements, ce qui serait bête, mais sur sa danse et son passé, et son avenir. Je n'avais pas encore idée d'une pareille enragée. Et elle veut que ce soit de suite. Et elle vous prendrait dans ses bras avec une couverture et vous porterait à l'Opéra, si elle pouvait.'[4] Halévy's efforts were apparently only partly successful, for although Josephine Chabot was also re-engaged for a period of three years, the salary of 2,400 frs. rising by 300 frs. each year did

[1] *Lettres de Degas*, 1945, *op. cit.*, p. 20.

[2] *L'Etoile*. Opera-bouffe in 3 Acts; libretto by Literrier and Vanloo; music by Chabrier. Produced Bouffes Parisiens, November 1877.

La Burgonde. Opera in 4 Acts; libretto by Bergerat and de Saint-Croix; music by Vidal. Produced Théâtre de l'Opéra, December 1898. Ballet in 2nd Act, choreography by J. Hansen.

La Ronde des Saisons. In 3 Acts and 7 Scenes; music by Henri Büsser; argument by J. Hansen. Produced Théâtre de l'Opéra, 1905.

[3] *Figaro Illustré*, numéro spécial, *l'Opéra*, February 1895, p. 36.

[4] *Lettres de Degas*, 1945, *op. cit.*, pp. 72–73.

not satisfy her. She had been a *sujet* for the past three years, had had an increase after each examination, and thought she now merited more than was offered to her. Degas wrote all this to Halévy, again asking his friend to help the young dancer, whereas he might easily have lost patience, thinking he had done enough. In 1890 Chabot appeared as *premier sujet* in Saint-Saëns' *Ascanio*, in which Désiré and Lobstein also danced; in Gastinel's *Le Rêve* of the same year, and with Zambelli in *Hellé* in 1896.[1]

One other dancer whose name Degas mentions with enthusiasm is Mlle Alice Biot.[2] It was she who created Andrikes in Petipa's *Namouna* of 1882, the ballet in which Sangalli danced the title role, Mérante the *jeune premier*—at the age of fifty-four!—and Pluque the 'gorgeous pirate'.

It would not be unreasonable to suppose, on the contrary it seems highly probable, that some or all of these dancers posed for Degas on more than one occasion. But despite much research and comparison with identified photographs, it has only been possible to suggest a few pictures for which they acted as models. M. André Levinson writes that as well as Mérante and Pluque, other dancers may be recognised in Degas' work, and he quotes 'l'espiègle Mlle Salle, la mime Salandri et la fringante Mlle Hirsch, personnages que le peintre place avec une visible prédilection au centre de ses toiles. . . .'[3] It is a great pity that M. Levinson has not gone further and cited the actual canvases in which these dancers may be found.

Mlle Mante is of the opinion that the dancer who appears in the group of pastels, *Danseuses aux cheveux longs* (Pls. 160–5), is the Belgian, Mlle van Goeuthen who, as well as Mlle Lobstein, had such a beautiful head of hair that she always danced with it hanging down her back. These pastels were painted between the years 1884 and 1888, and *Ces Demoiselles de l'Opéra*,[4] published in 1883, gives strength to Mlle Mante's suggestion, for of Mlle van Goeuthen it is said: 'Un modèle, pour les peintres. Elle fréquentait volontiers la brasserie des Martys, le café de la Nouvelle-Athènes et l'estaminet du Rat-Mort.' Moreover, Coquiot speaks of her as an illustrious dancer who often posed for Degas.[5] Both Mlles van Goeuthen and Lobstein became *sujets* at the Opéra where they remained until 1914 and 1910 respectively.

During the 'eighties and 'nineties, Rosita Mauri was the Parisians' favourite ballerina. Her most famous role was Yvonette in *La Korrigane* which, originally presented in 1880, was subsequently performed more than a hundred times. It was the unaccustomed realism of this ballet which at first caused such dismay among the *corps de ballet*, some of whom burst into tears, protesting that they would look like servants when their charming Breton peasant caps were shown to them in the place of their usual flower or butterfly fantasies.[6] In 1885 Mauri created the role of Gourouli in *Les Deux Pigeons*, concerning which *le Figaro* wrote: 'By good fortune we find her (Mauri) again in the second act, with her magnificent black tresses flowing over her

---

[1] *Ascanio*. Opera in 5 Acts and 6 Scenes; libretto by Gallet; music by Saint-Saens; ballet in 3rd Act, choreography by J. Hansen. Produced 1890

Le Rêve. Ballet in 2 Acts and 3 Scenes, choreography by J. Hansen. Produced l'Opéra, 1890.

Hellé. Opera in 4 Acts; libretto by du Locle and Nuitter; music by Duvernoy; ballet in 2nd Act, choreography by J. Hansen. First produced 1896.

[2] *Lettres de Degas*, 1945, *op. cit.*, p. 104.

[3] *Comœdia*, 26th September, 1931. (Melanie Hirsch, born Paris, 15th October, 1868. Entered the Opéra at age of eight.)

[4] Written by Jane Hugard after Prod'homme, p. 195.

[5] Gustav Coquiot, *op. cit.*, p. 76.   [6] *Figaro Illustré*, *op. cit.*

shoulders, whose whiteness emerges from a firecoloured bodice. . . .'[1] So it seems that the fashion of dancing with hair flowing instead of neatly piled upon the head was one of the period rather than of the individual dancer.

.   .   .   .   .   .

In a minor role in his ballet *Les Deux Pigeons*, Mérante, after the closest association with the Opéra for a period of thirty-eight years, danced his adieu to Paris audiences. His death brought to its final close the great chapter of French ballet of the nineteenth century. Too young to have participated in the height of its glory, and not big enough to have stayed its decline, he continued its traditions and upheld its dignity despite the many difficulties which beset a fast changing era. Of this time Mlle Berthe Bernay, a former dancer at the Opéra, wrote: 'A few years ago the ballet was the greatest of delights to the playgoer. Today it holds a very subordinate position. The ballet seems no longer in request and its place in our principal theatre is becoming more and more restricted. . . . Elsewhere it has had to make way for the singular, but sometimes charming dances introduced by artistes such as the Barrison sisters, the Martyns, Mlle Englantine and many others. . . .'[2] The scene had changed indeed, from the Opéra to the Folies Bergères, the Jardin de Paris and the Moulin Rouge; the idols of the Parisian *galants* were no longer stars of the classical ballet, but Loie Fuller, Eglantine, Jane-Avril and La Goulue. The faithful Degas had no eyes for these newcomers, but nevertheless they found their own apostle—if a somewhat unorthodox one—in the person of his passionate admirer, Toulouse-Lautrec. And while Degas continued to make authentic ballet 'un pretexte pour le dessin', Lautrec flung himself into the world of wild eccentricities of which these new dancers were a telling expression.

But Degas had one final tribute to pay to ballet itself. In 1909, Diaghilev's company took Paris by storm. The great impresario had gathered around him such an incredible assemblage of dancers, choreographers, composers and designers, that although its appearance was awaited with the keenest anticipation, it actually surpassed the wildest of hopes, and even the critics admitted the inadequacy of words with which to express their full admiration. That Degas was equally moved by the strength of the performance is proved by his immediate response. For after a period of more than twenty years when he painted no actual *Scène de Ballet*, and despite the infirmities of blindness and old age, he could not resist a last pictorial appreciation.

The season opened at the Théâtre de Chatelet on the 19th May with three of Fokine's ballets, *Le Pavillon d'Armide*, *The Polovtsian Dances* from *Prince Igor*, and *Le Festin*. The latter was included because *Cléopatre* was not ready and because it was thought advisable to present one entirely Russian production on the opening night. In June *Les Sylphides* and *Cléopatre* were performed, and in the following year the company, this time at the Opéra, enlarged its repertoire with *Schéhérazade*, *Carnaval*, *L'Oiseau de Feu* and *Giselle*.

All but the last named of the ballets were created by Fokine, but they serve only as an indication of this fine dancer's great achievement which places him as one of the greatest

---

[1] *Complete Book of Ballets*, by Cyril W. Beaumont, pub. London, 1937, p. 627.
[2] *La Danse au Théâtre*, Bernay, 1890.

choreographers of all time, and certainly the supreme master of his art in the first half of this century. Beyond all this, Fokine was a reformer whose status equalled Noverre's: he believed 'that ballet must have complete unity of expression, a unity which is made up of a harmonious blending of three elements, music, painting and plastic art', and as these ideals were shared by Diaghilev, ballet reached a state of such perfect integration that it seems doubtful whether it will ever again be achieved in a similar form.

The names of the dancers are breath-taking; they included Pavlova, Karsavina, Rubinstein, Fokina, Nijinska, Fedorova and Lopoukova; and amongst the men Nijinsky, Bolm, Fokine, Mordkin, Novikov, Volinin and Cecchetti. The music of Borodin, Chopin, Arensky, Schumann and Rimsky-Korsakov was used, that of *L'Oiseau de Feu* being especially composed by the young Igor Stravinsky. The two great designers Bakst and Benois were responsible for most of the décor and costumes, and so after a period of some seventy years Paris witnessed the revival of the Classical ballet, perfect in its parts and united in its whole.

In an article on ballet sculpture, M. Arsène Alexandre wrote of Degas' *Grande Danseuse*[1] (Pls. 96 and 97): 'Ce chef-d'œuvre est rentré à l'atelier de l'artiste. Espérons que son hautain dédain de son temps n'aura pas induit l'auteur à détruire ou à laisser se perdre son œuvre.' But Degas' 'hautain dedain de son temps' could not withstand the *Ballet Russe*. *Le Festin*, a suite of Russian dances in national costume and based on Russian folklore, with its fire and vitality the like of which he had never seen, prompted the group of pastels, *Danseuses Russes* (Pls. 242–3). M. Alexandre Benois and M. Serge Grigorieff, whose intimate knowledge gives authority to their opinion,[2] both confirm the fact. M. Benois writes: 'C'est très probable que votre supposition soit juste et que ce tableau ait été suggéré par l'impression produite sur le maître par un numéro du divertissement, le Festin, danse sur la musique du Hopak de Moussorgski, avec Mme Fedorova en tête.' But, M. Benois continues, Degas has certainly added something of his own 'puis qu'il a translaté l'action en plein air ''dans les steppes'', et les couleurs mêmes des costumes ne me paraissaient pas être identiques à ceux qui figuraient à notre spectacle.' While M. Grigorieff is quite certain, for he says: '. . . the movement—*pas*—and the costumes are definitely taken from the *Gopak* dance in the ballet *Le Festin*, as it was produced in Diaghilev's first season in Paris.'

And so these pastels of 1909 represent a swan-song in the long partnership of painter and dancer, and the latter may derive some satisfaction from the knowledge that, although the hour was late, Degas just lived to see the finest flowering of her art.

---

[1] M. Alexandre was referring to *La Petite Danseuse de Quatorze Ans.* which is the largest of Degas' sculpture.

[2] Alexandre Benois, the famous stage designer, was responsible for some of the costumes in *Le Festin*, whose production is said to have been his idea.

Serge Grigorieff, for many years Diaghilev's 'right-hand' in his capacity as *Régisseur*. A sympathetic description of him is given in *The Diaghilev Ballet in London* by Cyril W. Beaumont, pub. London, 1940, pp. 238–3.

Both M. Benois and M. Grigorieff stated their opinions in letters to the author as a result of her having sent them a coloured reproduction of one of the pastels in question.

DEGAS AND THE OPERA

T he Paris Opéra boasts an uninterrupted history of just under three hundred years. Despite various political vicissitudes and the loss of several of its homes—mostly occasioned by fire—it had become so important a part of cultural life that its performances were never allowed to lapse for long.

Introduced into France in 1650 by Mazarin, as a result of his visit to the principal theatres of Italy, it was established by Perrin and Cambert in 1671. The patent of the Royal Académie de Musique had originally been granted to the Abbé Perrin, but as he was deprived of his 'privilege' by the intrigues of Lully, Louis XIV in 1672 directed the latter to inaugurate a school for the training of dancers, singers and instrumentalists to be incorporated with the Académie Royale de Musique et de Danse. Since then opera and ballet have been so closely linked that it is almost impossible to speak of one without automatically including the other.

From its inception the Opéra's title has fluctuated in accordance with the varying regimes. It has been known by such names as Académie Royale, Opéra Nationale, Académie Nationale and Académie Impériale; and although today it is popularly called Théatre de l'Opéra, the name which appears on the structure of Garnier's building is L'Académie de Musique et de Danse.

. . . . . .

Before the advent of electricity, fire was the theatre's greatest enemy. The Opéra had already known many different homes when, situated in the Palais Royal, it was burnt down in 1763. Eighteen years later, when established in the Second Salle de Palais Royal on a site given by the Duke of Orléans, the building was again destroyed. It was this fire, on the night of the 8th June, 1781, which was the subject of Hubert Robert's painting now in the Musée de l'Opéra.

Until the Salle de la Porte-Saint-Martin was ready, the Opéra was temporarily housed in the Salle des Menus-Plaisirs where it made its home until 1794, when it was moved to the rue de Richelieu, on the site which is now the Square Louvois. It was in this theatre that, for the first time, the audience was seated *au parterre*.

After attending a performance in February 1820, the Duc de Berri was assassinated as he was handing his duchess into her carriage. The theatre was pulled down in accordance with the demands made by the Archbishop of Paris who, having administered the holy sacrament in a profane building, therefore required its immediate demolition. Once again the Opéra was homeless, and between April 1820 and August 1821 it gave its performances in the Salle Favart and Salle Louvois.

The August of 1821 saw the inauguration of the Salle de la rue Le Peletier, the theatre which was to witness the rise and fall of the Romantic ballet; the revolutionary development

E

65

of lighting and stage mechanism, as well as the historic events of 1870. It had been built by Debret in the gardens of the former l'Hôtel de Choiseul, and considering the haste with which it was erected, it is said to have been fairly presentable from the outside but with an interior rich and full of taste and with an especially splendid *foyer*.[1] Le Peletier was meant only as a temporary home for the Opéra, but as it lasted for over half a century it proved to be more permanent than most of its predecessors. By 1868 its foundations had begun to sink, so that the fire which eventually destroyed it on the night of the 28th October was not, despite the sorrow of its patrons, a great tragedy in itself. What was far more serious was the enormous loss of material: the *décors* of fifteen works—almost its entire repertoire, nearly twelve orchestral scores, just on six thousand costumes and all its musical instruments.[2] But fortunately the fire broke out just before midnight after the artists and personnel had gone, and although it became so violent as seriously to threaten the adjoining building, only one fireman lost his life.

But the Nouvel Opéra had already been in the course of construction for eleven years. For in 1858 an attack was made on the Emperor and Empress as their carriage drew up before the Salle de la rue Le Peletier, whose confined space made such attempts particularly dangerous. They escaped unharmed, but it was then and there decided no longer to postpone the building of the new Académie on a more appropriate site. The project was made an open competition and in 1862 the stone of Garnier's immense building was laid.

It was in the Salle de la rue Le Peletier, on the night of the 6th February 1822, that lighting by gas was first used in the Opéra, and indeed in the whole of France. The tallow candles of Lulli had been replaced by the wax candles of Rameau, the latter by the Argand lamps of Gluck, and these by the *Lampe Merveilleuse* whose brilliant light so shocked the amateurs of the theatre that for some time many of them regretted the progress of science and longed for the candles of past eras. Yet, despite the protection of wire cages, hardly a year passed that a fire more or less serious did not break out, in fact the danger continued so great a menace that in 1859 a solution was invented which, sprayed on costumes and scenery rendered them noninflammable. But this chemical discoloured everything and so detracted from the charm of the snowy *tutu*, that the brilliant young dancer, Emma Livry, whose name has already been mentioned, refused to submit to its spray and as a result was burnt to death at the age of twenty-one.

During a period when all kinds of mechanical devices were employed in order to make productions as spectacular as possible, accidents were by no means limited to outbreaks of fire. One of the most revolutionary experiments in both décor and lighting was that devised by M. Duponchel[3] for the third act of *Robert le Diable*. The scene (Pls. 8 and 9) represented a vaulted cloister lit by the eerie light of the moon, through the arches of which the nuns, dark and ghostly, rose from their tombs and danced. The then extraordinary effect of moonlight was obtained by enclosing gas jets in boxes suspended from the 'flies'. But one night the dramatic spell was broken. A box fell with a crash on to the stage narrowly missing Mme Dorus-Gras

---

[1] Eugène Lami painted a watercolour *Foyer de la Danse—rue Le Peletier* in 1841 which is reproduced in *Eugène Lami* by P. A. Lemoisne, 1912, p. 96.

[2] The bust of Gluck by Houdon, and another of Lully, both saved from the fire of 1781, were destroyed.

[3] The architect, M. Duponchel, succeeded Dr Véron as Director of the Opéra in 1835. He later shared his directorship first with M. Monnais, then with M. Léon Pillet, and finally, until 1849, with M. Nestor Roqueplan.

who was singing the role of Alice; later an enormous piece of 'cloud' broke loose and would have injured Taglioni, lying on her tombstone, had she not quickly noticed it and jumped aside; while in the fifth act, the singer Nourrit[1] disappeared by mistake through a trap door. These various accidents so unnerved Taglioni that she asked M. Véron[2] to find another dancer in her place.

Degas saw his first operas and ballets in the Salle de la rue Le Peletier, and engravings confirm that his *Répétitions* (Pls. 28, 30 and 31) show the stage of this theatre although the two later versions, at any rate, were painted after the building was burnt down. It is also certain that all the *Classe de Danse* pictures painted against a background of long french windows were done from studies made in the rue Le Peletier. As no architectural plans or engravings of the class-rooms seem to have been preserved, it is not possible to say—although it would appear likely—that a spiral staircase, connecting the lower rooms with those above, actually existed. But from the many engravings of the exterior it is clear that otherwise Degas' class-rooms coincide with all architectural details. Moreover, neither the Salle Ventadour—occupied temporarily by the Opéra for one year—nor the Nouvel Opéra, was built in garden surroundings; and while there is very little pictorial evidence as to the structure of the former, only one class-room in Garnier's building has windows at all, the rest being lit from sky-lights above. Contrary to general belief, it has only been possible to trace one *Classe de Danse* painted by Degas in the present opera house, and this was done in the circular room right at the top of the building which has round windows in the nature of a ship's portholes.[3] Of the later *Classe de Danse* pictures (Pls. 114, 116, 116a, 118, 120 and 120a) it is impossible to ascertain whether the narrow enclosed room opening out to a wider one with windows and posts actually existed or whether it was simply a creation of Degas'.

During the September Revolution the Opéra closed its doors; Perrin handed in his resignation to the new government; and, as in the days before the Empire, l'Académie Impériale again became l'Académie Nationale. Towards October 1870, several theatres reopened to give performances for charity, and the opera artists, having remained in Paris, formed themselves into a society with Perrin's co-operation and were given permission to hold a series of concerts, the first to be in aid of the victims of the Château fire. These concerts began on the 6th November, the singers were dressed in out-door clothes and for the first time in the Opéra's history, women members of the audience were seated in the orchestra stalls.

With the advent of the Commune the Opéra closed again and this time few of its artists remained behind in Paris. On the 1st May, 1871, Perrin was asked to organise a concert for the wounded of the Garde Nationale, but reluctant to put himself to much trouble on behalf of the so-called government of the Hôtel-de-Ville, he raised so many difficulties that he was summarily dismissed. M. Eugène Garnier was then elected director and with the help of foreign artists arranged the concert; but he left the Opéra in July when M. Halanzier provi-

---

[1] Adolphe Nourrit (1802–39). Celebrated singer. Made his début at the Opéra in 1821; committed suicide in 1839.

[2] Dr Véron, administrateur général de l'Opéra, 1831–5, was the first to lease the Opéra after the period of Royal subsidy had ended. He quickly made a fortune out of it and retired after four years. His first great success was *Robert le Diable*.

[3] Atelier Edgar Degas, Vente catalogue, 1ᵉ, No. 66.

sionally accepted the appointment, which the latter took up permanently in October of the same year. As co-directors, Halanzier and Dufrenoy acted until 1879, they were followed by Vaucorbeil until 1884, Ritt and Gailhard until 1891, Bertrand and Gailhard until 1893, Gailhard alone until 1908, and by M. Jacques Rouché then M. Lehmann the predecessors of the present director M. Hirsch.

. . . . . .

Just under thirteen years after the laying of the foundation stone, the Nouvél Opéra, built to the design of Charles Garnier and unanimously selected from among those of one hundred and seventy-one competitors, was opened. The occasion was one of great importance, and the audience correspondingly brilliant. Degas' name, however, does not appear in any of the contemporary lists of notables, but it is hardly likely that he did not make every effort to be present at such an auspicious ceremony.

This remarkable building, this complete little world on its island site right in the heart of Paris, from that time on became one of Degas' favourite haunts. He once said: 'Vous voulez me décorer, c'est donc que vous voulez me faire plaisir, eh bien, donnez moi mes libres entrées à l'Opéra ma vie durant.'[1] And he was given free access to every part of the enormous structure, a complete tour of which takes many hours to complete. How frequently he must have wandered along its labyrinth of corridors and up its innumerable double staircases; watched the lessons in its variety of class-rooms; heard as he did so the practice of voices and of orchestra echoing down the passages; and seen the *rats* darting out from their school-rooms to have a meal before appearing in front of their *professeur de danse*. Perhaps he became so familiar a figure that they clamoured about him with a 'bon jour, Monsieur Degas', as today they crowd around the kindly M. Lepelletier, their *régisseur de danse*, who is apparently very different from his predecessor, the formidable 'César' Pluque.

Degas seems to have had an especial feeling of tenderness for the *rats*, and many of his pictures (Pls. 74–78) show compassion for these pathetic young children obediently drilling their thin little bodies to take up, what must be admitted to be, the most unnatural of positions. They were christened by M. Roqueplan,[2] and according to him they were the waifs of the theatre, wearing other people's discarded and cut-down clothes, insufficiently fed, and always begging a few sous with which to buy sweets. As they mostly came from poor families it was imperative for them to earn their keep as soon as possible, so they were sent to the Opéra between the ages of seven and eight years and, as in M. Roqueplan's time no facilities for their education were provided, they grew into women ignorant of everything except that which concerned their work. Another writer says[3] that most of these children were unhappy in their disciplined and strenuous lives, for as yet they were far too young to know whether they would like the profession chosen for them, and it was not until their second year that they made even occasional appearances in a performance. After the third year the authorities decided

[1] *Degas*, by Paul Lafond, pub. Paris, 1918, Vol. I, p. 89.
[2] M. Roqueplan, Director of the Opéra 1849–54; then *Administrateur de la Liste Civile*, July-November, 1854.
[3] For a description of the *rats* in the early 'sixties, see Bernay, *op. cit.*, pp. 8–18; and for a contemporary one, see *Initiation à la Danse* by Pierre Tugal, pub. Paris, 1947, p. 33.

whether they should be given an engagement or dismissed; if they were lucky enough for it to be the former it meant untold wealth at the age of ten, nine hundred francs a year; after that, and with success in each examination, it was possible to become a *petit sujet* after a further eight or nine years.

. . . . . .

The *age of the danseuse* is generally accepted as having begun with the Romantic era, but the famous stars of that time did not enjoy more popularity or more lionisation than those of a century earlier. Wherever they went, the ballerinas of the eighteenth century were fêted and made the spoilt darlings of society. They commanded their own salaries, behaved with suitable 'temperament' towards the management, and—perhaps the greatest glory of all—set the fashions in dress. Marie Camargo is said to have made her shoemaker's fortune over night, for all the ladies of the court insisted on wearing shoes 'à la Camargo'; while Madeleine Guimard's advice on questions of dress was sought by no less a person than Marie Antoinette herself. This dancer was so conscious of her powers of attraction that she deliberately held her entertainments to clash with those of the king.

Little is known about the lesser *danseuses* of the eighteenth century, but when ballet became the rage in the third decade of the nineteenth, romantic and often brilliant futures were open to members of the corps de ballet as well as to the *premières danseuses*. Many of them were courted by the illustrious and titled men of the day; showered with costly jewels; kept in magnificent *hôtels* and sometimes married into noble and wealthy families. Under influential protection it was possible to rise in status to the rank of *sujet*, without it the task was difficult if not impossible. M. Charles de Boigne wrote: 'L'Armèe compte plus de soldats devenus maréchaux que la danse ne compte de figurantes devenues premiers sujets.'[1]

But how alluring seemed the profession at a time when careers for women were practically unknown; when a life of servitude faced those unfortunates who, having to earn their own living, were not lucky enough to find husbands. Shop-girls of today dream of becoming film-stars; the grisettes of the nineteenth century longed to be ballerinas. They could not visualise the strenuous and often heart-breaking struggles and failures but, like the public, saw only the glittering results. For their daughters, greengrocers, seamstresses and concierges all aspired to the material luxuries that life had denied them: to mansions, servants and, above all, to carriages, the height of gentility and hallmark of success. If these could be attained through conventional means, so much the better; if not . . . tant pis! M. Ludovic Halévy's delightful *La Famille Cardinal*[2] is based on this theme. The two daughters of a little bourgeois family started as *rats* at the Opéra. Pauline, to the pride of her parents, became the Marquise Cavalcanti; Virginie attained her riches with more variety but less respectability. The monotypes which Degas did to illustrate this story (Pls. 132a, 167a and 179a) are, apart from the class-room picture already mentioned, the only examples among his work which actually show the background of the Nouvel Opéra. In one of them the mother, presumably *la mère Cardinal*, is waiting in the wings for her daughters, attended by one of their admirers; in the others, one of which

[1] Charles de Boigne, *op. cit.*, p. 20.　　　[2] See p. 34 and note 5.

shows the corridor of the dressing rooms, the dancers are surrounded by an attentive group of *galants*. It was this side of the Opéra life which so attracted Forain and various other illustrators, but as might be expected was otherwise ignored by Degas who, only considered these mono-types in the light of a recreation.

.   .   .   .   .   .

In 1869, towards the close of the Second Empire, the opera ballet comprised about sixty artists apart from the *marcheuses* and the children; by the end of the century its personnel totalled more than two hundred, with M. Hansen *maître de ballet*, M. Pluque still *régisseur* and with six *professeurs de danse* under them. The two *sujets étoiles* were Mlles Mauri and Subra; while the thirty *sujets* included names already mentioned in connection with Degas: Mlles Hirsch, Désiré, Lobstein, Chabot, Van Goethen, Sandrini, Salle, and Mante.

In the special number of the *Figaro Illustré* of February 1895 there is, among others, a charming photograph of *Les Garçons, classe de M. Stilb*. Apart from its historical interest (for it shows that the age of the violinist-teacher had not yet passed) it depicts a crowd of tiny girls watching the master put their male counterparts through the five positions of the dance. These little boys, who look so appealing in their black knickerbockers and white shirts, apparently had no attraction for Degas. It seems that he chose to ignore their existence, for in all his hundreds of pictures and drawings of dancers they do not even creep in on one single occasion.

As far as Degas is concerned, ballet is unquestionably a feminine art in which men may only be tolerated in their capacity of teachers.

Degas occupies a special position, not only in the nineteenth century, but also in the history of French painting. Belonging to the Florentine tradition founded upon the Classical art of Greece, whose one concern was with the rendering of the human figure in terms of the deepest artistic reality, who regarded colour as of secondary importance and illustration of small consequence, he reached the highest value of his expression the further he receded from these two aspects. Then it was that, through his realisation of movement in form entirely by means of the human body, and surpassing Poussin and Ingres, he was able to approach the plastic achievements of Giotto and Leonardo.

Without attempting to exaggerate his stature by comparison with such giants, Degas in a more restricted way, belonging to a less heroic age, was a man of similar mettle. The Floren-tines of the Renaissance were renowned as personalities, their intellect, scientific curiosity, and exploration into all forms of expression set them apart from, for instance, the Venetians, who were essentially painters. Degas fitted into this conception as far as was possible according to the conditions of his time. Although he can only be regarded as potentially a great sculptor—using the qualification in relation to the world's finest achievements—the small number of his models which have been preserved and cast are sufficient to perpetuate his memory should the whole of his pictorial output disappear. One of his greatest regrets was the lack of opportunity for painting murals. 'It is the dream of my life to paint a fresco, but nobody has approached me to do so,'[1] he said, and his magnificent frieze of dancers in the Cleveland Museum of Art suggests the heights he might have attained in this field. His scientific researches into varying forms of pictorial expression have already been dwelt upon; he was acknowledged as having the greatest intellect of all the painters of his time; and his letters, and even his few sonnets,[2] testify to the telling simplicity with which he used the written as well as the spoken word.

Regarding Degas' letters, George Moore wrote: 'Il y a dans son style comme un parfum du XVe siècle,'[3] which observation is profoundly true both of the man and his art, and as most people feel instinctive ties with some particular period of the past, Degas undoubtedly must have recognised his to be with that of the fifteenth century.

There is the strong temptation to go just one step further, to seek an individual who, across the centuries, may be named as the spiritual counterpart. The great Renaissance painter of Central Italy, Piero della Francesca, comes at once to mind. His unemotional and objective conception, his austere and noble forms, his impassive generalisation of types are all echoed in the nineteenth century language of Degas. This impersonal approach, the link uniting these two great figures, is one of the highest yet humblest of virtues, for it effaces the mere man and his emotions, and allows him the freedom to stand aside leaving unimpeded the deepest appreciation of his artistic endeavours. Schopenhauer wrote: 'Art, like philosophy, with which it has much in common, with which it is intimately connected, exists solely in the disinterested contemplation of things; and the faculty of putting them before others in that aspect is the essence of genius.'

[1] Hans Graber, *op. cit.*, p. 94.
[2] *Huit Sonnets d'Edgar Degas*, preface de Jean Nepveu Degas, pub. Paris, 1945.
[3] *Lettres de Degas*, 1945, *op. cit.*, p. 261.

1. SEMIRAMIS CONSTRUISANT UNE VILLE, DE L'OPERA 'SEMIRAMIS'
1860–1, 59 × 102 *ins*.

1a. ETUDE DE LA FEMME A GENOUX POUR 'SEMIRAMIS
CONSTRUISANT UNE VILLE'
1860–1, $11\frac{7}{8} \times 9\frac{1}{4}$ *ins*.

2. ETUDE POUR 'LA SOURCE'. JEUNE FILLE A LA GUITARE
1866–7, 14 × 8½ ins.

3. MLLE FIOCRE DANS LE BALLET 'LA SOURCE'
1866–7, 52 × 57¾ ins.

3a. FEMME ASSISE AU BORD DE L'EAU. ETUDE POUR 'LA SOURCE'
1866–7, 14½ × 10 ins.

4. L'ORCHESTRE DE L'OPERA. LE PORTRAIT DE DESIRE DIHAU
1868–9, 21½ × 18 *ins*.

5. MUSICIENS DE L'ORCHESTRE
circa 1872, 25 × 19½ *ins.*

6. TROIS RELIGIEUSES. ETUDE POUR 'ROBERT LE DIABLE'
1871–2, 11 × 17 ins.

6a. DEUX RELIGIEUSES. ETUDE
POUR 'ROBERT LE DIABLE'
1871–2, 10¼ × 17 ins.

7. UNE RELIGIEUSE. ETUDE POUR 'ROBERT LE DIABLE'
1871–2, 17 × 13¼ *ins*.

8. LE BALLET DE 'ROBERT LE DIABLE'
1872, 26 × 21⅜ *ins*.

9. LE BALLET DE 'ROBERT LE DIABLE'
1874–6, 29¾ × 32 ins.

10. DANSEUSE EN 'QUATRIEME DERRIERE, POINTE TENDUE'
circa 1872, $16\frac{1}{8} \times 11\frac{1}{4}$ *ins.*

11. DANSEUSE DEBOUT, VUE DE DOS
circa 1872, size unknown.

12. JOSEPHINE GAUGELIN EN 'QUATRIEME DERRIERE POINTE TENDUE'
1872, 12 × 8 ins.

13. DANSEUSE DE DEGOURDISSANT A LA BARRE
circa 1875, 18 × 12 ins.

14. ETUDE DE DANSEUSE DE PROFIL
circa 1872, 11¼ × 9 ins.

15. DANSEUSE ASSISE
circa 1872, 11¼ × 9 ins.

16. LA CLASSE DE DANSE DE M. MERANTE
1872, 13 × 18½ ins.

16a. DEUX DANSEUSES DEBOUT A
BARRE. ETUDE
circa 1872, 8¼ × 10 ins.

II. LA LEÇON DE DANSE
circa 1872, 7¾ × 10⅝ *ins.*

17. LA LEÇON DE DANSE
circa 1872, $7\frac{3}{4} \times 10\frac{5}{8}$ *ins.*

17a. TÊTE DE MME GAUGELIN
circa 1867, $14\frac{1}{2} \times 9\frac{1}{4}$ *ins.*

18. DANSEUSE ASSISE
circa 1873, 16⅜ × 12⅞ *ins.*

19. DANSEUSE DEBOUT

circa 1873, 15 × 10¼ *ins.*

20. DANSEUSE RAJUSTANT SON CHAUSSON

circa 1873, 12$\frac{7}{8}$ × 9$\frac{5}{8}$ *ins.*

21. DEUX DANSEUSES EN REPOS.
1874, $17\frac{1}{4} \times 11\frac{7}{8}$ ins.

22. LA CLASSE DE DANSE DE M. PERROT
1873–4, 34 × 30 *ins*.

23. LA CLASSE DE DANSE DE M. PERROT
circa 1874–6, $33\frac{1}{4} \times 30\frac{1}{2}$ *ins.*

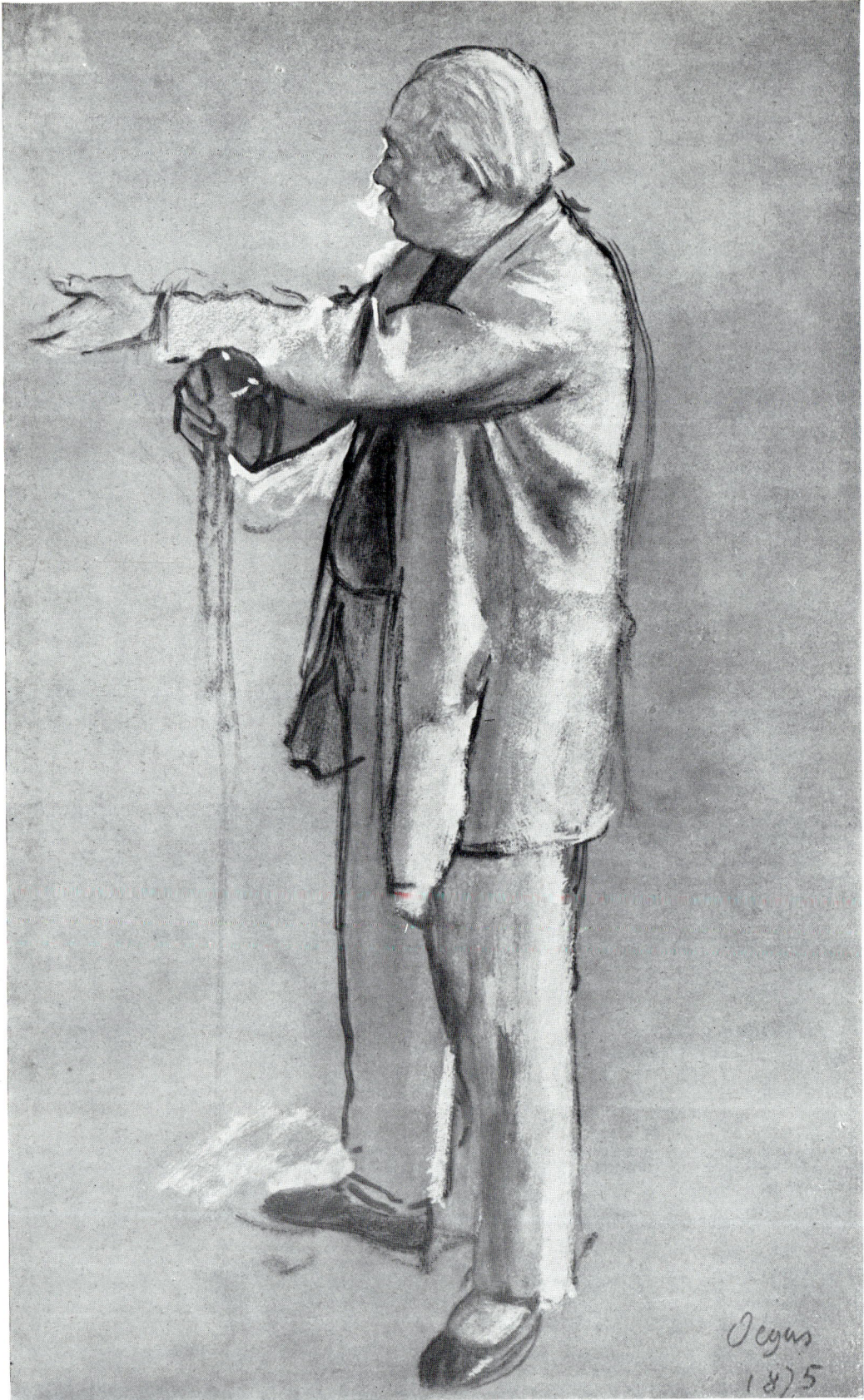

24. JULES PERROT DEBOUT. ETUDE

1875, 19¾ × 12 ins.

25. DANSEUSE AUX CHEVEUX LONGS, DEBOUT
circa 1874, 25½ × 20 *ins.*

26. DANSEUSE BAILLANT
circa 1873–4, 18 × 10 *ins.*

27. DANSEUSE DEBOUT

1873–4, 18 × 11¼ ins.

28. REPETITION D'UN BALLET SUR LA SCENE
1873–4, $26\frac{1}{2} \times 33$ *ins.*

28a. DANSEUSE ASSISE SE GRATTANT LE
DOS. ETUDE
circa 1874, $8\frac{1}{4} \times 10\frac{1}{4}$ *ins.*

29. DANSEUSE EN BLANC SUR LES POINTES
1873–4, $16\frac{1}{2} \times 11\frac{1}{2}$ *ins*.

30. REPETITION D'UN BALLET SUR LA SCENE
circa 1874–5, 21⅜ × 28¾ ins.

30a. LE MAITRE. ETUDE POUR 'LA REPETITION D'UN BALLET SUR LA SCENE'
circa 1874–5, 12 × 8 ins.

31. REPETITION D'UN BALLET SUR LA SCENE
circa 1876–7, 21 × 28½ ins.

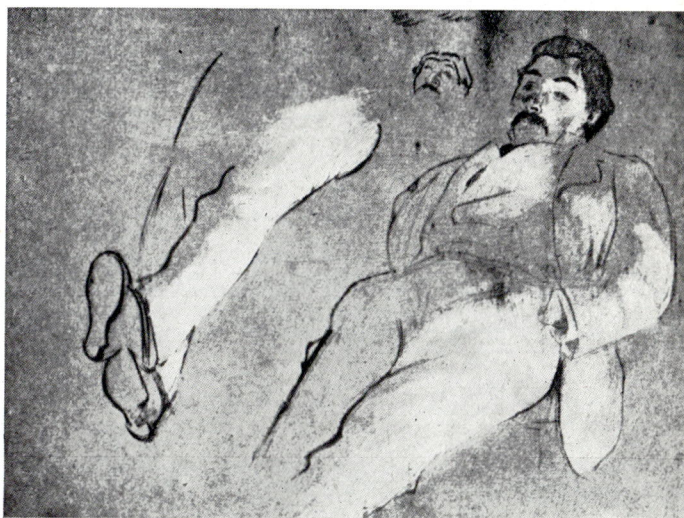

31a. HOMME ASSIS. ETUDE POUR 'LA REPETITION
D'UN BALLET SUR LA SCENE'
circa 1874–5, 8 × 12 ins.

32. DANSEUSE VUE DE DOS
circa 1876, 14½ × 10 *ins.*

33. DEUX DANSEUSES DEBOUT, VIS A VIS

circa 1876, $24\frac{1}{8} \times 15\frac{1}{2}$ *ins.*

34. LA CLASSE DE DANSE. 'ADAGE'
circa 1876, 22 × 32 *ins*.

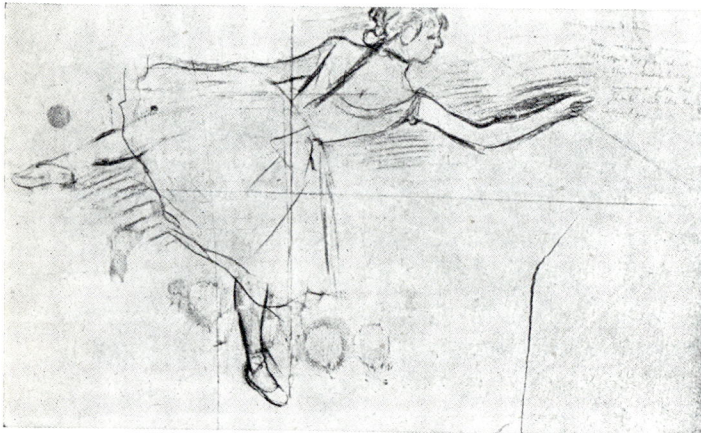

34*a*. 'ARABESQUE CROISEE.' ETUDE POUR 'LA
CLASSE DE DANSE'
14 × 20 *ins*.

35. TROIS DANSEUSES EXECUTANT 'DEVELOPPE A LA SECONDE'
    circa 1877, 18½ × 24 *ins*.

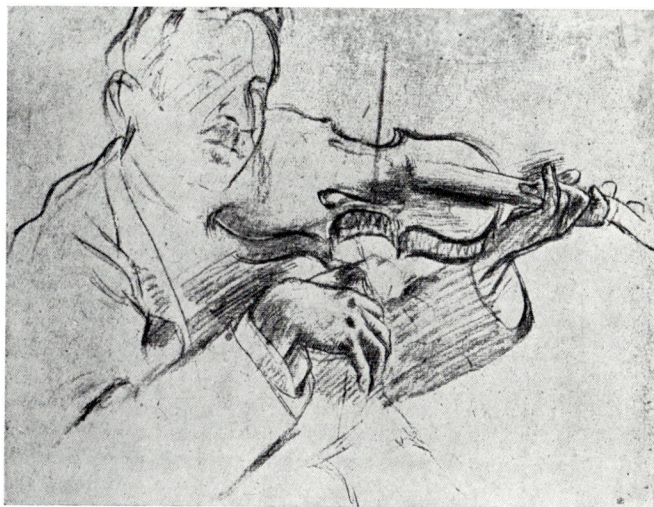

5a. LE VIOLINISTE. ETUDE
    circa 1877, 10 × 12¼ *ins*.

36. ECOLE DE DANSE. 'ADAGE'
circa 1876, $17\frac{1}{4} \times 23$ *ins.*

36a. LE VIOLINISTE VU DE DOS. ETUDE
circa 1876, $17\frac{1}{2} \times 12$ *ins.*

37. ECOLE DE DANSE. 'ADAGE'
   circa 1877, 18⅝ × 24¼ ins.

37a. 'L'ADAGE.' ETUDE
   circa 1876, 17 × 12¼ ins.

38. LA LEÇON DE DANSE
circa 1878–80, $16 \times 21\frac{1}{2}$ *ins.*

38*a*. DANSEUSE MONTANT UN ESCALIER
circa 1878–80, $18\frac{1}{4} \times 12\frac{1}{4}$ *ins.*

III. PREPARATION POUR LA CLASSE
circa 1877, 24 × 37 ins.

39. PREPARATION POUR LA CLASSE
circa 1877, 24 × 37 ins.

39a. MLLE S . . . (SANGALLI) PREMIERE DANSEUSE A L'OPERA
circa 1876, 15¼ × 8 ins.

40. LA LEÇON DE DANSE
circa 1879, 22 × 27¾ *ins.*

40a. LE MAITRE DE DANSE VU DE DOS
circa 1879, 17½ × 10 *ins.*

IV. DANSEUSE BLEUE
circa 1878–9, 13 × 10 *ins.*

41. GROUPE DE CINQ DANSEUSES AVEC PAYSAGE CLASSIQUE
    circa 1878–9, 16 × 22 *ins*.

41a. DANSEUSE BLEUE. ETUDE
    circa 1878–9, 16¼ × 10¼ *ins*.

42. DANSEUSE POSANT

1878–9, 18 × 11¼ *ins*.

43. DANSEUSE POSANT CHEZ UN PHOTOGRAPHE
1878–9, 26 × 20 ins.

44. DANSEUSE SUR LES POINTES
circa 1878–9, 12 × 8½ *ins.*

45. LA CLASSE DE DANSE. TEMPS DE POINTES
circa 1879–80, $18\frac{3}{4} \times 24\frac{1}{2}$ *ins.*

45a. DANSEUSE SUR L'ESCALIER. ETUDE
circa 1880, $19\frac{1}{4} \times 25$ *ins.*

46. DANSEUSES A LA BARRE
1876–7, 29¾ × 32 *ins.*

7. DEUX DANSEUSES A LA BARRE. ETUDE
   1876-7, $15\frac{1}{2} \times 25$ ins.

a. DANSEUSE SE DEGOURDISSANT A LA BARRE. ETUDE
   circa 1876, 12×10 ins.

48. DANSEUSE SE DEGOURDISSANT A LA BAR[RE]
circa 1876–7, $6\frac{3}{4} \times 8\frac{3}{4}$ *ins.*

48a. 'GRAND BATTEMENT A LA SECON[D]
A LA BARRE'
circa 1880, 19×21 *ins.*

49. DANSEUSE REPOSANT
circa 1880–2, $18\frac{7}{8} \times 24\frac{1}{2}$ *ins.*

49*a*. 'PLIE A LA SECONDE A LA BARRE.' DEUX
DANSEUSES
circa 1880, $13 \times 20\frac{1}{4}$ *ins.*

50. LE 'PAS DE DEUX' SUR LA SCENE
1873–4, $24\frac{1}{4} \times 18\frac{1}{4}$ ins.

V. LE 'PAS DE DEUX' SUR LA SCENE
1873–4, $24\frac{1}{4} \times 18\frac{1}{4}$ ins.

51. LE 'PAS DE DEUX' SUR LA SCENE
circa 1878, 12 × 10½ *ins.*

52. SCENE DE BALLET—'PAS DE DEUX'
    circa 1876, $10\frac{1}{4} \times 8\frac{1}{4}$ *ins*.

53. DANSEUSE SUR LA SCENE
circa 1878–9, $14\frac{1}{4} \times 8\frac{3}{4}$ *ins.*

54. DANSEUSE SUR LA POINTE
circa 1876, $22\frac{1}{4} \times 30$ *ins.*

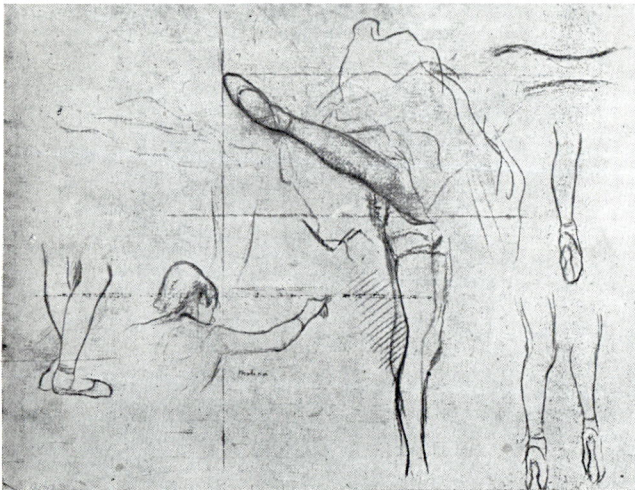

54a. ETUDES DE JAMBES ET DE BRA
circa 1876, $19 \times 24\frac{1}{4}$ *ins.*

55. DANSEUSE SUR LA SCENE. 'L'ETOILE

circa 1876, 23 × 17 *ins.*

56. DANSEUSE, UN BOUQUET A LA MAIN
1876–7, 30 × 31 *ins*.

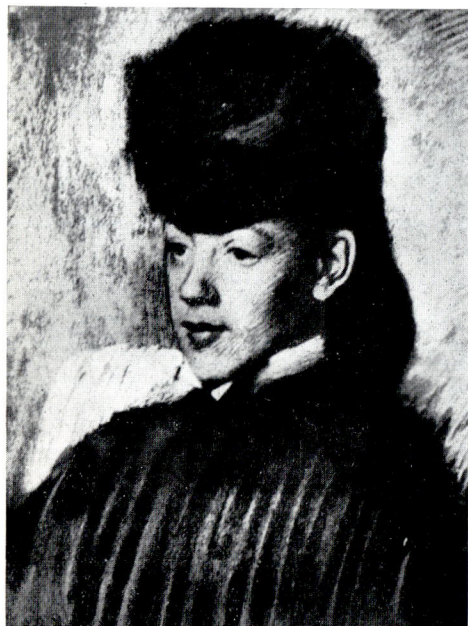

56a. PORTRAIT DE MLLE MALO. BUSTE
circa 1869, 18¼ × 15 *ins*.

57. DANSEUSE, UN BOUQUET A LA MAIN
circa 1878–80, $20\frac{1}{4} \times 26$ *ins*.

57a. DANSEUSE DEBOUT A L'EVENTAIL
circa 1878–80, $19\frac{1}{4} \times 12\frac{1}{4}$ *ins*.

58.   DANSEUSE SALUANT
circa 1882–5, 30 × 22½ *ins.*

59. DANSEUSE SALUANT, UN BOUQUET A LA MAIN
circa 1885, 24 × 18 *ins.*

60. LA LOGE DE DANSEUSE
1878–9, $23\frac{1}{4} \times 17\frac{3}{4}$ ins.

61. LA LOGE DE DANSEUSE
1878–9, 24 × 17 ins.

62. LA LOGE DE DANSEUSE
1878–9, $11\frac{7}{8} \times 20\frac{1}{2}$ ins.

63. DANSEUSE EN JUPE ROUGE
circa 1878–80, 16 × 12¾ ins.

64. DEUX DANSEUSES DERRIERE UN PORTANT
circa 1880, 27½ × 19 *ins.*

65. ETUDE DE DANSEUSE ALLONGEE
circa 1877, 18 × 12 ins.

66. DANSEUSE RAJUSTANT SA CHAUSSURE. MELINA DARDE
1878, 16¼ × 12 ins.

67. DANSEUSE ASSISE. MELINA DARDE
circa 1878, 17 × 12 *ins.*

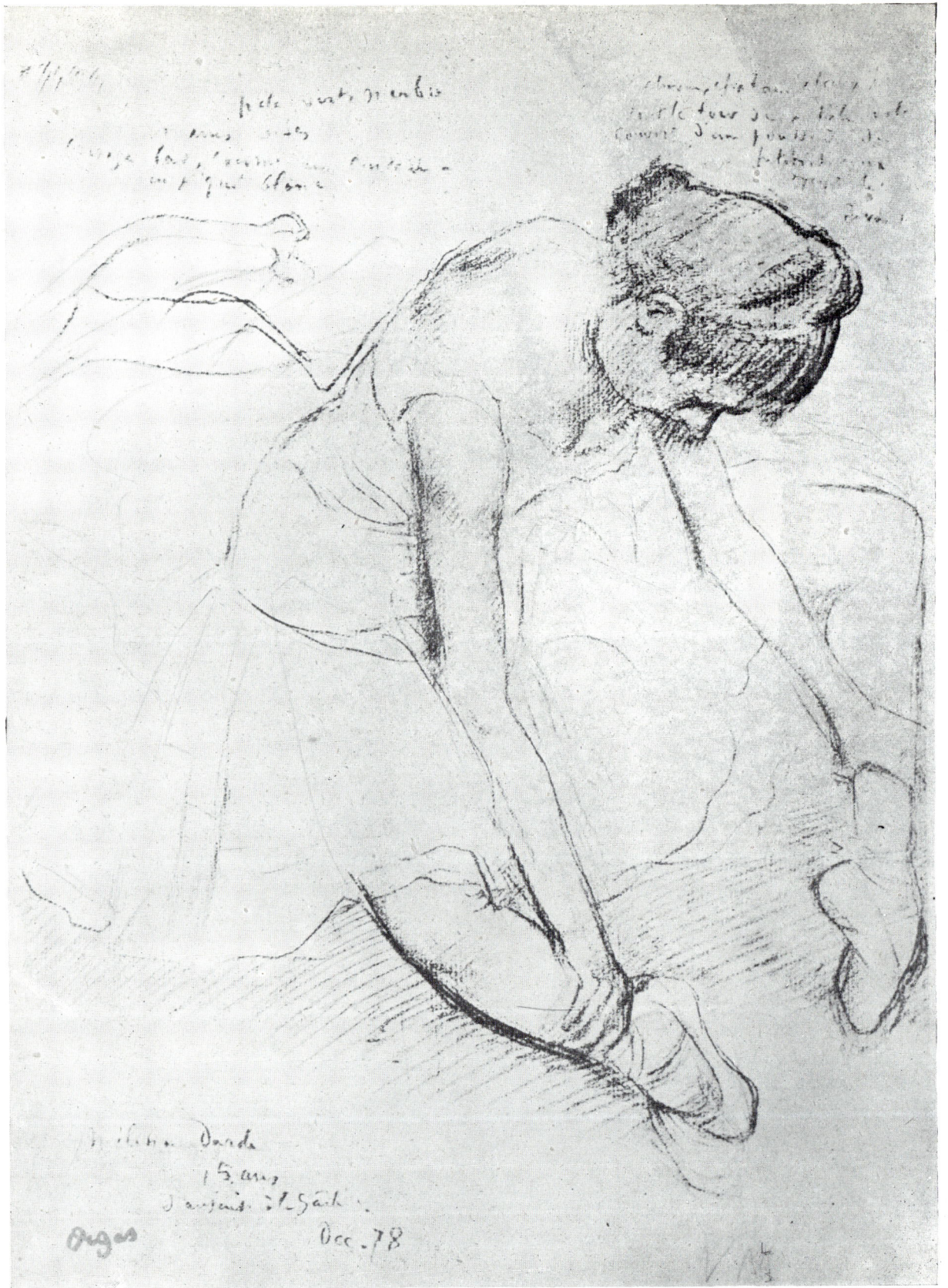

68. MELINA DARDE ASSISE
1878. 12 × 9¾ ins.

69. MELINA DARDE A 'SON ADAGE'
1878, 18 × 12 ins.

70. DANSEUSE SE MASSANT LA CHEVILLE
circa 1878, 25 × 20 ins.

71. L'ATTENTE
   circa 1879–80, 19 × 24 ins.

71a. DANSEUSE ASSISE SE MASSANT LA CHEVILLE
DU PIED. ETUDE
   circa 1879–80, 18¼ × 24 ins.

72. LA FAMILLE MANTE
1880, $35\frac{1}{2} \times 19\frac{3}{4}$ ins.

73. LA FAMILLE MANTE
circa 1882, *size unknown*

74. JEUNE DANSEUSE A LA BARRE
circa 1880, 26¼ × 18½ *ins.*

75. DANSEUSE EN BLEU A LA BARRE
circa 1880–2, $26\frac{3}{4} \times 18\frac{7}{8}$ *ins.*

76. 'BATTEMENTS SUR LES POINTES A LA BARRE'
circa 1883–5, *size unknown*

77. 'BATTEMENTS A LA SECONDE A LA BARRE'
circa 1883–5, 12¾ × 11½ ins.

Rond de jambe à terre
Dessin de Degas
N. Bonnet

78. 'RONDS-DE-JAMBE-A-TERRE A LA BARRE'
circa 1883–5, 12 × 9½ *ins.*

79. PENDANT LE REPOS

circa 1880–2, $29\frac{5}{8} \times 21\frac{5}{8}$ *ins.*

80. JEUNE DANSEUSE EN CINQUIEME POSITION
circa 1878–80, 17½ × 12 ins.

81. DANSEUSE SE DEGOURDISSANT A LA BARRE
circa 1880–2, 12 × 9 *ins.*

82. LA LEÇON DE DANSE
circa 1876–8, 17 × 31½ ins.

82a. LE PAS 'BATTU'
circa 1880, 10½ × 11¾ ins.

83. GROUPE DE DANSEUSES EN DIVERSES ATTITUDES
circa 1880–3, 24 × 19¾ *ins.*

84. GROUPE DE DANSEUSES DANS UNE SALLE
circa 1880–2, $29\frac{1}{2} \times 29\frac{1}{2}$ *ins.*

85. 'PAS DE TROIS'. UNE REPETITION
circa 1880, 20 × 24 *ins*.

86. DANSEUSES PRATIQUANT DANS UNE SALLE A COLONNES
circa 1882–3, 28½ × 36 *ins*.

I. AVANT LA REPRESENTATION
circa 1882–3, $19\frac{1}{4} \times 25$ *ins.*

87. 'GRAND BATTEMENT A LA SECONDE'
circa 1880–2, 12½ × 9½ *ins.*

88. LA REPETITION AVANT LE BALLET
circa 1883–5, 22 × 27 ins.

88*a*. DEUX DANSEUSES DANS LA COULISSE
circa 1875–80, 4½ × 4¼ ins.

VII. DANSEUSES SUR LA SCENE AVANT LA REPRESENTATION

circa 1875–80, 6⅜ × 11⅝ *ins.*

89. LA CLASSE DE DANSE. MOMENT DE PAUSE
   circa 1884, 22¾ × 33¾ *ins*.

89a. DANSEUSE EN 'QUATRIEME CROISEE'
   circa 1885, 12¾ × 8¼ *ins*.

90. DANSEUSE DEBOUT VUE DE DOS, ET ETUDES DE PIEDS
circa 1878–80, 19 × 24 *ins.*

90*a*. DANSEUSE DEBOUT VUE DE DOS
circa 1878–80, 13 × 19 *ins.*

91. TROIS ETUDES DE DANSEUSE 'EN QUATRIEME'
    circa 1878–80, 19 × 24 ins.

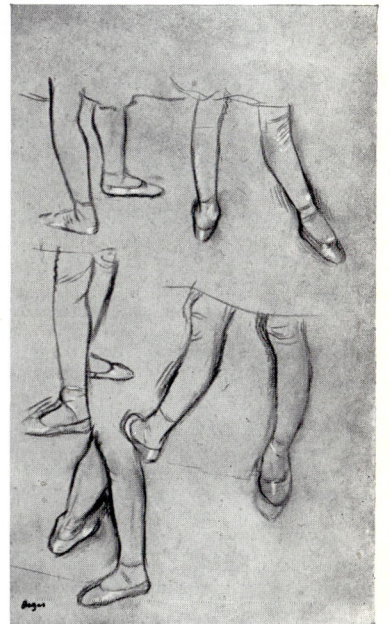

91a. CINQ ETUDES D'UNE PAIRE DE JAMBES
    circa 1878–80, 19 × 12 ins.

92. DEUX ETUDES D'UNE DANSEUSE DEBOUT
circa 1878–80, $25\frac{1}{8} \times 19\frac{1}{4}$ *ins.*

93. TROIS ETUDES DE DANSEUSE DEBOUT
circa 1878–80, 18 × 24 *ins.*

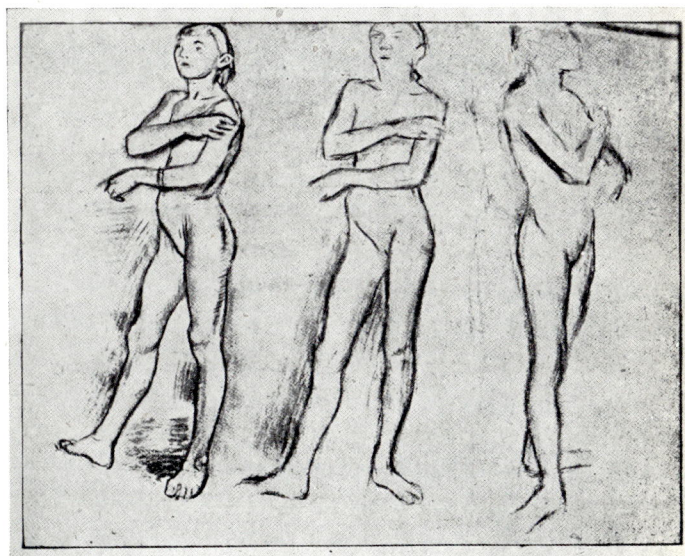

93*a*. TROIS ETUDES D'UNE JEUNE DANSEUSE NUE
circa 1878–80, 19 × 25 *ins.*

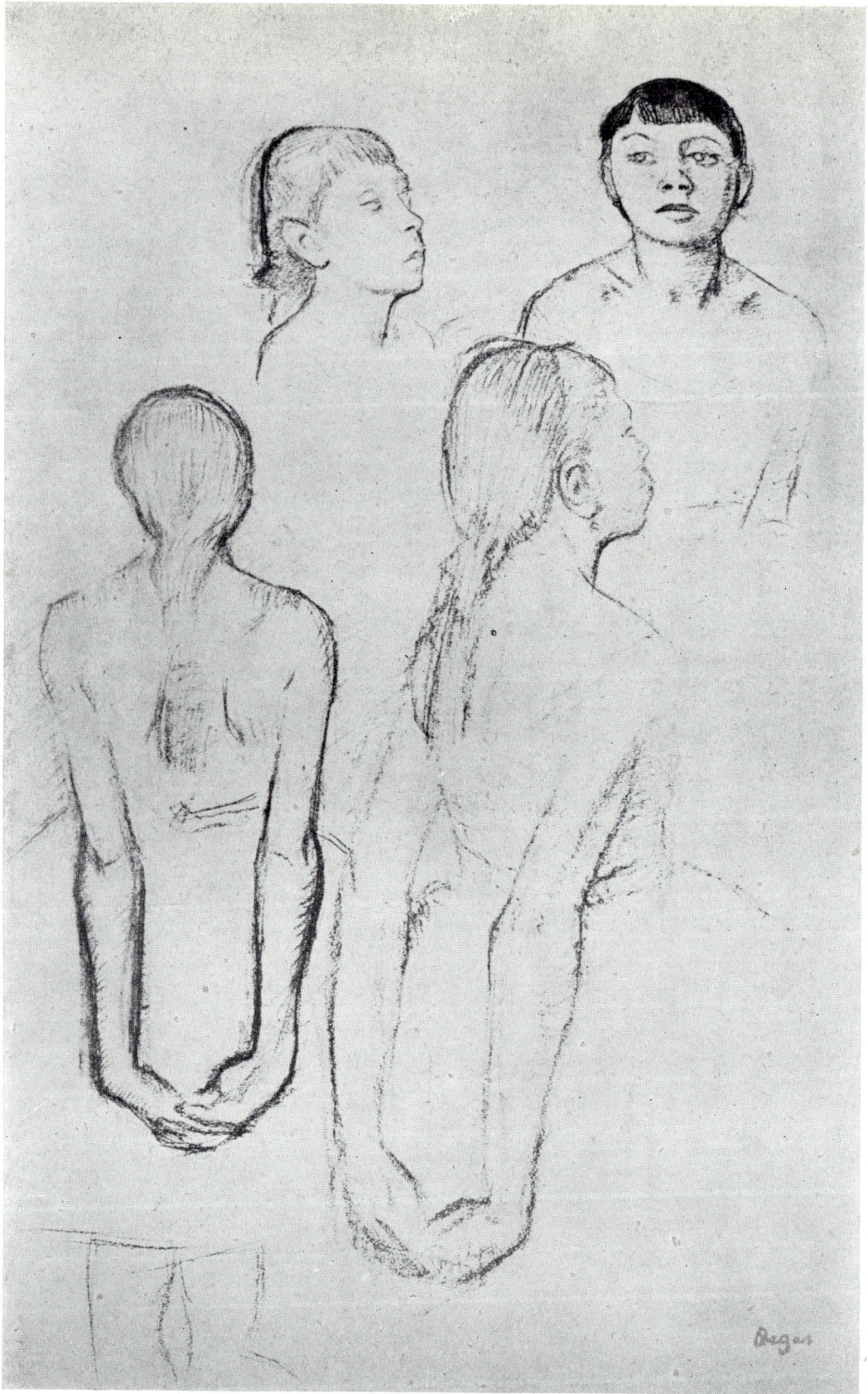

94. ETUDES DE TETE ET DE BRAS POUR 'LA PETITE DANSEUSE DE QUATORZE ANS'
circa 1878–80, 19 × 12 ins.

95. ETUDE DE NUE POUR 'LA PETITE DANSEUSE DE QUATORZE ANS'
1879–80, *height* 28¾ *ins.*

96. LA PETITE DANSEUSE DE QUATORZE ANS
1880, *height* 39½ *ins.*

97. LA PETITE DANSEUSE DE QUATORZE ANS
1880, height 39½ ins.

98. LA REPETITION DANS LA SALLE D'UN 'PAS DE TROIS'
circa 1880, 32 × 29½ *ins.*

. LE REPOS. DEUX DANSEUSES ASSISES
circa 1880–2, 19¾ × 23 *ins.*

a. DEUX DANSEUSES ASSISES. ETUDE
circa 1880–2, 11⅞ × 18 *ins.*

100. VIOLINISTE JOUANT

circa 1882–4, $15\frac{1}{2} \times 11\frac{7}{8}$ *ins.*

101. EXERCICES A LA BARRE AU VIOLON
circa 1882–4, 27 × 23½ *ins*.

102. AVANT LA CLASSE
circa 1882, $24\frac{1}{2} \times 18\frac{1}{2}$ *ins*.

103. DEUX DANSEUSES EXECUTANT 'GRANDS BATTEMENTS A LA SECONDE A LA BARRE'
circa 1882–4, $25\frac{1}{4} \times 18\frac{3}{4}$ *ins*.

104. JEUNE DANSEUSE AUX BRAS ETENDUS
circa 1882–5, 25 × 19 ins.

abandon du corps

bras droit [...]
allongé

Degas

105. 'PORTE DE BRAS'
circa 1880–5, 14 × 9 *ins.*

106. DANSEUSE AU BOUQUET DERRIERE U
FEMME A L'EVENTAIL
circa 1878–80, 16 × 19¾ *ins.*

106a. ETUDE DE MAIN GANTEE TENANT
JUMELLES DE THEATRE
circa 1883–5, 12 × 7¼ *ins.*

107. LOGE D'AVANT SCENE. FEMME A L'EVENTAIL
circa 1883, 9 × 8 *ins.*

108. LE BALLET VU D'UNE LOGE DE THEATRE
circa 1883–5, 27 × 23¼ *ins*.

VIII. DEUX DANSEUSES A MI-CORPS A L'EVENTAIL
circa 1883–5, 22$\frac{1}{4}$ × 32$\frac{1}{4}$ *ins*.

109. AU BALLET. LA FEMME A L'EVENTAIL
circa 1883–5, $18\frac{7}{8} \times 24\frac{1}{2}$ *ins.*

110. AU THEATRE. LE BALLET VU D'UNE LOGE
circa 1885, 24 × 18 *ins.*

III. DANSEUSES EN SCENE

circa 1884–6, 25½ × 19½ *ins.*

112. DANSEUSES PENDANT LE REPOS
circa 1880–3, 19 × 25½ *ins.*

112a. ETUDE DE DEUX DANSEUSES
circa 1884–5, 18¼ × 24 *ins.*

113. TROIS DANSEUSES ASSISES
circa 1880–3, 18¼ × 24½ *ins.*

113a. TROIS ETUDES DE LA TETE D'UNE DANSEUSE
circa 1886–90, 7½ × 22¼ *ins.*

114. LA CLASSE DE DANSE. FRISE
circa 1884–5, $15 \times 34\frac{1}{2}$ *ins.*

114a. QUATRE DANSEUSES DANS LA SALLE DE DANSE
circa 1884, $15\frac{1}{4} \times 29$ *ins.*

115. QUATRE DANSEUSES ATTACHANT LEURS CHAUSSONS. FRISE
circa 1885–90, 28 × 80 ins.

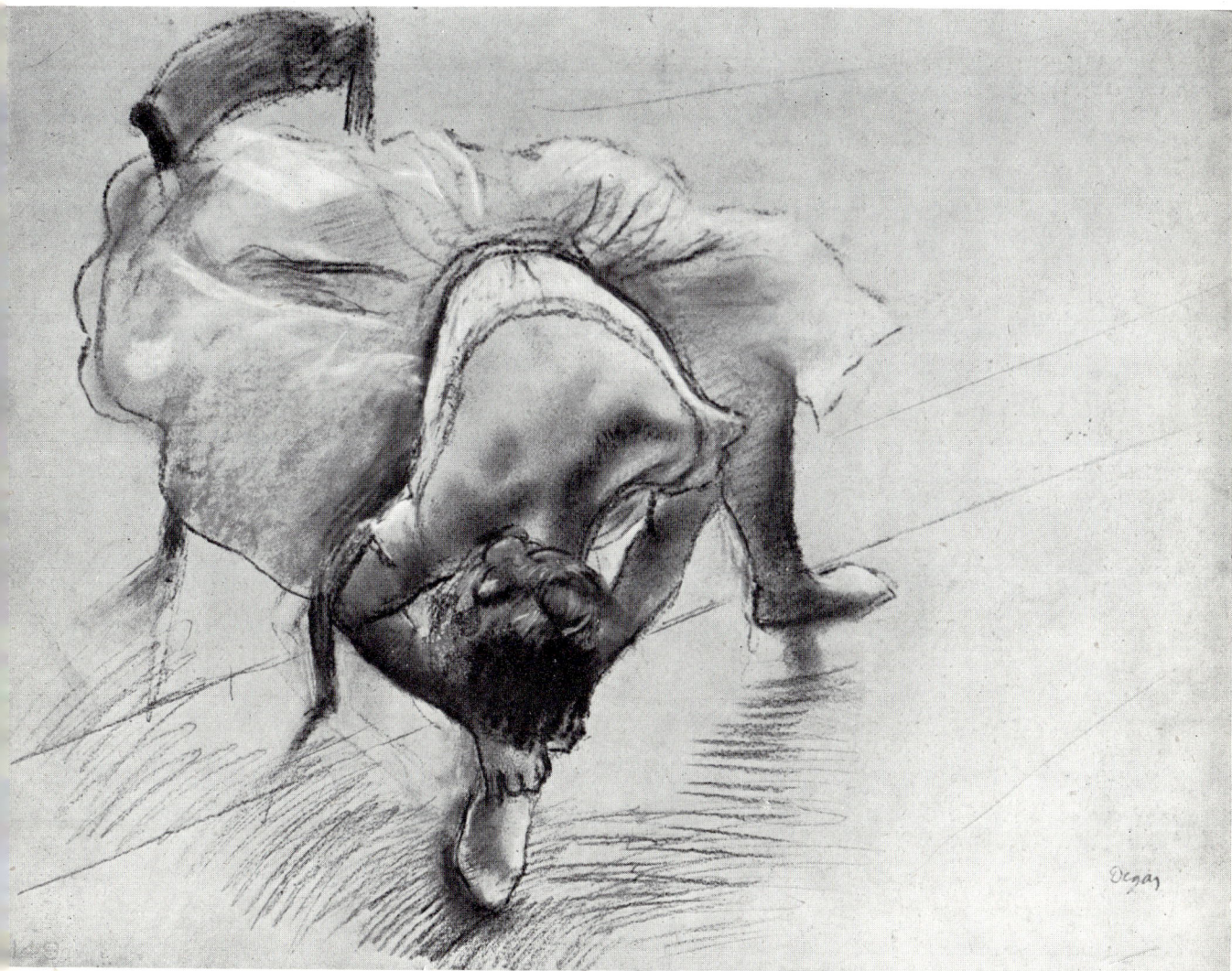

115a. DANSEUSE ATTACHANT SES RUBANS
circa 1880, 25 × 19 ins.

116. SEPT DANSEUSES DANS UNE SALLE DE CLASSE. FRISE
circa 1883, $15\frac{1}{2} \times 34\frac{3}{4}$ *ins.*

116*a*. SIX DANSEUSES DANS UNE SALLE DE CLASSE. FRISE
circa 1884–6, $16 \times 35\frac{1}{2}$ *ins.*

Degas

117. DANSEUSE DEBOUT A L'EVENTAIL

circa 1883, 24 × 16½ *ins.*

118. DANSEUSES AVEC CONTREBASSE. FRISE
circa 1880–3, $15\frac{1}{8} \times 35\frac{1}{4}$ *ins.*

118a. DEUX DANSEUSES SE REPOSANT
circa 1880–3, $18\frac{1}{2} \times 26\frac{1}{4}$ *ins.*

119. DANSEUSE ATTACHANT SES RUBANS

circa 1880, $17\frac{1}{4} \times 16$ *ins.*

120. DANSEUSES AVEC CONTREBASSE DANS LA SALLE DE DANSE. FRISE
circa 1880–3, $17\frac{1}{2} \times 35\frac{1}{4}$ *ins.*

120*a*. DANS LA SALLE DE DANSE. FRISE
circa 1880–3, $15 \times 35\frac{1}{2}$ *ins.*

121. DANSEUSE DEBOUT ATTACHANT SA CEINTURE

circa 1880–3, 19 × 12 *ins.*

122. 'DEVELOPPE EN AVANT, FONDU'
circa 1885, 12 × 9 ins.

123. DANSEUSE EN 'QUATRIEME', VUE DE PROFIL
circa 1885, 12 × 9 ins.

Ballet de Faust
Egyptiennes

Degas

124. ETUDE—BALLET DE 'FAUST'
circa 1885, 12 × 10 ins.

125. 'DEGAGE EN QUATRIEME OUVERTE'
circa 1885, 12 × 9 *ins*.

126. 'PORTE DE BRAS'. DANSEUSE VUE DE DOS
circa 1885, 12 × 10 *ins.*

7. PREPARATION POUR UNE 'PIROUETTE EN DEHORS'
    circa 1885, 9 × 12 ins.

a. DANSEUSE EN 'QUATRIEME DEVANT'
    circa 1885, 11¾ × 9 ins.

128. DEUX ETUDES D'UNE DANSEU[
circa 1885, 18 × 24 *ins.*

128a. DANSEUSE AJUSTANT SON CHAUSSON. ETUD[
circa 1885, 24 × 18¼ *ins.*

129. ETUDE DE DANSEUSE SALUANT
circa 1885–7, 12 × 8¾ *ins.*

130. DANSEUSE ASSISE TIRANT SON MAILLOT
circa 1883–5, $9\frac{1}{2} \times 12\frac{1}{2}$ *ins.*

130a. DANSEUSE ASSISE TIRANT SON MAILLOT
circa 1883–5, $9\frac{1}{4} \times 11\frac{7}{8}$ *ins.*

131. DANSEUSE ASSISE TIRANT SON MAILLOT

circa 1883–5, $15\frac{3}{4} \times 10\frac{3}{4}$ *ins.*

132. L'ENTRÉE DES MASQUES
circa 1884–6, 20 × 26 *ins.*

132a. 'LA FAMILLE CARDINAL'. DANS LES COULISSE
circa 1880–3, 6¼ × 8¼ *ins.*

133. DANSEUSE AU CORSELET, SE REPOSANT
circa 1884–6, $24\frac{3}{8} \times 18\frac{1}{2}$ *ins.*

134. TROIS DANSEUSES EN LIGNE DIAGONALE SUR LA SCENE
    circa 1884–6, 24½ × 18½ *ins.*

IX. TROIS DANSEUSES EN LIGNE DIAGONALE SUR LA SCENE
circa 1884–6, 24½ × 18½ *ins.*

135. TROIS DANSEUSES A GENOUX SUR LA SCENE
circa 1884–6, *size unknown*

136. DANS LES COULISSES. DEUX DANSEUSES EN ROSE
circa 1884–6, $19\frac{5}{8} \times 15\frac{3}{4}$ *ins.*

137. TROIS DANSEUSES EN CORSELETS, DEBOUT
circa 1884–6, 32 × 20 ins.

138. DANSEUSE VERTE VUE DE DOS
circa 1884–6, 18 × 12 ins.

139. EN ATTENDANT L'ENTREE
circa 1884–6, 12¼ × 10 *ins*.

140. LE COMMENCEMENT DES 'PIROUETTES SUR LA POINTE EN DEDANS'
circa 1880–3, 18 × 14 *ins.*

141. DANSEUSE AU BOUQUET
circa 1882–4, 26 × 14½ *ins.*

142. LE PAS SEUL SUR LA SCENE
circa 1880–3, 14½ × 10½ *ins.*

143. LE BALLET SUR LA SCENE
circa 1883–5, 22½ × 16 *ins.*

144. DANSEUSE BLEUE
circa 1884, 28½ × 15¼ ins.

145. LE PAS SEUL SUR LA SCENE

circa 1884–6, $28\frac{1}{2} \times 15$ *ins*.

146. 'ECHAPPE SUR LES POINTES A LA SECONDE A LA BARRE'
circa 1885, size unknown

147. 'PLIE A LA SECONDE A LA BARRE'
circa 1885, 12 × 9 *ins.*

148. DANSEUSE SE DEGOURDISSANT A LA BARRE
circa 1885–90, 12 × 9 *ins*.

149. DANSEUSE EXERÇANT A LA BARRE
circa 1885–90, 12 × 9¼ *ins*.

150. 'RELEVE SUR LA POINTE A LA BARRE'
circa 1885, 12 × 9 *ins.*

151. DANSEUSE PRATIQUANT A LA BARRE
circa 1885–90, 12 × 9 ins.

152. DANSEUSE EN FACE DE LA BARRE
circa 1885–90, 12 × 9 *ins.*

153. DANSEUSE DEGOURDISSANT LES TENDONS DES TALONS
circa 1885–90, 12 × 9 *ins*.

154. DANSE ESPAGNOLE
circa 1884, height 17 ins.

155. DANSEUSE NUE EN GRANDE ARABESQUE
circa 1882–6, height 16 ins.

156. DANS LA SALLE DE DANSE
circa 1880–3, 20 × 25¼ *ins.*

156a. DANSEUSES MONTANT UN ESCALIER. FRISE
circa 1880–3, 15½ × 36 *ins.*

157. DANSEUSE NUE EN ARABESQUE
circa 1882–6, height 19 ins.

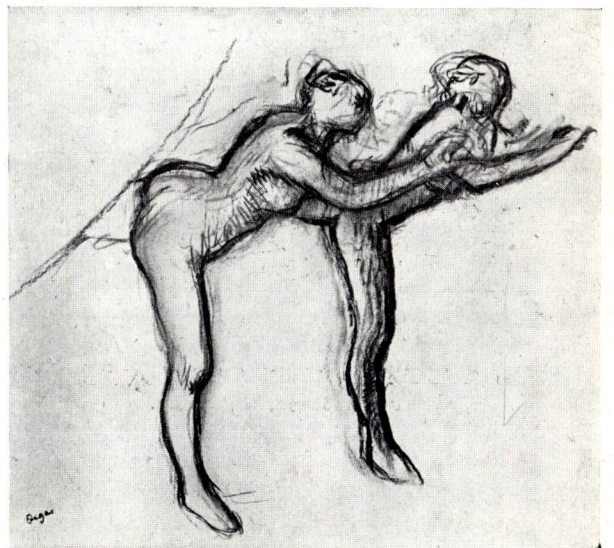

157a. DEUX DANSEUSES NUES EN ARABESQUE
circa 1885–90, 18 × 21¾ ins.

158. 'DEVELOPPE EN AVANT'
circa 1882–90, height 23 ins.

159. DANSEUSE NUE 'EN QUATRIEME DEVANT'
circa 1882–90, height 22 ins.

160. DANSEUSE AUX CHEVEUX LONGS SALUANT
circa 1884–8, 30¼ × 17½ ins.

161. DANSEUSE EN JAUNE SALUANT
circa 1884–8, 28 × 15 ins.

162. DEUX DANSEUSES AUX CHEVEUX LONGS
circa 1884–8, 28 × 15½ *ins.*

163. TROIS DANSEUSES VERTES AUX CHEVEUX LONGS
circa 1884–8, $28\frac{1}{2} \times 15\frac{1}{2}$ *ins.*

164. DANSEUSE ROSE SALUANT
circa 1884–8, $28\frac{1}{2} \times 15\frac{3}{4}$ *ins.*

165. DANSEUSE ROSE SALUANT
circa 1884–8, 28 × 15 *ins.*

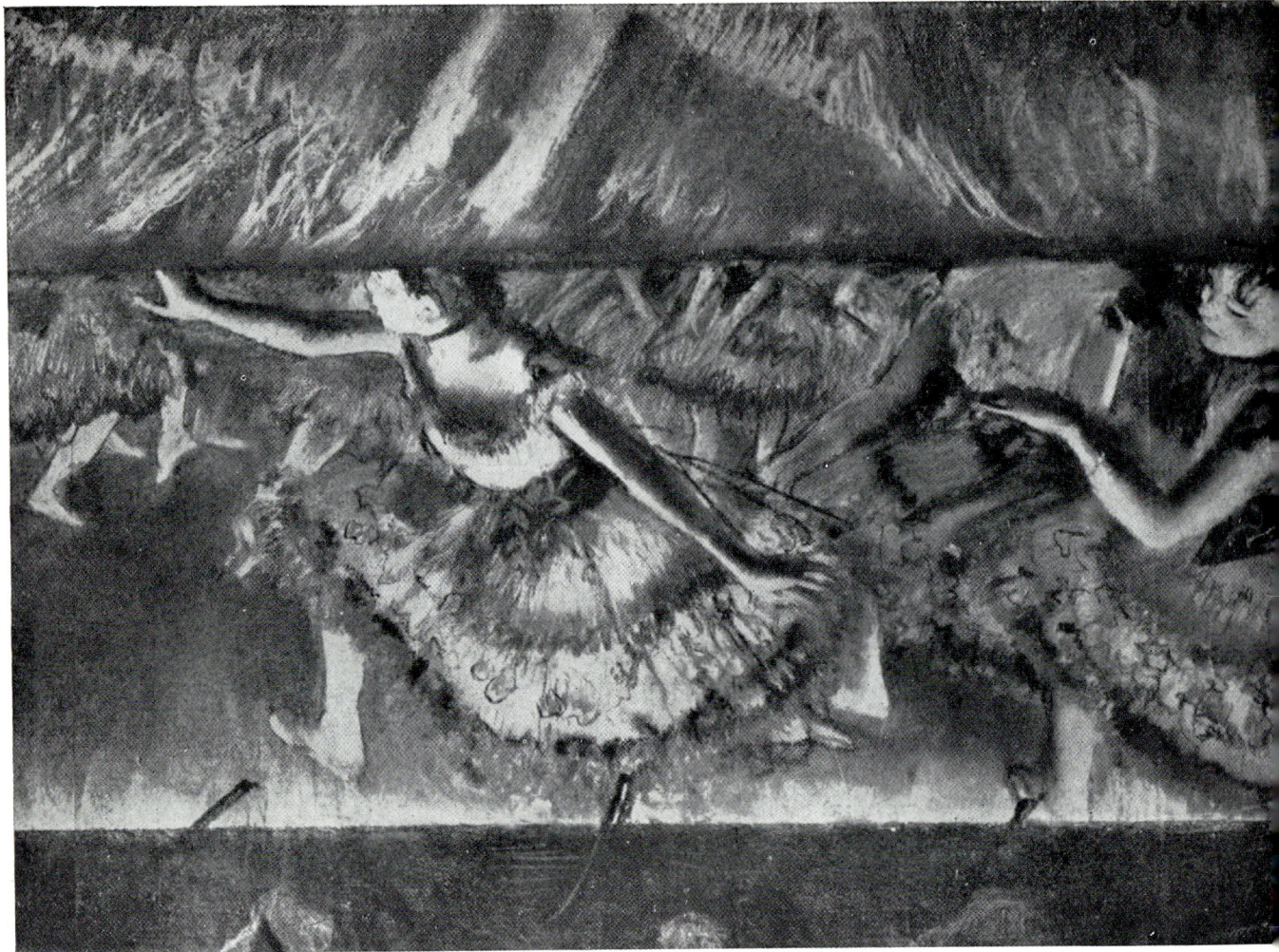

166. LE BAISSER DU RIDE
circa 1880–2, 22 × 30 i.

166a. DEUX DANSEUSES A GENOUX. ETU
circa 1880–2, 18 × 24 *ins.*

167. LES DEUX 'SUJETS' SUR LA SCENE
circa 1880–2, 14 × 19 ins.

167a. 'LA FAMILLE CARDINAL'.
LE CORRIDOR DES LOGES
circa 1880–3, 6 × 8 ins.

168. SUR LA SCENE. DANSEUSE VERTE

circa 1884–6, $24\frac{1}{2} \times 14$ *ins*.

169. ARLEQUINADE
1886, $20\frac{1}{2} \times 25\frac{1}{2}$ ins.

169a. DANSEUSE SALUANT. ETUDE
circa 1884–6, 24 × 18 ins.

170. LES DEUX ARLEQUINS
1886, 20 × 15 ins.

171. ARLEQUIN MENAÇANT COLOMBINE
1886, $16\frac{1}{4} \times 16\frac{1}{4}$ ins.

172. DANS LA COULISSE. DEUX DANSEUSES
circa 1885, $9\frac{1}{2} \times 7$ ins.

73. MLLE SALLE EN COSTUME DU 'FANDANGO', ET ETUDES DE BRAS ET DE JAMBES
    1884, 23 × 27 *ins.*

73a. BUSTE DE MLLE SALLE
    circa 1888–90, 25 × 18¼ *ins.*

174. TROIS DANSEUSES DANS LES COULISSES
circa 1883–6, 29 × 23¼ *ins.*

175. DANSEUSE AVEC UN HOMME DANS LES COULISSES
circa 1883–6, 24½ × 18½ *ins.*

176. DANSEUSE EN ARABESQUE SUR LA SCEN
circa 1883–6, $35\frac{1}{2} \times 46\frac{1}{2}$ *ins.*

176a. DANSEUSE A L'ADAGE. ETUD
circa 1885–90, $20\frac{1}{4} \times 20\frac{1}{4}$ *ins.*

177. SEPT DANSEUSES DANS LA SALLE DE DANSE
circa 1883–6, $21\frac{1}{2} \times 16$ *ins.*

178. PAS SEUL. 'LE GRAND JETE'
circa 1883–6, 24 × 16¾ *ins*.

179. DANS LES COULISSES. DANSEUSE AU TAMBOURIN
  circa 1883–6, 13 × 16½ *ins.*

179a. 'LA FAMILLE CARDINAL'. AU FOYER
  circa 1880–3, 6¼ × 5 *ins.*

180. DANSEUSES ROSES ET VERTES
circa 1885–7, 32⅜ × 29¾ *ins.*

181. LES DANSEUSES ROSES AVANT LE BALLET
circa 1885–7, 15 × 18 ins.

182. TROIS DANSEUSES EN ROSE DANS LES COULISSES

circa 1885–7, 40 × 21¾ ins.

183. GROUPE DE DANSEUSES DANS UNE SALLE DE DANSE
circa 1888–90, 26 × 21 *ins.*

184. DEUX DANSEUSES DANS LA LOGE
circa 1886–8, 17 × 25 ins.

184*a*. MLLE SALLE. TROIS ETUDES DE LA TETE
1886, 20 × 20 ins.

185. TROIS DANSEUSES SE PREPARANT A LA CLASSE
circa 1886–8, 21½ × 20½ *ins.*

186. AVANT LA CLASSE. TROIS DANSEUSES
circa 1886–8, 21 × 20 *ins.*

187. LA PREPARATION A LA CLASSE

circa 1886–8, $25\frac{5}{8} \times 19\frac{3}{8}$ *ins.*

188. LA REPETITION SUR LA SCENE. CINQ DANSEUSES
circa 1888–90, 29¼ × 31¾ *ins.*

189. DANSEUSES A UNE REPETITION. ETUDE
circa 1888–90, 24 × 19 *ins*.

190. DANSEUSE VUE DE DOS. 'GRAND BATTEMENT A LA SECONDE'
circa 1885–90, 12 × 9 *ins.*

191. DANSEUSE DEBOUT, LES MAINS SUR LE CORSAGE
circa 1885–90, 18⅛ × 12 *ins*.

oreille
transparent

trop cru!

degas

192. DANSEUSE DEBOUT, LES MAINS DANS LES EMMANCHURES
circa 1885–90, 12 × 10 ins.

193. DANSEUSE DEBOUT, LES MAINS DANS LES EMMANCHURES
circa 1885–90, 12 × 10 ins.

194. DANSEUSE DEBOUT, LES MAINS DANS LES EMMANCHURES
circa 1885–90, $18\frac{5}{8} \times 11\frac{3}{4}$ *ins.*

195. DEUX DANSEUSES EN JUPES JAUNES, POSANT SUR LA SCENE
circa 1888–90, 24 × 17 *ins*.

196. DANSEUSE EN 'QUATRIEME', LES MAINS SUR LES REINS
circa 1882–90, height 17¼ ins.

197. DEUX DANSEUSES NUES DEBOUT
circa 1900, 24 × 18½ *ins.*

198. LE REPOS. QUATRE DANSEUSE
circa 1888–90, 20 × 29 *ins*.

198a. QUATRE DANSEUSES NUES EN REPO
circa 1888–90, 24½ × 30 *ins*.

X. LE REPOS. TROIS DANSEUSES
circa 1888–90, 20 × 24½ *ins.*

199. LE REPOS. TROIS DANSEUSES
circa 1888–90, 20 × 24½ *ins.*

200. DANSEUSE ROSE SE DEGOURDISSANT LE COU-DE-PIED
circa 1885–8, $23\frac{1}{2} \times 17\frac{1}{2}$ *ins.*

XI. DANSEUSE ROSE SE DEGOURDISSANT LE COU-DE-PIED

circa 1885–8, 23½ × 17½ *ins.*

201. TROIS DANSEUSES EN TETE A TETE
circa 1895–1900, 23 × 16 ins.

202. LA JUPE VERTE. DANSEUSE SE DEGOURDISSANT LE COU-DE-PIED
circa 1890–1900, 16 × 13 ins.

203. DANSEUSE EN JAUNE ASSISE
circa 1890–1900, 22 × 18 *ins.*

204. DEUX DANSEUSES SUR UNE BANQUETTE
circa 1890–1900, $31\frac{1}{4} \times 43$ *ins.*

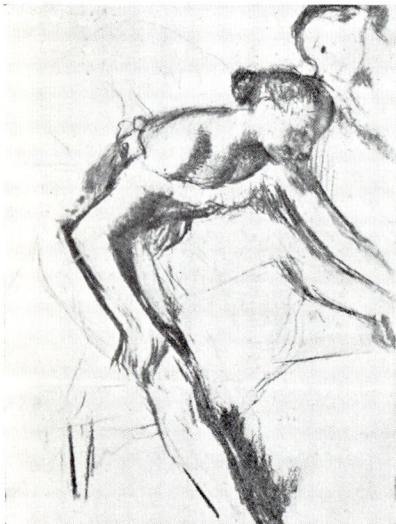

204*a*. DANSEUSE ASSISE. ETUDE
circa 1890–1900, 25×23 *ins.*

205. DEUX DANSEUSES SUR UNE BANQUETTE
circa 1890–1900, $34\frac{1}{2} \times 17\frac{1}{2}$ *ins.*

206. DEUX DANSEUSES CAUSANT SUR UNE BANQUETTE
circa 1890–1900, $23\frac{1}{4} \times 20$ *ins.*

207. DEUX DANSEUSES AUX CORSAGES JAUNES, ASSISES
circa 1890–1900, 33 × 27⅜ ins.

208. DANSEUSE A L'EVENTAIL, DANS LES COULISSES
circa 1900–5, 21⅞ × 19¼ *ins.*

209. DANSEUSE DEBOUT S'APPUYANT CONTRE UN PORTANT

circa 1900–5, 20 × 12 ins.

210. DEUX DANSEUSES DEBOUT DANS LES COULISSES
circa 1900–5, $23\frac{1}{4} \times 18\frac{1}{4}$ *ins.*

XII. TROIS DANSEUSES, DECOR D'ARBRES
circa 1900–5, 19½ × 18 ins.

211. DEUX DANSEUSES DEBOUT, DECOR D'ARBRES
circa 1900–5, 28 × 21⅜ ins.

212. QUATRE DANSEUSES SE REPOSANT DANS LES COULISSES
circa 1900—5, 28 × 26 *ins.*

213. QUATRE DANSEUSES SE REPOSANT DANS LES COULISSES
circa 1900–5, $24\frac{1}{2} \times 27\frac{1}{2}$ *ins.*

214. DEUX DANSEUSES EN CORSAGES VIOLETS AUX BRAS LEVES
circa 1900, 31½ × 19¾ *ins.*

215. DANSEUSES ROSES AUX BRAS LEVES
circa 1900, $33\frac{1}{8} \times 22\frac{7}{8}$ *ins.*

216. ETUDE DE TROIS DANSEUSES AUX BRAS LEVES
circa 1900, 18½ × 24 *ins*.

216*a*. DEUX DANSEUSES AUX BRAS LEVES. ETUDE
circa 1900, 17 × 13 *ins*.

217. TROIS DANSEUSES EN JUPES VIOLETTES AUX BRAS LEVES
circa 1900, 28 × 19 *ins*.

218. DANSEUSE NUE. 'DEVELOPPE EN AVANT'
circa 1882–90, height 22⅜ ins.

219. DANSEUSE SE DEGOURDISSANT A LA BARRE, LE BRAS DERRIERE LE DOS
circa 1900–5, 44 × 25 ins.

220. DEUX DANSEUSES SE DEGOURDISSANT A LA BARRE
circa 1900–5, 51 × 38 ins.

221. DEUX DANSEUSES SE DEGOURDISSANT A LA BARRE
circa 1900–5, 50 × 43¼ *ins.*

222. DANSEUSE AUX BAS ROUGES

circa 1900, 24¼ × 18½ *ins.*

223. QUATRE DANSEUSES A MI-CORPS

circa 1900, $26\frac{3}{8} \times 18\frac{3}{8}$ *ins.*

224. QUATRE DANSEUSES DANS LES COULISSES, DECOR DE PAYSAGE
circa 1900, 59¼ × 71¼ *ins*.

225. QUATRE DANSEUSES SUR LA SCENE
circa 1900–5, 29 × 37 ins.

226. QUATRE DANSEUSES BLEUES A MI-CORPS
  circa 1900–5, 25½ × 26 ins.

227. TROIS DANSEUSES A MI-CORPS
circa 1900–5, 24¼ × 26 *ins*.

228. DEUX DANSEUSES ROSES, TROIS-QUARTS

circa 1905–12, 25 × 23 ins.

229. QUATRE DANSEUSES, JUPES SAUMON
circa 1900–12, 36 × 26 *ins.*

230. DANSEUSES DANS LES COULISSES OBSERVANT LE SPECTACLE
circa 1905–12, 30 × 24 *ins*.

231. TROIS DANSEUSES DANS LES COULISSES
circa 1905–12, 37½ × 32 ins.

232. SIX DANSEUSES SUR LA SCENE
circa 1905–12, 30 × 44 *ins.*

232a. 'PORT DE BRAS'
circa 1885–90, 12¼ × 21½ *ins.*

233. DANSEUSES DEBOUT SUR LA SCENE
circa 1905–12, $29\frac{1}{2} \times 22\frac{1}{2}$ *ins.*

233*a*. DEUX DANSEUSES DEBOUT. ETUDE
circa 1905–12, 21 × 23 *ins.*

234. DANS LES COULISSES, TROIS DANSEUSES DEBOUT
circa 1905–12, 36 × 34 *ins*.

235. TROIS ETUDES D'UNE DANSEUSE
circa 1900–12, 19 × 25 *ins.*

235a. BLANCHISSEUSES ET CHEVAUX
circa 1885–1900, 42 × 48½ *ins.*

236. DANSEUSE A MI-CORPS SE COIFFANT
circa 1900–12, 14½ × 11 *ins.*

237. DEUX DANSEUSES A MI-CORPS, DOS-A-DOS
circa 1900–12, 18 × 14⅜ *ins.*

238. TROIS DANSEUSES À MI-CORPS, DÉCOR D'ARBRES
circa 1900–12, 25¾ × 20 ins.

239. TROIS DANSEUSES VUES A MI-CORPS
circa 1900–12, 26 × 20 *ins*.

240. DANSEUSES A MI-CORPS S'ARRANGEANT LES EPAULETTES
circa 1900–12, 24 × 25¼ *ins.*

241. QUATRE DANSEUSES VUES A MI-CORPS
circa 1900–12, 29 × 28 *ins.*

242. DANSEUSE RUSSE. LE 'HOPAK' DU BALLET 'LE FESTIN'
1909, $24\frac{3}{8} \times 18$ *ins.*

243. TROIS DANSEUSES RUSSES. LE 'HOPAK' DU BALLET 'LE FESTIN'
1909, 25 × 27 ins.

244. TROIS DANSEUSES, LES CHEVEUX EN TRESSE
1905–12, 26 × 21 *ins.*

245. TROIS DANSEUSES DEBOUT DANS LES COULISSES
1905–12, 23 × 28 ins.

246. DANSEUSES DANS LA SALLE DE DANSE. FRISE
circa 1905–12, 18 × 34 *ins.*

246a. TROIS DANSEUSES EN ARABESQUE
circa 1905–12, 16 × 26 *ins.*

247. TROIS DANSEUSES NUES
circa 1905–12, $34\frac{1}{2} \times 30\frac{1}{2}$ *ins.*

248. DEUX DANSEUSES, L'UNE A L'EVENTAIL
circa 1905–12, 24 × 15 *ins*.

249. DEUX DANSEUSES NUES, L'UNE A L'EVENTAIL
circa 1905–12, 22½ × 19 *ins.*

250. TROIS DANSEUSES EN MAILLOT
circa 1905–12, $34\frac{1}{2} \times 30\frac{1}{2}$ *ins.*

251. DEUX DANSEUSES NUES SUR UNE BANQUETTE
circa 1905–12, $18\frac{1}{2} \times 24$ *ins.*

252. DEUX DANSEUSES NUES DOS-A-DOS
circa 1900–12, 25 × 19 *ins.*

253. DEUX DANSEUSES EN MAILLOT
circa 1905–12, 20 × 16 ins.

254. QUATRE DANSEUSES NUES
circa 1905–12, 22½ × 19 ins.

255. GROUPE DE TROIS DANSEUSES DEBOUT
circa 1905–12, 23 × 21½ ins.

256. DEUX DANSEUSES EN 'QUATRIEME DERRIERE POINTE TENDUE'
circa 1905–12, 25 × 19 *ins*.

NOTES ON THE PLATES

NOTES ON THE PLATES

As so few of Degas' pictures are dated and very little documentary evidence—especially of the later working years—exists as to when his pictures were painted, the question of placing them in chronological order rests almost entirely upon stylistic grounds. I have therefore stated the actual year only when it could be done with certainty, otherwise I have suggested the approximate year or period of years within which the work appears to me to have been done. In some instances I have deliberately avoided chronological arrangement of the plates in order to trace the development of a particular idea or to demonstrate the recurrence of similar themes.

All criticisms of dancing positions are based on modern standards; and in many cases, chiefly when they have proved unacceptable or inexplicit from the balletic angle, I have taken the liberty of changing titles given me by the owners.

Many of the pictures reproduced have been shown in exhibitions too numerous to mention; I have therefore confined myself to the exhibitions which I feel to be of the greatest importance and whose catalogues I have been able to study myself. I have only referred to reproductions in journals when the pictures in question have not been reproduced in standard works. M. Lemoisne's *Catalogue Raisonné* of paintings and pastels could not be quoted as at the time of going to press it had not been published.

The unacknowledged photographs have been taken primarily from the Degas Sale catalogues. The pictures reproduced in these catalogues were in Degas' studio at the time of his death, and though a few among them had already been signed by Degas, all were subsequently stamped with his signature.

Some of the pictures have been reproduced in colour as well as in black-and-white in order to show the exact function which colour fulfils in Degas' painting.

As the plates, irrespective of the sizes of the originals, have to be uniformly reproduced, and as it is difficult to visualise the wide divergence of measurements even though the individual sizes are stated, I have thought it might be useful to students to give a chart (which is placed at the end of the Notes on the Plates) showing in scale the range within which Degas worked.

COLOUR PLATES

I. AU THEATRE. LE BALLET VU D'UNE LOGE (*Frontispiece*)

A reproduction in colour of Plate 110.

II. LA LEÇON DE DANSE (*opposite Pl. 17*)

A reproduction in colour of Plate 17.

III. PREPARATION POUR LA CLASSE (*opposite Pl. 39*)

A reproduction in colour of Plate 39.

IV. DANSEUSE BLEUE (*opposite Pl. 41*)

She stands on the right of the picture facing right. Her arms are *en couronne*, her left foot is *sur la pointe en quatrième devant*, the knee of that leg being bent.

Oil on canvas. 13 × 10 ins. Signed lower left. *Circa* 1878–9.

Owned by M. Alfred Vallotton, Lausanne.

Reproduced through the courtesy of Adam Bros., London.

For a drawing study of the picture see Pl. 41*a*. See also Pls. 40–3.

V. LE 'PAS DE DEUX' SUR LA SCENE (*opposite Pl. 50*)

A reproduction in colour of Plate 50.

VI. AVANT LA REPRESENTATION (*opposite Pl. 86*)

Against a set of trees and foliage, dancers in yellow and orange ballet skirts are seen stretching and doing exercises before the performance.

Oil on canvas. $19\frac{1}{4}$ × 25 ins. Stamp of the Degas sale lower right. *Circa* 1882–3.

Collections. Atelier Degas ; David Eccles ; Edward Molyneux.

Reproduced. Catalogue vente Degas, I (1918), No. 77.

Owned by Mr and Mrs Alexander Maitland, Edinburgh.

Reproduced by courtesy of the owners.

For a pastel of a similar composition see *Catalogue vente Degas*, I (1918), No. 122; see also IV (1919), No. 190.

VII. DANSEUSES SUR LA SCENE AVANT LA REPRESENTATION

(*opposite Pl. 88*)

They are standing in yellow *tutus*, some partly hidden by the 'foliage'.

Oil on silk. $6\frac{3}{8}$ × $11\frac{5}{8}$ ins. Signed lower right. *Circa* 1875–80.

Collection. La Duchesse de Montmorency. Paris.

Owned by Reid & Lefevre. London.

Reproduced by courtesy of the owners.

Following the example of some 18th century French painters, and like other of his contemporaries, Degas painted a series of fans, probably between the years 1875 and 1885.
These were done on silk, parchment and board, and five were exhibited in the 4th Impressionist Exhibition in 1879. It is evident that the above picture was originally designed by
Degas as a fan, not only because it is painted on silk with the markings of the positions of the
ribs visible, but also because the top left-hand corner clearly shows the original peripheral
boundary which is also borne out by the composition.

VIII. DEUX DANSEUSES A MI-CORPS A L'EVENTAIL (*opposite Pl. 109*)

They are facing each other, talking. One rests on what appears to be a tall stick, the other
holds an open fan behind her head.

> *Pastel.* $22\frac{1}{4} \times 32\frac{1}{4}$ ins. Stamp of the Degas sale lower left. *Circa* 1883–5.
> *Collection.* Atelier Degas; Sir William Burrell.
> *Reproduced.* *Catalogue vente Degas*, I (1918), No. 134.
> *Owned* by the Glasgow Art Gallery and Museum. (Sir William Burrell Collection.)
> *Reproduced* by courtesy of the Glasgow Art Gallery.

IX. TROIS DANSEUSES EN LIGNE DIAGONALE SUR LA SCENE
(*opposite Pl. 134*)

A reproduction in colour of Plate 134.

X. LE REPOS. TROIS DANSEUSES (*opposite Pl. 199*)

A reproduction in colour of Plate 199.

XI. DANSEUSE ROSE SE DEGOURDISSANT LE COU-DE-PIED
(*opposite Pl. 200*)

A reproduction in colour of Plate 200.

XII. TROIS DANSEUSES, DECOR D'ARBRES (*opposite Pl. 211*)

They are standing in a group behind a 'tree', their hands on their hips, and looking to the left.

> *Pastel.* $19\frac{1}{2} \times 18$ ins. Signed twice, lower left and right. *Circa* 1900–5.
> *Collection.* Sir William Burrell.
> *Reproduced.* Ambroise Vollard, *98 Reproductions signed by Degas* (Bernheim Jeune, 1918),
> Pl. 48; Julius Meier-Graefe, *Degas* (1927), Pl. 103.
> *Owned* by the Glasgow Art Gallery and Museum. (Collection of Sir William Burrell.)
> *Reproduced* by courtesy of the Glasgow Art Gallery.

See also *Catalogue vente Degas*, I (1918), Nos. 137, 203, 245, 273; II (1918), No. 284; III
(1919), Nos. 222, 240, 257, 258, 261, 325 and 381.

MONOCHROME PLATES

1. SEMIRAMIS CONSTRUISANT UNE VILLE, DE L'OPERA 'SEMIRAMIS'

The group surrounding the queen is seen on the right of the picture; on the left the Hanging Gardens of Babylon.

> *Oil on canvas.* 59 × 102 ins. Unfinished. Painted 1860–1.
> *Collection.* Atelier Degas.
> *Exhibition.* Salon, 1861.
> *Reproduced. Catalogue vente Degas*, I (1918), No. 7; Paul Lafond, *Degas*, Vol. I (1918), p. 19; Paul Jamot, *Degas* (1924), Pl. 6; J. B. Manson, *The Life and Work of Edgar Degas* (1927), Pl. 2; Georges Rivière, *Mr. Degas (Bourgeois de Paris)* (1935), p. 31; Georges Grappe, *Degas* (1936), p. 5; Camille Mauclair, *Degas* (1941), p. 71; Marguerite Rebatet, *Degas* (1944), Pl. 7; John Rewald, *History of Impressionism* (1946), p. 53.
> *Owned* by the Musée du Louvre, Paris (transferred from the Musée du Luxembourg in 1929).
> *Photograph.* Archives photographiques.

There are several sketches for this picture, one of which was shown in the *Exposition Degas*, Galerie Georges Petit, 1924, No. 5. Also there are many studies for individual figures (see Pl. 1*a*) and for the composition; two of these small drawings belong to M. Nepveu Degas and another in the *Croquis Degas*, Cabinet des Estampes. See also *Catalogue vente Degas*, I (1918), Nos. 21 and 219.

The opera, from which Degas took his subject was first produced in July 1860. See p. 50.

1*a*. ETUDE DE LA FEMME A GENOUX POUR 'SEMIRAMIS CONSTRUISANT UNE VILLE'

The figure is nude, kneeling on one leg with hand supporting chin and facing left. Also studies for arms and foot.

> *Pencil.* 11⅞ × 9¼ ins. Stamp of the Degas sale lower left; also signature and collector's stamp 'M. N.' on lower right. Inscribed at top with remarks about the light. Squared for painting. Drawn 1860–1.
> *Collection.* Atelier Degas.
> *Exhibitions. Degas*, Galerie Georges Petit, Paris, 1924, No. 76*a*; *Degas*, Pennsylvania Museum of Art, Philadelphia, 1936, No. 60 (reproduced).
> *Reproduced. Catalogue vente Degas*, I (1918), No. 7*b*; *Degas—Vingt Dessins*, Albumn Manzi (1896), Pl. I; Paul Lafond, *Degas*, Vol. I (1918), opp. p. 20; Georges Grappe, *E. Degas* (1936), p. 4.
> *Owned* by the Musée du Louvre, Paris (transferred from the Musée du Luxembourg).
> *Photograph.* Archives photographiques.

2. ETUDE POUR 'LA SOURCE'. JEUNE FILLE A LA GUITARE

She kneels facing quarter left, her head seen in profile.

Pencil. 14 × 8½ ins. Stamp of the Degas sale lower right. Drawn 1866–7.
Collection. Atelier Degas.
Reproduced. *Catalogue vente Degas*, IV (1919), No. 79a.
Owned by the Art Institute of Chicago. Gift of Robert Allerton.
Photograph. The Art Institute of Chicago.

See also pencil drawing, *Catalogue vente Degas*, IV, No. 247a, and notes Pl. 3.

3. MLLE FIOCRE DANS LE BALLET 'LA SOURCE'

She is sitting on a 'rock' with her toes in the water. On her left a horse and a seated woman; on her right a girl playing a guitar.

Oil on canvas. 52 × 57¾ ins. Unsigned. Painted 1866–7.
Collection. Atelier Degas.
Exhibitions. Paris Salon, 1868, No. 686; *Degas, Portraitiste, Sculpteur*, Musée de l'Orangerie, Paris, 1931, No. 37a; *French Art*, Royal Academy, London, 1932, No. 391; *Degas*, Pennsylvania Museum of Art, Philadelphia, 1936, No. 9 (reproduced); *Degas*, Cleveland Museum of Art, 1947, No. 12 (reproduced).
Reproduced. *Catalogue vente Degas*, I (1918), No. 8a; P. A. Lemoisne, *Degas* (1912), p. 39; Paul Lafond, *Degas*, Vol. I (1918), p. 87; Ambroise Vollard, *Degas* (1924), p. 8; Paul Jamot, *Degas* (1924), Pl. 18; J. B. Manson, *The Life and Work of Edgar Degas* (1927), p. 8; Georges Grappe, *Degas* (1936), p. 18; Camille Mauclair, *Degas* (1941), p. 72; Marguerite Rebatet, *Degas* (1944), Pl. 15; John Rewald, *History of Impression* (1946), p. 153.
Owned by the Brooklyn Museum, Brooklyn.
Photograph. Durand Ruel, Paris.

For studies for this picture apart from Pls. 2 and 3a see *Catalogue vente Degas*, I (1918), Nos. 8b and 38; II (1918), Nos. 10 and 96; IV (1919), No. 77a.

'La Source' was first produced in November 1866. See p. 51.

3a. FEMME ASSISE AU BORD DE L'EAU. ETUDE POUR 'LA SOURCE'

She is sitting with one leg tucked under her, the other bent close to her body. Her hair falls over her shoulders and she supports herself with her right hand on the floor.

Charcoal. 14½ × 10 ins. Stamp of the Degas Sale since added to original. Drawn 1866–7.
Collection. Atelier Degas.
Reproduced. *Catalogue vente Degas*, IV (1919), No. 77b.
Owner unknown.

See notes Pl. 3, also *Catalogue vente Degas*, IV (1919), No. 77a.

4. L'ORCHESTRE DE L'OPERA. LE PORTRAIT DE DESIRE DIHAU

Oil on canvas. 21½ × 18 ins. Signed lower right. Painted 1868–9.
Collections. Désiré Dihau; Mlle Marie Dihau.

Exhibitions. Lille, during the war of 1870–1; *Degas*, Galerie Georges Petit, Paris, 1924, No. 30 (reproduced); *Art Français*, Amsterdam, 1926, No. 40 (reproduced); *Degas*, *Portraitiste*, *Sculpteur*, Musée de l'Orangerie, Paris, 1931, No. 44; *French Art*, Royal Academy, London, 1932, No. 502; *Degas*, Pennsylvania Museum of Art, Philadelphia, 1936, No. 12 (reproduced); *Degas*, Musée de l'Orangerie, 1937, No. 9.

Reproduced. Paul Jamot, *Degas* (1924), Pl. 19; Georges Grappe, *Degas* (1936), p. 15; Camille Mauclair, *Degas* (1941), p. 159; Marguerite Rebatet, *Degas* (1944), Pl. 20; John Rewald, *History of Impressionism* (1946), p. 202.

Owned by the Musée du Louvre, Paris (bought 1923, but not taken over until Mlle Dihau's death in 1935).

Photograph. Archives photographiques.

Degas originally intended the picture as a portrait of Désiré Dihau, who appears as the most prominent figure in the picture, playing his bassoon. But he enlarged his idea and included other members of the orchestra as well as his own friends who had nothing to do with the orchestra itself. He has also rearranged the places of the musicians—Dihau, for instance, occupies that of the first violin. In the stage box, on the extreme left, is the head of the composer, Chabrier; on extreme right, the back of Gouffe, the double-bass player; the flautist is Altes, future leader of the orchestra; behind him Lancien and Gout, first violins; on the left, the cellist, Pillet; and among Degas' friends, the painter Piot-Normand; the composer, Souquet; Dr. Pillot (all amateur violinists) and Gard, *metteur en scène de la danse de L'Opéra*.

For a study of Dihau between two musicians see *Catalogue vente Degas*, I (1918), No. 9.

5. MUSICIENS DE L'ORCHESTRE

In the lower half of the picture are seen the backs of three musicians' heads; in the upper half, dancers on the stage.

Oil on canvas. 25 × 19½ ins. Signed lower right. *Circa* 1872.

Exhibition. *Degas*, Musée de l'Orangerie, Paris, 1937, No. 15 (reproduced).

Reproduced. Georges Grappe, *E. Degas* (1909), opp. p. 56; P. A. Lemoisne, *Degas* (1912), Pl. 14; Paul Lafond, *Degas*, Vol. I (1918), p. 111; Knut Hoppe, *Degas* (1922), p. 43; Ambroise Vollard, *Degas* (1924), p. 104; Paul Jamot, *Degas* (1924), Pl. 104; J. B. Manson, *The Life and Work of Edgar Degas* (1927), p. 15; Camille Mauclair, *Degas* (1941), p. 155; Marguerite Rebatet, *Degas* (1944), Pl. 74.

Owned by the State Museum, Frankfort (bought 1912).

Photograph. Durand Ruel, Paris.

Perhaps this is *L'Orchestre* which Degas exhibited in the second 'Impressionist Exhibition' of 1876; it is unlikely to have been the Dihau picture, because the family would almost certainly have passed this important information on to the Louvre authorities.

6. TROIS RELIGIEUSES. ETUDE POUR 'ROBERT LE DIABLE'

The three dancers are seen standing in varying positions.

Peinture à l'essence. 11 × 17 ins. Stamp of the Degas sale lower left. Drawn 1871–2.

Collection. Atelier Degas.

Reproduced. *Catalogue vente Degas*, III (1919), 364*b*.

Owned by the Victoria and Albert Museum, London.

Photograph. Victoria and Albert Museum.

See also Pls. 6a and 7; finished pictures Pls. 8 and 9, and notes; as well as *Catalogue vente Degas*, III (1919), No. 364a.

6a. DEUX RELIGIEUSES. ETUDE POUR 'ROBERT LE DIABLE'

The two dancers are standing, the one facing the audience, the other bending sideways towards it.

Peinture à l'essence. $10\frac{1}{4} \times 17$ ins. Stamp of the Degas sale lower left. Drawn 1871–2.

Collection. Atelier Degas.

Reproduced. Catalogue vente Degas, III (1919), No. 363a.

Owned by the Victoria and Albert Museum, London.

Photograph. Victoria and Albert Museum.

See Pls. 8 and 9 and notes.

7. UNE RELIGIEUSE. ETUDE POUR 'ROBERT LE DIABLE'

The dancer is standing bending sideways towards the audience.

Peinture à l'essence. $17 \times 13\frac{1}{4}$ ins. Stamp of the Degas sale lower left. Drawn 1871–2.

Collection. Atelier Degas.

Reproduced. Catalogue vente Degas, III (1919), No. 363a.

Owned by the Victoria and Albert Museum, London.

Photograph. Victoria and Albert Museum.

See also Pls. 6 and 6a; finished pictures Pls. 8 and 9, and notes.

8. LE BALLET DE 'ROBERT LE DIABLE'

In the foreground members of the audience and orchestra; in the background, the ballet is in progress on the stage.

Oil on canvas. $26 \times 21\frac{3}{8}$ ins. Signed lower right and dated '1872'.

Collection. Mme Albert Hecht.

Reproduced. Georges Grappe, *E. Degas* (1909), p. 53; Paul Lafond, *Degas*, Vol. I (1918), p. 50; Julius Meier-Graefe, *Degas* (1927), Pl. 14; Georges Grappe, *Degas* (1936), p. 39; Camille Mauclair, *Degas* (1941), p. 160; John Rewald, *History of Impressionism* (1946), p. 231.

Owned by the Metropolitan Museum of Art, New York. (Havemeyer bequest, 1929).

Photograph. Metropolitan Museum of Art.

The bearded man, turning and looking through his glasses, is M. Helch, the collector and friend of Manet and Degas (the former painted him in *Jardin des Tuileries*); next to him, on the left, Désiré Dihau is seen playing the bassoon. It is from this picture that Faure ordered his canvas, see Pl. 9.

For studies of the dancers see Pls. 6, 6a and 7.

Towards the end of 1871 'Robert le Diable' was again revived. In this presentation Laure Fonta led the 'Ballet of the Nuns'. See p. 52.

NOTES ON THE PLATES

9. LE BALLET DE 'ROBERT LE DIABLE'

Members of the audience and orchestra are seen in the foreground; in the background the ballet on the stage.

> *Oil on canvas.* 29¾ × 32 ins. Signed lower left. Painted 1874–6.
> *Collections.* Faure; Ionides.
> *Reproduced.* P. A. Lemoisne, *Degas* (1912), Pl. 13; Paul Jamot, *Degas* (1924), Pl. 25; J. B. Manson, *The Life and Work of Edgar Degas* (1927), Pl. 14.
> *Owned* by the Victoria and Albert Museum, London. (Ionides Bequest.)
> *Photograph.* Victoria and Albert Museum.

On extreme left M. Helch holding his glasses, may be seen; behind him, Désiré Dihau, in profile; and third from the right, with beard, le Vicomte Lepic.

For studies of the dancers see Pls. 6, 6a and 7; and for earlier version, Pl. 8. See also notes Pl. 8.

10. DANSEUSE EN 'QUATRIEME DERRIERE, POINTE TENDUE'

She is standing facing the spectator with head turned a quarter to the right.

> *Pencil and crayon heightened with white chalk on pink paper, and squared for painting.* 16⅛ × 11¼ ins. Signed lower right. Drawn *circa* 1872.
> *Collections.* Atelier Degas; De Hauke; Paul Sachs.
> *Exhibitions. Degas,* Fogg Art Museum, Cambridge, 1931, No. 23; *Degas,* Pennsylvania Museum of Art, Philadelphia, 1936, No. 75 (reproduced); *Degas,* Musée de l'Orangerie, Paris, 1937, No. 81.
> *Reproduced. Vingt Dessins de Degas,* Albumn Manzi (1896), Pl. 10; *Catalogue vente Degas,* I (1918), No. 328; Paul Jamot, *Degas* (1924), Pl. 18.
> *Owned* by the Fogg Museum, Cambridge, Mass. (Paul J. Sachs Collection.)
> *Photograph.* The Fogg Museum.

In his early pictures, when he was only attempting dancers in static positions, Degas frequently used this 'quatrième derrière', which is a preparatory position for 'enchainements'. The drawing is a study for the 'danseuse' in *La Classe de Danse de M. Perrot* (Pl. 22) and has also been used for one of the figures in the *Répétition sur la Scène* pictures (Pls. 28, 30 and 31). For the same position, with arms differently placed, see Pls. 12, 14, 16 and 17. It is interesting to note that, contrary to his usual practice, Degas does not, at any later date, again refer to this position. The model bears a close facial resemblance to Mlle Chabot, but the dates do not coincide and no other suggestion as to identification has been found possible.

11. DANSEUSE DEBOUT, VUE DE DOS

She is facing three-quarters left, apparently arranging her bodice.

> *Pencil and chalk.* Size unknown. Signed lower left, with plumb-line running through the centre of the figure. *Circa* 1872.
> *Owner* unknown.
> *Photograph.* Sir Robert Witt Library, London.

12. JOSEPHINE GAUGELIN EN 'QUATRIEME DERRIERE POINTE TENDUE'

She is seen front view, her head turned a quarter to the right.

> *Pencil.* 12 × 8 ins. Stamp of the Degas sale lower right. Two plumb-lines containing the figure. Inscribed lower left, 'Josephine Gaugelin, autrefois danseuse à l'Opéra, puis actrice au Gymnase', and dated 1872.
> *Collections.* Atelier Degas; D. Kelekian; F. Koenigs.
> *Exhibition.* Boymans Museum, Rotterdam, 1933–4.
> *Reproduced.* Catalogue vente Degas, III (1919), No. 156.
> *Owned* by the Boymans Museum, Rotterdam (presented 1940).
> *Photograph.* Boymans Museum.

This particular study does not seem to have been used in any picture. For a portrait study of Mme Gaugelin, see Pl. 17a, also note to Pl. 20.

13. DANSEUSE SE DEGOURDISSANT A LA BARRE

She is facing the *barre*, holding it with both hands, and with right leg upon it. On the same page, the back view of two feet in first position; and beneath them, a study of legs in fourth position 'sur les trois-quarts-pointes'.

> *Charcoal heightened with white and pastel.* 18 × 12 ins. Stamp of Degas sale lower left. The figure is squared for painting. Remarks about the position written by Degas at the top of the sheet. *Circa* 1875.
> *Collection.* Atelier Degas.
> *Reproduced.* Catalogue vente Degas, III (1919), No. 367a.
> *Owner* unknown.
> *Photograph.* Durand Ruel, Paris.

The drawing is a study for one of the dancers in the classroom pictures, Pls. 35 and 37.

It is a dancer's practice to stretch herself either before a class or a performance, and she usually begins with a few minutes at the *barre*. From the position which Degas shows, the foot is slid along the *barre* away from the standing leg as far as possible, and with both knees kept straight, the groins and tendons behind the knees are slowly pulled. Degas has written 'un peu loin le pied' reminding himself of the subsequent move. The dancer's position is imperfect in that her body should be nearly touching the *barre*, with the leg so well turned and the 'pointe' so forced, that the foot lies flat upon it.

14. ETUDE DE DANSEUSE DE PROFIL

She is standing, facing the right in 'quatrième derrière, pointe tendue'.

> *Pencil and gouache on pink paper.* 11¼ × 9 ins. Stamp of the Degas sale lower right. Inscribed '93 rue du Bac; d'Hugues'. *Circa* 1872.
> *Collections.* Atelier Degas; René de Gas.
> *Exhibitions.* French Painting of the 19th and 20th Centuries, Fogg Art Museum, Cambridge, 1929, No. 21 (of drawings); Rhode Island School of Design, Providence; Degas, Pennsylvania Museum of Art, Philadelphia, 1936, No. 73 (reproduced).

Reproduced. Degas—Vingt Dessins, Album Manzi (1896); *Catalogue vente Degas*, II (1918), No. 231*a*; *Catalogue vente René Degas* (1927), No. 23*a* (reproduced).
Owned by John Nicholas Brown, Providence.
Photograph. John Nicholas Brown.

The drawing is a study for *La Classe de Danse de M. Mérante*, Pl. 16. Hugues was evidently the name of the dancer.

15. DANSEUSE ASSISE

She is sitting with her skirts spread around her, legs outstretched, facing three-quarters left.

Pencil and gouache on pink paper. $11\frac{1}{4} \times 9$ ins. Stamp of the Degas sale faintly visible lower left. *Circa* 1872.

Collections. Atelier Degas; René de Gas.

Exhibitions. French Painting of the 19th and 20th Centuries, Fogg Art Museum, Cambridge, 1929, No. 22 (of drawings); Rhode Island School of Design, Providence; *Degas*, Pennsylvania Museum of Art, Philadelphia, 1936, No. 74 (reproduced).

Reproduced. Catalogue vente Degas, II (1918), No. 231*b*; *Catalogue vente René Degas* (1927), No. 23*b* (reproduced).

Owned by John Nicholas Brown, Providence.

Photograph. John Nicholas Brown.

The drawing is a study for *La Classe de Danse de M. Mérante*, Pl. 16, but Degas has altered the angle of the sitter in the oil painting.

16. LA CLASSE DE DANSE DE M. MERANTE

In the opera-house, rue Le Peletier, M. Mérante is seen conducting a class.

Oil on canvas. $13 \times 18\frac{1}{2}$ ins. Signed lower left. Painted 1872.

Collections. Manzi; H. Vever; Isaac de Camondo.

Reproduced. Engraved by Martinez in 1873 for Durand Ruel; Georges Grappe, *E. Degas* (1909), p. 17; P. A. Lemoisne, *Degas* (1912), Pl. 16; Paul Lafond, *Degas*, Vol. I (1918), p. 149; Paul Jamot, *Degas* (1924), Pl. 23; Julius Meier-Graefe, *Degas* (1927), Pl. 17; Georges Rivière, *Mr. Degas (Bourgeois de Paris)* (1935), p. 119.

Owned by the Musée du Louvre, Paris (bequeathed in 1911 by Camondo).

Photograph. Archives photographiques.

In the Louvre catalogue the picture is known as *Le Foyer de la Danse à l'Opéra*. There are various studies for the figures in this picture (Pls. 14, 15 and 16*a*); the study for the violinist is reproduced in the *Catalogue vente Degas*, III (1919), 113*b*, but Degas has changed the head considerably, for in the oil-painting the violinist strongly resembles Pagans the guitarist, of whom Degas painted at least two pictures. For a study of the two dancers at the *barre* see *Catalogue vente Degas*, II (1918), No. 224. See also p. 53.

16*a*. DEUX DANSEUSES DEBOUT A LA BARRE. ETUDE

One is leaning her back against the *barre*, the other stands with the *pointe* of one foot crossed over the supporting one.

Peinture à l'essence ?. $8\frac{1}{4} \times 10$ ins. Stamp of the Degas sale lower right. *Circa* 1872.

Collections. Atelier Degas; F. Koenigs.

Reproduced. *Catalogue vente Degas*, III (1919), No. 395*b*; H. Rivière, *Les Dessins de Degas* (1922–3).

Owned by the Boymans Museum, Rotterdam.

Photograph. Boymans Museum.

This is one of the studies for *La Classe de Dance de M. Mérante*, Pl. 16.

17. LA LEÇON DE DANSE

In the opera-house rue Le Peletier. In this picture only the violinist, and not the *professeur* is seen.

Oil on panel. $7\frac{3}{4} \times 10\frac{5}{8}$ ins. Signed lower right. *Circa* 1872.

Collections. Manzi; H. O. Havemeyer.

Reproduced. John Rewald, *History of Impressionism* (1946), p. 232, also a detail in colour.

Owned by The Metropolitan Museum of Art, New York. (H. O. Havemeyer bequest 1929.)

Photograph. Metropolitan Museum of Art.

See also Colour Plate II.

17a. TETE DE MME GAUGELIN

She is seen full face wearing a bonnet tied under the chin.

Pencil. $14\frac{1}{2} \times 9\frac{1}{4}$ ins. Stamp of the Degas sale on the original. Inscribed with title lower right. *Circa* 1867.

Collection. Atelier Degas.

Exhibitions. *Degas*, Galerie Georges Petit, Paris, 1924, No. 95; *Degas—Portraitiste, Sculpteur*, Musée de l'Orangerie, Paris, 1931, No. 114.

Reproduced. *Catalogue vente Degas*, III (1919), No. 405*b*.

Owned by A. M. Olivier Senn, Paris.

For a drawing of Mme Gaugelin full length and in ballet skirt see Pl. 12; see also note to Pl. 20. The drawing is a study for the portrait of Mme Gaugelin, *La Femme aux raisins dorés* which belonged to Mrs. Gardner of Boston.

18. DANSEUSE ASSISE

Her feet, the soles touching, are resting 'sur les pointes'; her body is turned a quarter to the right; and with her fingers she is working out an *enchainement*.

Charcoal heightened with white chalk on pink paper. $16\frac{3}{8} \times 12\frac{7}{8}$ ins. Signed lower right. The plumb line is visible, also rectangle into which the figure has been fitted. *Circa* 1873.

Collection. H. O. Havemeyer.

Owned by the Metropolitan Museum of Art, New York. (H. O. Havemeyer bequest 1929.)

Photograph. Metropolitan Museum of Art.

A teacher will often call out the steps of an *enchainement* while indicating with the fingers the positions through which the feet pass. The pupil, in order to make sure that she has memorised the steps, goes through the same procedure with her own fingers. This is the habit that Degas has indicated in his drawing, sometimes called, erroneously, *La Danse de la Chatte*. The figure appears in both the paintings Pls. 22 and 23, but the arms and head are differently placed.

19. DANSEUSE DEBOUT

She is standing with head bent forward and turned a quarter right, tucking in her bodice with her right hand.

Charcoal heightened with white chalk on pink paper. 15 × 10¼ ins. Stamp of the Degas sale lower right. Plumb line through the centre of the figure. *Circa* 1873.
Collection. Atelier Degas.
Reproduced. Catalogue vente Degas, II (1918), No. 332.
Owned by John S. Newbury, Jr., Michigan.
Photograph. Bucholz Gallery, New York.

The drawing is a study for one of the figures in the earlier version of *La Classe de Danse de M. Perrot.* See also *Catalogue vente Degas*, II (1918), No. 326.

20. DANSEUSE RAJUSTANT SON CHAUSSON

She is standing on her left leg while she raises the other and arranges her shoe-ribbons. With her right hand she supports herself and turns her head towards it.

Pencil and white chalk on pink paper. 12⅞ × 9⅝ ins. Signed lower left. Inscribed on the right 'le bras est enfoncé un peu dans la mousseline'. Squared for painting. *Circa* 1873.
Collection. H. O. Havemeyer.
Owned by the Metropolitan Museum of Art, New York. (H. O. Havemeyer bequest 1929.)
Photograph. Metropolitan Museum of Art.

The drawing is a study for *Deux Danseuses en Repos*, Pl. 21. See also *Catalogue vente Degas*, IV (1919), No. 261*b*, which is inscribed 'd'après Gaugelin, 1873'. It seems that Gaugelin posed for most of Degas' drawings in the early 'seventies, so it is presumably she who figures in the paintings of the same time.

21. DEUX DANSEUSES EN REPOS

One sits on the piano scratching her back; the other supports herself against it while arranging her shoe-ribbons.

Pastel. 17¼ × 11⅞ ins. Signed lower left and dated 1874.
Reproduced. Paul Lafond, *Degas*, Vol. I (1918), p. 63; Julius Meier-Graefe, *Degas* (1927), Pl. 25; Marguerite Rebatet, *Degas* (1944), Pl. 95.
Owned by Mr and Mrs J. Watson Webb, New York.
Photograph. The owners.

The dancer on the piano is a study for the figure which is said to have been added to the first version of *La Classe de Danse de M. Perrot*, Pl. 22. It is one of the earliest of dancing subjects to have been executed by Degas in pastel.
See also *Catalogue vente Degas*, III (1919), No. 341; and IV (1919), No. 271.

22. LA CLASSE DE DANSE DE M. PERROT

The dancer about to perform before M. Perrot, is standing waiting in a preparatory position; many others are grouped about.

Oil on canvas. 34 × 30 ins. Signed lower left. Painted 1873–4.
Collections. M. Brandon (1874); English collection, Brighton; Manzi (1893); Isaac de Camondo.

Exhibitions. 1er *Exposition des Impressionistes,* 1874, No. 55; and perhaps again in 3ème *Exposition des Impressionistes,* 1877, No. 48; *Degas,* Galerie Georges Petit, 1924, No. 46; *Degas,* Musée de l'Orangerie, Paris, 1937, No. 21.

Reproduced. P. A. Lemoisne, *Degas* (1912), Pl. 22; Paul Lafond, *Degas,* Vol. I (1918), p. 41; Gustave Coquiot, *Degas* (1924), opposite p. 80; Paul Jamot, *Degas* (1924), Pl. 35; Julius Meier-Graefe, *Degas* (1927), Pl. 15; Georges Rivière, *Mr Degas (Bourgeois de Paris)* (1935), p. 117; Georges Grappe, *Degas* (1936), p. 36.

Owned by the Musée du Louvre (bequeathed in 1911 by Camondo).

Photograph. Archives photographiques.

The dancer seated on the piano is said to have been added to the picture later. For a study of M. Perrot see Pl. 24. See also p. 54.

It is quite possible that in Degas' time, the mothers were allowed to watch classes, a procedure which is strictly forbidden at the Opéra nowadays.

23. LA CLASSE DE DANSE DE M. PERROT

Showing the performing dancer passing through the position of 'attitude'.

Oil on canvas. 33¼ × 30½ ins. Signed lower left. *Circa* 1874–6.

Reproduced. Georges Grappe, *E. Degas* (1909), p. 21; Ambroise Vollard, *Degas* (1924), p. 96; Paul Jamot, *Degas* (1924), Pl. 40; Julius Meier-Graefe, *Degas* (1927), Pl. 16; Marguerite Rebatet, *Degas* (1944), Pl. 77.

Owned by Mr Payne Bingham, New York.

Photograph. Metropolitan Museum of Art.

This is one of the earliest pictures in which Degas shows a dancer in the middle of a movement. The picture is said (by M. Guerin, *Lettres de Degas,* 1931) to have been the *Examen de Danse* belonging to M. Faure and exhibited in the Impressionist Exhibition of 1876, No. 37. But Degas knew very well that the examinations took place only on the Opéra stage, and though he later paid little attention to such details it is unlikely that he would have taken liberties at this early date regarding a subject in which so eminent a person as Jules Perrot figured. See also Pls. 22 and 24, and p. 54.

24. JULES PERROT DEBOUT. ETUDE

The celebrated dancer is seen leaning on his stick as he conducts a class.

Peinture à l'essence on greenish-grey paper. 19¾ × 12 ins. Signed and dated lower right 1875.

Collections. Petitdidier; Exsteens; Ochsé.

Exhibitions. *Art français of the 19th and 20th centuries,* Copenhagen, 1914, No. 703; *Degas,* Galerie Georges Petit, Paris, 1924, No. 54; *Degas,* Pennsylvania Museum of Art, Philadelphia, 1936, No. 78 (reproduced); *Degas,* Cleveland Museum of Art, 1947, No. 67 (reproduced).

Reproduced. H. Rivière, *Les Dessins de Degas,* 1922, Pl. 26.

Owned by Henry P. McIlhenny, Philadelphia.

Photograph. The owner.

The study is probably done from the oil-painting (Pl. 22) and, with the position of the hands altered, used for (Pl. 23). There is a charcoal drawing for it (*Catalogue vente Degas,* III (1919),

No. 157*b*), and on the same page, No. 157*c* a drawing of Perrot seated, which is a study for a painting (*Catalogue vente Degas*, I (1918), No. 54).

Of this sketch A. S. Hartrick writes: 'He (Renouard) spoke also of a portrait of a ballet master by Degas done in the school against a whitewashed wall, which he considered the most wonderful painting ever done by the master. I have never heard of it from any other source nor seen a reproduction; so I sometimes wonder if it belonged to the kind which John Sargent once referred to when he said 'Every portrait is another enemy', and whether it has been destroyed because of the vanity of the sitter. (*A Painter's Pilgrimage through Fifty Years*, pub. 1939, p. 87.)

25. DANSEUSE AUX CHEVEUX LONGS, DEBOUT

She is standing in fourth position facing right, with left hand holding on to edge of flat above her head.

Peinture à l'essence. 25½ × 20 ins. Stamp of the Degas sale lower left. Painted *circa* 1874.
Collection. Atelier Degas.
Exhibitions. Der Unbekannte Winterthurer Privatbesitz, 1500–1900. Kunstmuseum Winterthur, 1942, No. 83 (reproduced, Pl. 48).
Reproduced. Catalogue vente Degas, II (1918), No. 345.
Owned by private collector. Winterthur.
Photograph. Leicester Galleries, London.

A study for one of the figures in the two later versions of *Répétition d'un Ballet sur la Scène* (Pls. 30 and 31).

26. DANSEUSE BAILLANT

She stands in first position with hands clasped behind her head.

Charcoal heightened with white. 18 × 10 ins. Stamp of the Degas sale lower left. *Circa* 1873–4.
Collection. Atelier Degas.
Reproduced. Catalogue vente Degas, II (1918), No. 331.
Owner unknown.
Photograph. Durand Ruel, Paris.

The drawing is a study for the first version of *La Répétition d'un Ballet sur la Scène* (Pl. 28).

27. DANSEUSE DEBOUT

She stands facing the right, her left hand resting on the flat above her head, the other on her waist.

Charcoal heightened with white on pink paper. 18 × 11¼ ins. Stamp of the Degas sale lower left. Drawn 1873–4.
Collections. Atelier Degas; Dr Viau.
Exhibition. Degas, Galerie Georges Petit, Paris, 1924, No. 112.
Reproduced. Catalogue vente Degas, III (1919), No. 338; *Les Dessins de Degas*, Demotte Edition, p. 68.
Owned by Lt. Comdr. and Mrs C. Mitchell, Jr.
Photograph. Jacques Seligmann & Co., Inc., New York.

The drawing is a study for one of the figures in the first version of *La Répétition d'un Ballet sur la Scène* (Pl. 28). It is interesting to compare it with a similar study (Pl. 25) used in the two later pictures; and with *Catalogue vente Degas*, III (1919), 163c.

28. REPETITION D'UN BALLET SUR LA SCENE

The stage is in the opera house, rue Le Peletier.

Oil on canvas (grisaille). 26½ × 33 ins. Signed lower right. Painted 1873–4.

Collections. Mulbacher (1874); Isaac de Camondo (1893).

Exhibitions. 1ᵉʳ *Exposition des Impressionistes,* 1874, No. 60; *Degas,* Galerie Georges Petit, Paris, 1924, No. 47.

Reproduced. P. A. Lemoisne, *Degas* (1912), Pl. 21; Paul Lafond, *Degas,* Vol. I (1918), p. 45; Gustave Coquiot, *Degas* (1924), opposite p. 168.

Owned by the Musée du Louvre (bequeathed in 1911 by Camondo).

Photograph. Archives photographiques.

There are numerous studies for the figures in this picture, see Pls. 10, 26, 27 and 29; for the dancers performing a *pas de Deux* see also Pl. 52. For the two later versions, see Pls. 30 and 31. See as well *Catalogue vente Degas,* II (1918), Nos. 244, 327 and 333.

28a. DANSEUSE ASSISE SE GRATTANT LE DOS. ETUDE

She is seen facing three-quarter right scratching the back of her neck with her right hand.

Peinture à l'essence. 8¼ × 10¼ ins. Stamp of the Degas sale on the original. *Circa* 1874.

Collections. Atelier Degas; M. Gaston Migeon, Paris.

Reproduced. Catalogue vente Degas, III (1919), No. 132c; Paul Lafond, *Degas,* Vol. II (1919), between pp. 36 and 37.

Owner unknown.

This figure is a study for *Répétition sur la Scène,* Pls. 30 and 31; for the same figure in the earliest version of the picture see *Catalogue vente Degas,* II (1918), No. 333. See as well *Catalogue vente Degas,* III (1919), Nos. 25, 83b and 132b.¶

29. DANSEUSE EN BLANC SUR LES POINTES

Pastel. 16½ × 11½ ins. Signed lower right. Painted 1873–4.

Collection. Atelier Degas.

Reproduced. Catalogue vente Degas, I (1918), No. 114.

Owner unknown.

The pastel is a study for one of the figures in the first version of *La Répétition d'un Ballet sur la Scène* (Pl. 28); see also *Le Pas de Deux* (Pl. 52).

30. REPETITION D'UN BALLET SUR LA SCENE

With the 'maître de ballet', two onlookers on the far side of the stage, and scrolls of two double-basses in foreground.

Peinture à l'essence on paper mounted on canvas. 21⅜ × 28¾ ins. Signed upper left. *Circa* 1874–5.

Collections. Mrs Cobden Sickert; H. O. Havemeyer.

Exhibitions. *Centennale de l'Art Français*, 1900, No. 210; *Degas*, Musée de l'Orangerie, Paris, 1937, No. 22 (reproduced); *Degas*, Cleveland Museum of Art, 1947, No. 23 (reproduced).

Owned by the Metropolitan Museum of Art. (H. O. Havemeyer Collection, 1929.)

Photograph. Metropolitan Museum of Art.

From stylistic evidence this picture seems to come in date between the other two versions. For studies of figures see Pls. 25, 28*a* and 31*a*. The 'maître' in this picture, as well as in Pl. 31, is probably Eugène Coralli. See p. 55.

30*a*. LE MAITRE. ETUDE POUR 'LA REPETITION D'UN BALLET SUR LA SCENE'

He is standing facing three-quarters right with both hands raised in front of him and the right foot forward.

Pencil. 12 × 8 ins. Stamp of the Degas sale on the original. *Circa* 1874–5.

Collection. Atelier Degas.

Reproduced Catalogue vente Degas, III (1919), No. 113*a*.

Owner unknown.

The drawing is a study for both Pls. 30 and 31.

31. REPETITION D'UN BALLET SUR LA SCENE

With 'maître de ballet' and two onlookers, but with fewer dancers than earlier versions and scroll of only one double-bass in left foreground.

Pastel. 21 × 28½ ins. Signed upper left. *Circa* 1876–7.

Collections. May; H. O. Havemeyer.

Exhibition. Probably the version in the 1er *Exposition des Impressionistes*, 1877, No. 61.

Reproduced. Paul Jamot, *Degas* (1924), Pl. 36; Georges Rivière, *Mr Degas (Bourgeois de Paris)* (1935), p. 133; Camille Mauclair, *Degas* (1941), p. 145; Marguerite Rebatet, *Degas* (1944), Pl. 75.

Owned by the Metropolitan Museum of Art. (H. O. Havemeyer Bequest, 1929.)

Photograph. Metropolitan Museum of Art.

As this is the mostly freely handled and simplified version of the subject, it would seem to have been the latest in date. For studies of the figures see note on Pl. 30. See also *Catalogue vente Degas*, III (1919), No. 80*a*.

31*a*. HOMME ASSIS. ETUDE POUR 'LA REPETITION D'UN BALLET SUR LA SCENE'

He is facing a quarter left, sprawling on a chair with hands in his pockets. On the left a study of his legs.

Sepia heightened with white. 8 × 12 ins. Stamp of the Degas sale on the original. *Circa* 1874–5.

Collection. Atelier Degas.

Reproduced Catalogue vente Degas, III (1919), No. 164*a*.
Owner unknown.

The drawing is a study for one of the two men seated on the right of both the *Répétition sur la Scène* pictures. As is frequent with Degas, both the appearance and the character of the figure, as well as that of the Maître de ballet (Pl. 30*a*) differ considerably between the studies and finished pictures.

32. DANSEUSE VUE DE DOS

She is standing with hands on her hips, looking to the left.

Chinese ink and gouache on pink paper. 14½ × 10 ins. Signed faintly lower right. *Circa* 1876.
Collections. Armand Guillaumin; Jack Aghion; Isaac de Camondo.
Exhibition. Degas, Musée de l'Orangerie, Paris, 1937, No. 94.
Owned by the Musée du Louvre (bequeathed in 1911 by Camondo).
Photograph. Archives photographiques.

See figure on extreme left, *Répétition d'un Ballet sur la Scène* (Pl. 31).

33. DEUX DANSEUSES DEBOUT, VIS A VIS

One is tucking in the frill of her bodice, the other arranging her dress at the shoulder.

Peinture à l'essence on pink paper. 24⅛ × 15½ ins. Signed lower right. *Circa* 1876.
Collection. H. O. Havemeyer.
Owned by the Metropolitan Museum of Art. (H. O. Havemeyer Collection.)
Photograph. The Metropolitan Museum of Art.

34. LA CLASSE DE DANSE. 'ADAGE'

The spiral staircase is seen on the left; the dancers are meant to be in the position of 'arabesque'. The 'maître de danse' in right distance is probably M. Pluque; the 'mère' with group of dancers on extreme right is Sabine Neyt, Degas' housekeeper. The classroom, like all those with long French windows, is in the opera-house rue Le Peletier.

Oil on canvas. 22 × 32 ins. Signed lower left. *Circa* 1876.
Collections. Jacques-Emile Blanche; Sir Wm. Burrell.
Exhibitions. Degas, Galerie Georges Petit, Paris, 1924, No. 48; *French Art*, Royal Academy, London, 1932, No. 481.
Reproduced. Georges Grappe, *E. Degas* (1909), p. 47; Paul Lafond, *Degas*, Vol. I (1918), p. 151; Paul Jamot, *Degas* (1924), Pl. 38; Meier-Graefe, *Degas* (1927), Pl. 30; Camille Mauclair, *Degas* (1941), p. 126; Marguerite Rebatet, *Degas* (1944), Pl. 83.
Owner. Glasgow Art Gallery and Museum. (Sir William Burrell Collection.)
Photograph. Glasgow Art Gallery.

For another version of this subject see Pl. 45; for study of one of the dancers, Pl. 34*a*. See also note on that position.

Adage is the generic term given to slow balancing exercises done in the 'centre', that is without the support of the *barre*. (Ital. *ad agio*, at leisure.)

NOTES ON THE PLATES

34a. 'ARABESQUE CROISEE'. ETUDE POUR 'LA CLASSE DE DANSE'

She is seen back view, facing right, and balancing on the right leg.

Charcoal. 14 × 20 ins. Stamp of the Degas sale on the original. Plumb and horizontal lines through the figure. Inscribed upper right with criticism regarding the position and the name 'Arabesque en dedans'.

Collection. Atelier Degas.

Reproduced. Catalogue vente Degas, III (1919), No. 362b.

Owner unknown.

The drawing is a study for one of the figures in Pl. 34. The term 'arabesque en dedans' is meaningless unless it is an abbreviation of 'arabesque en tournant en dedans'. In any case this position—which occurs frequently in Degas' work—is a faulty one, being a cross between the 'attitude', in that the raised leg is bent, and an 'arabesque', in the placing of the arms. For the same position of the legs see Pls. 54 and 54a; for correct 'arabesque', Pl. 157.

35. TROIS DANSEUSES EXECUTANT 'DEVELOPPE A LA SECONDE'

The violinist is seen in the left foreground looking to the right; the class-room is in the rue Le Peletier.

Oil on canvas. 18½ × 24 ins. Signed lower right. *Circa* 1877.

Collection. Henri Rouart.

Exhibition. Probably the *Ecole de Danse* app. *à Mon. H. R. . . .* in 4ᵉᵐᵉ *Exposition des Impressionistes*, 1879, No. 66.

Reproduced. Album of 15 Lithographs after Degas by G. W. Thornley (done under Degas' supervision, 1895–1900); Paul Lafond, *Degas*, Vol. I (1918), p. 9; Henri Hertz, *Degas* (1920), Pl. 14; Julius Meier-Graefe, *Degas* (1927), Pl. 64; Georges Rivière, *Mr Degas (Bourgeois de Paris)* (1935), p. 73; Camille Mauclair, *Degas* (1941), p. 123; Marguerite Rebatet, *Degas* (1944), Pl. 93.

Owner unknown.

Photograph. Knoedler & Co., London.

Thornley was working on these lithographs at the end of the 'nineties; for a letter written by Degas to him from Cauterets, see *Lettres de Degas*, 1945, *op. cit.*, p. 152–3.

For a study of the violinist see Pl. 35a.

The dancers might equally well be doing 'grands battements à la seconde', as they also might in Pls. 36 and 37 and in many of the drawings.

See also *Catalogue vente Degas*, II (1918), No. 247; and III (1919), Nos. 146, 161a and 161b.

35a. LE VIOLINISTE. ETUDE

He is seen, half length, facing right and playing his instrument.

Charcoal heightened with white. 10 × 12¼ ins. Stamp of the Degas sale on the original. *Circa* 1877.

Collection. Atelier Degas.

Reproduced. Catalogue vente Degas, III (1919), No. 164*b*.

Owner unknown.

The drawing is a study for Pl. 35. See also *Catalogue vente Degas*, III (1919), No. 161*a* and 161*b*. It is interesting to note that Degas has used the head of these two latter studies and the pose of the one reproduced on Pl. 35*a*.

36. ECOLE DE DANSE. 'ADAGE'

The dancers in the 'centre' are doing *developpé à la seconde*; the violinist sits in the left foreground, his back to the spectator; the head of the *maître* is seen on extreme left.

Distemper. $17\frac{1}{4} \times 23$ ins. Signed lower right. *Circa* 1876.

Collections. May (vente May, 1890); H. O. Havemeyer.

Exhibitions. 4ème *Exposition des Impressionistes*, 1879, No. 65; *Degas*, Pennsylvania Museum of Art, Philadelphia, 1936, No. 25 (reproduced).

Reproduced. Paul Lafond, *Degas*, Vol. I (1918), p. 123; Julius Meier-Graefe, *Degas* (1927), Pl. 29; Georges Rivière, *Mr Degas (Bourgeois de Paris)* (1935), p. 71; Camille Mauclair, *Degas* (1941), p. 122.

Owned by Mr and Mrs J. Watson Webb, New York.

Photograph. Durand Ruel, Paris.

The class-room is in the rue Le Peletier. For another version see Pl. 37; and for study of the violinist, Pl. 36*a*.

Ernest May (1845–1925) was a banker and collector, and an acquaintance of both Manet and Degas. He appears in Degas' *La Bourse*, a picture which also belonged to him, and which was exhibited as well in the Impressionist exhibition of 1879.

The *maître* in the picture is probably Eugène Coralli. See p. 55.

36*a*. LE VIOLINISTE VU DE DOS. ETUDE

He is seated on a chair and is playing his instrument.

Charcoal heightened with white. $17\frac{1}{2} \times 12$ ins. *Circa* 1876. Stamp of the Degas sale lower left. Inscribed with a remark about the light underneath the violin. Squared for painting.

Collection. Atelier Degas.

Reproduced. Catalogue vente Degas, III (1919), No. 157*a*.

Owned by J. N. Bryson, Esq., Oxford.

Photograph. The owner.

The drawing is a study for Pl. 36.

37. ECOLE DE DANSE. 'ADAGE'

The dancers in the 'centre' are holding *developpé à la seconde*; part of the violinist's body can be seen on extreme left.

Distemper? $18\frac{5}{8} \times 24\frac{1}{4}$ ins. Signed lower right. *Circa* 1877.

Collection. Whittemore.

Owned by Maurice Wertheim, New York.

Photograph. National Gallery of Art, Washington.

For another version of this picture see Pl. 36. Through the window, the gardens of the former Choiseul mansion can be seen.

See also *Catalogue vente Degas*, II (1918), No. 227.

37*a*. 'L'ADAGE'. ETUDE

Charcoal on pink paper. 17 × 12¼ ins. Stamp of the Degas sale lower left. *Circa* 1876.
Collections. Atelier Degas; Kelekian; Koenigs.
Reproduced. Catalogue vente Degas, III (1919), No. 326*b*.
Owned by the Boymans Museum, Rotterdam.
Photograph. Boymans Museum.

38. LA LEÇON DE DANSE

One of the upper class-rooms in the rue Le Peletier. The master is demonstrating a step which the pupil is imitating. On the right a dancer leans over the stair-rail watching another coming up from below.

Oil on canvas. 16 × 21½ ins. Signed lower right. *Circa* 1878–80.
Collection. Prince de Wagram, Paris.
Reproduced. Georges Grappe, *E. Degas* (1909), p. 25; Julius Meier-Graefe, *Degas* (1927), Pl. 28.
Owned by Mr Payne Bingham, New York.
Photograph. John Rewald, New York.

Degas often made use of a ruler for architectural details, as he has apparently done in this picture. Towards the end of the 'seventies he was much interested in the silhouetting of shapes against the light, and whether he invented the pillars for this purpose or whether they actually existed, it is difficult to say.

38*a*. DANSEUSE MONTANT UN ESCALIER

Holding her skirt in front of her, she mounts the stairs to the right.

Charcoal heightened with white. 18¼ × 12¼ ins. Stamp of the Degas sale lower left. *Circa* 1878–80.
Collection. Atelier Degas.
Reproduced Catalogue vente Degas, III (1919), No. 151.
Owned by Jais Nielsen, Copenhagen.
Photograph. The owner.

See also Pl. 45*a* and p. 60; also *Catalogue vente Degas*, III (1919), No. 49.

The drawing is a study for Pl. 156*a*.

39. PREPARATION POUR LA CLASSE

A group of dancers in various stages of their toilette, two of whom are with their mothers.

Pastel. 24 × 37 ins. Signed lower right. *Circa* 1877.
Collection. Sir William Burrell.
Owned by the Glasgow Art Gallery and Museum. (Sir William Burrell Collection.)
Photograph. Glasgow Art Gallery.

39a. MLLE S . . . (SANGALLI) PREMIERE DANSEUSE A L'OPERA

She is seated holding a closed umbrella across her knees and wearing a coat and hat.

Charcoal heightened with pastel. 15¼ × 8 ins. Stamp of the Degas sale on original. *Circa* 1876.
Collections. Atelier Degas; Dr Viau.
Exhibition. Degas—Portraitiste, Sculpteur. Musée de L'Orangerie, Paris, 1931, No. 127.
Reproduced. Catalogue vente Degas, II (1918), No. 248.
Owner unknown.

It is certainly Mlle Sangalli who posed for this portrait, as apart from facial resemblance there was no other 'première danseuse' at the Opéra in 1876 whose name began with an 'S'. See p. 61.

40. LA LEÇON DE DANSE

The dancer is standing in position in the 'centre' facing a quarter left; the 'maître' is silhouetted against the window on the extreme left, while a dancer watches from right.

Pastel and gouache. 22 × 27¾ ins. Signed lower right. *Circa* 1879.
Collection. D. W. T. Cargill, Esq.
Owner unknown.
Photograph. Reid and Lefevre, London.

This position, in which the dancer stands with arms *en couronne* and front foot fully arched from a bent knee, was apparently a favoured one of dancers of that time. It is hardly ever used in contemporary ballet. It appears in many of Degas' pictures of varying dates. See Pls. 41–4 and Colour Plate IV opposite Pl. 41

40a. LE MAITRE DE DANSE VU DE DOS

He is standing with feet apart and holding a stick in his right hand.

Pencil and watercolour. 17½ × 10 ins. Stamp of the Degas sale on original. *Circa* 1879.
Collection. Atelier Degas.
Reproduced. Catalogue vente Degas, IV (1919), No. 206b.
Owner unknown.

See also *Catalogue vente Degas,* IV (1919), No. 206a.

41. GROUPE DE CINQ DANSEUSES AVEC PAYSAGE CLASSIQUE

The dancer in the centre of the group is standing with arms *en couronne*, and foot forced on the *pointe*. She is facing quarter left, the other four dancers are looking at her.

Charcoal. 16 × 22 ins. Stamp of the Degas sale lower left. *Circa* 1878–9.
Collections. Atelier Degas; René de Gas.
Reproduced. Catalogue vente Degas, III (1919), No. 180; *Catalogue vente René de Gas,* 1927, No. 36.
Owned by Capt Arthur Peto, Isle of Wight.
Photograph. Owner.

For an oil-painting of a similar subject see *Catalogue vente Degas,* II (1918), No. 33. See also Pls. 40, 41a, 42, 43 and Colour Plate IV.
The landscape back-cloth is reminiscent of *Jeunes Spartiates s'excerçant à la Lutte.*

41a. DANSEUSE BLEUE. ETUDE

She stands facing right, with arms *en couronne* and left foot *sur la pointe en quatrième devant* with knee bent.

Pencil. 16¼ × 10¼ ins. Stamp of the Degas sale on the original. *Circa* 1878–9.
Collection. Atelier Degas.
Reproduced. Catalogue vente Degas, IV (1919), No. 268.
Owner unknown.

This drawing is a study for the Colour Plate IV. See also Pls. 40–3, as well as *Catalogue vente Degas*, III (1919), No. 122a; and IV (1919), No. 263a.

42. DANSEUSE POSANT

Arms *en couronne*, left foot forced on the *pointe* in *quatrième devant*. Facing quarter right.

Charcoal heightened with white. 18 × 11¼ ins. Stamp of the Degas sale lower left, squared for painting. Drawn 1878–9.
Collections. Atelier Degas; Viau.
Exhibition. Degas, Galerie Georges Petit, Paris, 1924, No. 112.
Reproduced. Catalogue vente Degas, III (1919), No. 338b.
Owner unknown.
Photograph. Leicester Galleries, London.

The drawing is a study for the painting, Pl. 43, and it is interesting to note how faithfully Degas has adhered to it. See also Pls. 40, 41, 41a and Colour Plate IV.

43. DANSEUSE POSANT CHEZ UN PHOTOGRAPHE

With the large windows behind her and edge of mirror seen on extreme right, she stands before it with arms *en couronne* and left foot forced on the *pointe* in *quatrième devant*.

Oil on canvas. 26 × 20 ins. Signed lower right. Painted 1878–9.
Collections. Brame (who owned it in 1879); Sardnal (1919); Comte Doria; S. I. Schukin.
Exhibition. 4ème *Exposition des Impressionistes*, 1879, No. 72.
Reproduced. Paul Lafond, *Degas*, Vol. II (1919), between pp. 36 and 37; Camille Mauclair, *Degas* (1941), p. 125.
Owned by the Museum of Modern and Western Art, Moscow.
Photograph. S. C. R., London.

For the drawing of this picture see Pl. 42; also Pls. 40, 41, 41a and Colour Plate IV.

44. DANSEUSE SUR LES POINTES

She is standing with feet in fifth position and arms raised in fifth *en haut*. Behind her to the right two dancers and the *maître* are visible.

Pastel. 12 × 8½ ins. Signed lower left. *Circa* 1878–9.
Collection. Mrs Tweed.
Exhibition. Perhaps this is the *Portrait de Danseuse à la Leçon* in the 4ème *Exposition des Impressionistes*, 1879, No. 74.
Owner unknown.
Photograph. Durand Ruel, Paris.

For dancer in similar position see Pl. 45.

45. LA CLASSE DE DANSE. TEMPS DE POINTES

On the extreme left, dancers are coming down the twisting stair-case; on the right they are grouped around a bench; in the centre they are finishing their class with *pointe work*, and in right distance another class-room can be seen with dancers at the *barre*.

> *Oil on canvas.* $18\frac{3}{4} \times 24\frac{1}{2}$ ins. Signed lower right. *Circa* 1879–80.
> *Collections.* Manzi; Senator William A. Clark.
> *Reproduced.* John Rewald, *History of Impressionism* (1946), p. 233.
> *Owned* by the Corcoran Gallery of Art, Washington (bequest of Senator Clark).
> *Photograph.* Corcoran Gallery of Art.

For an earlier version of this picture see Pl. 34. See also Pl. 44.

According to Mlle Bernay (*op. cit.*, p. 161) classes of that time followed much the same procedure as they do today. The pupils began with exercises at the *barre*, which lasted for some twenty minutes. Then came *adage*, followed by *exercises sautés, enchainements, temps battus, temps de pointes*. The lesson ended with these last exercises, the whole lasting about an hour and a half.

45a. DANSEUSE SUR L'ESCALIER. ETUDE

One dancer is seen going up the stairs; two other studies of dancers are on the same sheet.

> *Charcoal heightened with pastel.* $19\frac{1}{4} \times 25$ ins. Stamp of the Degas sale on the original. *Circa* 1880.
> *Collection.* Atelier Degas.
> *Reproduced.* Catalogue vente Degas, III (1919), No. 399.
> *Owner* unknown.

See also Pl. 38a and note.

46. DANSEUSES A LA BARRE

Two dancers stretching at the *barre* before their class.

> *Distemper on canvas.* $29\frac{3}{4} \times 32$ ins. Signed lower left. Painted 1876–7.
> *Collections.* Henri Rouart (reproduced Sale catalogue, 1917, No. 177); H. O. Havemeyer.
> *Exhibitions.* 3ème *Exposition des Impressionistes*, 1877, No. 41.
> *Reproduced.* *Fifteen Lithographs after Degas* by G. W. Thornley (*circa* 1895–1900); P. A. Lemoisne, *Degas* (1912), Pl. 28; Paul Lafond, *Degas*, Vol. I (1918), opp. p. 150; Georges Grappe, *Degas* (1936), p. 61; Camille Mauclair, *Degas* (1941), p. 149; Hans Graber, *Edgar Degas* (1942), opp. p. 140; Marguerite Rebatet, *Degas* (1944), Pl. 91.
> *Owned* by the Metropolitan Museum of Art. (H. O. Havemeyer Collection.)
> *Photograph.* Metropolitan Museum of Art.

Mlle Bernay says (*op. cit.*, p. 160) that serious students used to be in the class-room a quarter of an hour before the lesson began in order to stretch and 'turn themselves out' at the *barre*. This is, of course, a practice which dancers always follow not only before a lesson but, even more important, before a performance.

A watering-can is frequently used to lay the dust and prevent the dancers from slipping. It was this can which Degas afterwards found 'idiotic' and wished to be allowed to remove.

See also Pls. 47, 47a and 48, as well as *Catalogue vente Degas*, II (1918), No. 234a; and IV (1919), Nos. 177 and 278a.

47. DEUX DANSEUSES A LA BARRE. ETUDE

Peinture à l'essence on green paper. 15½ × 25 ins. Signed lower right. Painted 1876–7.
Collections. Atelier Degas; Pellet; Whittemore.
Exhibitions. Degas, Pennsylvania Museum of Art, Philadelphia, 1936, No. 80 (reproduced).
Reproduced. Degas, vingt Dessins, Album Manzi (1896), No. 13; *Catalogue vente Degas,* II (1918), No. 338; H. Rivière, *Les Dessins de Degas* (1922), No. 86.
Owned by Cesar M. de Hauke, New York.
Photograph. Knoedler & Co., London.
This is a study for Pl. 46; for a drawing of one of the figures see Pl. 47*a*.

47*a*. DANSEUSE SE DEGOURDISSANT A LA BARRE. ETUDE

She is facing the *barre* with her right leg stretched upon it.

Charcoal. 12 × 10 ins. Stamp of the Degas sale lower left. *Circa* 1876.
Collection. Atelier Degas.
Reproduced. Catalogue vente Degas, III (1919), No. 133*d*.
Owner unknown.
The drawing is a study for Pl. 46.

48. DANSEUSE SE DEGOURDISSANT A LA BARRE

She is standing on the left with her leg raised on the *barre* in front of her; her hand on her ankle.

Pastel. 6¾ × 8¾ ins. Signed upper left. *Circa* 1876–7.
Owner unknown.
Photograph. Knoedler & Co., London.
See also Pls. 46, 47 and 47*a*.
This position is remarkable for the 'over-turn' of the supporting leg.

48*a*. 'GRAND BATTEMENT A LA SECONDE A LA BARRE'

The dancer, facing right, is working with her right leg. She looks down intently at her supporting leg which, in an effort to 'turn out', has the foot rolling over.

Charcoal heightened with pastel. 19 × 21 ins. Stamp of the Degas sale on the original. *Circa* 1880.
Collection. Atelier Degas.
Reproduced. Catalogue vente Degas, II (1918), No. 339, and Georges Rivière, *Mr Degas (Bourgeois de Paris)* (1935), p. 14.
Owner unknown.

49. DANSEUSE REPOSANT

She is seated on a bench with one foot on it, elbow resting on the knee and hand supporting head.

Pastel. 18⅞ × 24½ ins. Signed upper right. *Circa* 1880–2.
Owned by the John G. Johnson Art Collection, Philadelphia.
Photograph. Owners.

49a. 'PLIE A LA SECONDE A LA BARRE'. DEUX DANSEUSES

They are facing right and holding the *barre* with their left hands. The one in front is in a deeper *plié* than the dancer behind.

Crayon heightened with colour. 13 × 20¼ ins. Stamp of the Degas sale on the original. *Circa* 1880.

Collection. Atelier Degas.

Reproduced. Catalogue vente Degas, I (1918), No. 323.

Owner unknown.

The first dancer's position is a bad one, for the line of the thigh should not go further than parallel with the ground. A correct *plié à la seconde* would be halfway between those of the two dancers in its depth.

See also Pl. 147 and *Catalogue vente Degas*, III (1919), No. 138c.

50. LE 'PAS DE DEUX' SUR LA SCENE

One dancer is *sur les pointes*, the other is standing next to her in fourth position with arms in *demi-seconde*.

Oil on canvas. 24¼ × 18¼ ins. Signed lower left. Painted 1873–4.

Collections. Gallimard; Sir James Murray (sold 1927).

Exhibitions. Aberdeen, 1925; *Degas*, Musée de l'Orangerie, Paris, 1937, No. 26 (reproduced).

Reproduced. J. B. Manson, *The Life and Work of Edgar Degas* (1927), Pl. 19.

Owned by the Home House Trustees, Courtauld Institute, London.

Photograph. Courtauld Institute.

The *pas* is the one being rehearsed in the *Répétition sur la Scène*, Pls. 28, 30 and 31. The ballet is unidentifiable.

51. LE 'PAS DE DEUX' SUR LA SCENE

The dancer behind is in *posé sur la pointe*; over her head she holds some flowers which her partner seems to be refusing.

Pastel on monotype. 12 × 10½ ins. Signed lower left. *Circa* 1878.

Collection. Grenville L. Winthrop.

Reproduced. Ambroise Vollard, 98 Reproductions signed by Degas (pub. Berheim Jeune, 1918) in colour between Pls. 33 and 34; Paul Lafond, *Degas*, Vol. I (1918), opp. p. 42, in colour.

Owned by the Fogg Museum of Art, Cambridge, Mass. (Grenville L. Winthrop Bequest.)

Photograph. Fogg Museum of Art.

52. SCENE DE BALLET—'PAS DE DEUX'

The danseuse stands in front of the footlights looking into the auditorium; in the right foreground the large scroll of the double-bass; and in the right distance the 'male' dancer. The heads of the orchestra are just visible.

Oil on canvas. 10¼ × 8¼ ins. Signed lower left. *Circa* 1876.

Collections. Jules Claretie (sold 1914, reproduced in catalogue); Adolphe Lewisohn.

Exhibition. Degas, Musée de l'Orangerie, Paris, 1937, No. 29 (reproduced).
Reproduced. Camille Mauclair, *Degas* (1941), p. 154; Marguerite Rebatet, *Degas* (1944), Pl. 98.
Owner unknown.
Photograph. Durand Ruel, Paris.
The male role was obviously being danced by a woman.

53. DANSEUSE SUR LA SCENE

The scroll of the double-bass looms up dark in the left foreground; the heads of the musicians in the orchestra pit are just visible.

Pastel. $14\frac{1}{4} \times 8\frac{3}{4}$ ins. Signed lower left. *Circa* 1878–9.
Owner unknown.
Photograph. Knoedler & Co., London.
The dancer's position is similar to that of the one holding flowers in *Pas de Deux sur la Scène* (Pl. 51).

54. DANSEUSE SUR LA POINTE

The dancer is doing a *pas seul*; she is the only figure visible on the stage, the backcloth of which represents rocks and sea.

Pastel. $22\frac{1}{4} \times 30$ ins. Signed lower left. *Circa* 1876.
Collections. Alexis Rouart; Sir William Eden, Bt; Mrs Workman.
Reproduced. P. A. Lemoisne, *Degas* (1912), Pl. 25; Henri Hertz, *Degas* (1920), Pl. 17; J. B. Manson, *The Life and Work of Edgar Degas* (1927), Pl. 40; Marguerite Rebatet, *Degas* (1944), Pl. 78.
Owner unknown.
Photograph. Sir Robert Witt Library, London.
For a study for this picture see Pl. 54a; see also *Catalogue vente Degas*, II (1918), Nos. 3 and 246; III (1919), Nos. 181 and 226; and IV (1919), No. 180.
The position, which is discussed in the note to Pl. 34a, appears to be an *arabesque*.

54a. ETUDES DE JAMBES ET DE BRAS

On the left is a study of feet in fifth position as well as the head and shoulders of a dancer seen back view. On the right are various studies *sur les pointes*.

Black chalk. $19 \times 24\frac{1}{4}$ ins. Stamp of the Degas sale on the original. Squared for painting. *Circa* 1876.
Collection. Atelier Degas.
Reproduced. Catalogue vente Degas, IV (1919), No. 181.
Owner unknown.
The drawing is a study for Pl. 54. See also note to Pl. 34a.

55. DANSEUSE SUR LA SCENE. 'L'ETOILE'

The dancer is alone on the stage and suggests the completion of the *enchainement*—*chassé, coupé, jeté en tournant*.

Pastel. 23×17 ins. Signed upper left. *Circa* 1876

Collection. Caillebotte.

Exhibition. Degas, Musée de l'Orangerie, Paris, 1937, No. 88.

Reproduced. Georges Grappe, *E. M. Degas* (1909), opp. p. 32; Paul Lafond, *Degas*, Vol. I (1918), p. 47; Julius Meier-Graefe, *Degas* (1927), Pl. 38; Georges Rivière, *Mr Degas (Bourgeois de Paris)* (1935), Frontispiece; Georges Grappe, *Degas* (1936), p. 41; Camille Mauclair, *Degas* (1941), p. 144; Denis Rouart, *Degas à la Recherche de sa Technique* (1945), p. 58 and detail, p. 59.

Owned by the Musée du Louvre (bequeathed by Caillebotte in 1894 it was housed in the Luxembourg until its transference in 1929).

Photograph. Archives photographiques.

This is probably the best known of all Degas' pictures, and is one of the first in which he shows the dancer executing a *pas sauté*. For the various other versions see Pls. 141–5 and 178. See also *Catalogue vente Degas*, II (1918), No. 336; III (1919), Nos. 151*b* and 166*c*.

56. DANSEUSE, UN BOUQUET A LA MAIN

She is seen taking a bow. On the left other dancers are standing, and in the background two men in Eastern costumes hold large sunshades around one of whom three dancers with fans are grouped.

Pastel on paper mounted on canvas. 30 × 31 ins. Signed lower left. Painted 1876–7.

Collection. Isaac de Camondo.

Exhibitions. 3ème *Exposition des Impressionistes*, 1877, No. 40; *Degas*, Galerie Georges Petit, Paris, 1924, No. 121; *Degas*, Musée de l'Orangerie, Paris, 1937, No. 89.

Reproduced. P. A. Lemoisne, *Degas* (1912), Pl. 30; Paul Lafond, *Degas*, Vol. I (1918), p. 57; Julius Meier-Graefe, *Degas* (1927), Pl. 43; Camille Mauclair, *Degas* (1941), p. 145, in colour; Hans Graber, *Edgar Degas*, opp. p. 156; Denis Rouart, *Degas, à la Recherche de sa Technique* (1945), p. 21.

Owned by the Musée du Louvre (bequeathed in 1911 by Camondo).

Photograph. Archives photographiques.

Degas has taken amusing liberties with the subject of this picture, for while the dancers in the right background are posing before the audience, those in the left are 'standing at ease' and apparently chatting with people in the wings; the latter are also wearing orange and white striped stockings with their *tutus*, a costume too incongruous to have been factual.

For another version see Pl. 57, and for other pictures on the same theme, but different in composition, see Pls. 58, 59 and 106. For studies of the dancer with bouquet see *Catalogue vente Degas*, III (1919), No. 284; and IV (1919), No. 165.

56a. PORTRAIT DE MLLE MALO. BUSTE

She is seen facing a quarter left, wearing a cap tilted low over her forehead and her hair below the nape of her neck.

Pastel. 18¼ × 15 ins. Signed lower left. *Circa* 1869.

Collection. J. E. Blanche.

Exhibition. Degas, Galerie Georges Petit, Paris, 1924, No. 102 (reproduced).

Reproduced. Paul Lafond, *Degas*, Vol. I (1918), p. 36; Julius Meier-Graefe, *Degas* (1927), Pl. 42; Camille Mauclair, *Degas* (1941), p. 47; Hans Graber, *Edgar Degas* (1942), opp. p. 84.

Owner unknown.

Of the dancer Mlle Malo, Degas also did a similar head in oil-paint which belonged to Mme Friedmann and is reproduced in *Catalogue vente Degas*, II (1918), No. 48. Another, and larger painting of the same sitter, is reproduced in *Catalogue vente Degas*, I (1918), No. 86.

57. DANSEUSE, UN BOUQUET A LA MAIN

She is taking a bow with members of the *corps de ballet* on either side of her up stage.

Pastel. $20\frac{1}{4} \times 26$ ins. Signed lower left. *Circa* 1878–80.

Owner unknown.

Photograph. Knoedler & Co., London.

For the earlier version of this subject see Pl. 56; and for studies of the dancer with bouquet see *Catalogue vente Degas*, III (1919), No. 284; and IV (1919), No. 165.

57a. DANSEUSE DEBOUT A L'EVENTAIL

She is seen full-face holding an open fan.

Charcoal heightened with white. $19\frac{1}{4} \times 12\frac{1}{4}$ ins. Stamp of the Degas sale lower left. Plumb-line through the figure, and horizontal line beneath the feet. *Circa* 1878–80.

Collections. Atelier Degas; Dr Viau; F. Koenigs.

Reproduced. Catalogue vente Degas, III (1919), No. 339a.

Owned by the Boymans Museum, Rotterdam (presented by Mr D. G. van Beuniggen).

Photograph. The Boymans Museum.

See also Pl. 117 and note.

58. DANSEUSE SALUANT

The view is taken across stage from the wings. The dancer on the left is standing in third position blowing a kiss to her audience, while the *corps de ballet* is grouped along the right of the picture.

Pastel. $30 \times 22\frac{1}{2}$ ins. Signed lower right. *Circa* 1882–5.

Collections. Mme X (Sale, Paris, Feb. 1919, reproduced); Roger G. Gompel.

Exhibitions. Degas, Galerie Georges Petit, Paris, 1924, No. 152 (reproduced); *Degas*, Musée de l'Orangerie, Paris, 1937, No. 113 (reproduced).

Reproduced. Denis Rouart, *Degas, à la Recherche de sa Technique* (1945), p. 17.

Owned by Diego Suarez.

It would be nice to think that this picture represented Rosita Mauri who, as première danseuse, appeared with her long dark hair flowing over her shoulders in the first production of *Les Deux Pigeons* in 1885. From the point of view of facial resemblance the dancer in this pastel could easily be reconciled with existing photographs of the ballerina, but Degas evidently used the same model in his *Danseuse, un Bouquet à la Main* of 1877, and Mauri did not make her debut at the Opéra until 1879.

For another version of the pastel see Pl. 59.

59. DANSEUSE SALUANT, UN BOUQUET A LA MAIN

Occupying most of the picture, she acknowledges her greetings to the audience while the corps de ballet stand about in a diagonal line behind her.

> *Pastel.* 24 × 18 ins. Signed upper right. *Circa* 1885.
> *Owner* unknown.
> *Photograph.* Knoedler & Co., London.

For another version of this pastel see Pl. 58.

60. LA LOGE DE DANSEUSE

She stands behind an arm chair; on her left a dresser sews her *tutu*; on her right sits a man with a beard.

> *Pastel.* 23¼ × 17¾ ins. Signed lower right. Painted 1878–9.
> *Collections.* Blanc; H. O. Havemeyer.
> *Exhibition. Degas,* Pennsylvania Museum of Art, Philadelphia, 1936, No. 27 (reproduced).
> *Reproduced.* Paul Lafond, *Degas,* Vol. I (1918), p. 73; Camille Mauclair, *Degas* (1941), p. 118.
> *Owned* by Mr and Mrs Peter H. B. Frelinghuysen, New York.
> *Photograph.* Durand Ruel, Paris.

The dresser is Degas' housekeeper, Sabine Neyt. For a study of her see *Catalogue vente Degas,* IV (1919), No. 252, which is inscribed 'ma vieille bonne, Sabine Neyt. Morte à Paris, 21 rue Pigalle'. She died in 1884. The man bears a strong resemblance to Ludovic Halévy, whom Degas painted on several occasions. For other pastels on this theme see Pls. 61 and 62.

61. LA LOGE DE DANSEUSE

She stands between a dressing table on the left and a cupboard on the right; behind her the heads of a man and a dresser are just visible.

> *Pastel.* 24 × 17 ins. Signed middle left. Painted 1878–9.
> *Collections.* Viau; Wilhelm Hansen.
> *Reproduced.* P. A. Lemoisne, *Degas* (1912), Pl. 38; Paul Lafond, *Degas,* Vol. II (1919), between pages 36 and 37; Paul Jamot, *Degas* (1924), Pl. 46; Georges Riviére, *Mr Degas (Bourgeois de Paris)* (1935), p. 47; Camille Mauclair, *Degas* (1941), p. 120.
> *Owned* by Oskar Reinhart, Winterthur.
> *Photograph.* Kunsthistorik Pladearkiv, Copenhagen.

A pastel of this title was exhibited in the 4ème *Exposition des Impressionistes,* 1879, No. 71, as belonging to *Mme A. de C.* . . . But it is difficult to say if it is one of the pictures reproduced in this book, and if so, which one.

For other pastels on this theme see Pls. 60 and 62.

62. LA LOGE DE DANSEUSE

She is seen reflected in a mirror; standing full length and holding her skirts. Behind her can be distinguished the head of a man and the figure of the dresser.

> *Pastel.* 11⅞ × 20½ ins. Signed lower left. Painted 1878–9.
> *Reproduced. Fifteen Lithographs* by G. W. Thornley (1895–1900).

Owner unknown.

Photograph. Knoedler & Co., London.

For other pastels on this theme see Pls. 60 and 61.

63. DANSEUSE EN JUPE ROUGE

She is standing back view on the stage in front of a flat and on the left of the picture. Her hair is hanging down and she arranges her dress at the waist. In the upper right corner a figure of another dancer is just visible.

Oil on canvas. 16 × 12¾ ins. Signed lower right. *Circa* 1878–80.

Collection. Grenville L. Winthrop.

Owned by the Fogg Museum of Art, Cambridge, Mass. (Grenville L. Winthrop Bequest.)

Photograph. Fogg Museum of Art.

64. DEUX DANSEUSES DERRIERE UN PORTANT

The one on the left is holding on to the back of the flat while she adjusts her shoe-ribbons; the other, in costume of a butterfly, is cut in half by the right edge of the picture.

Pastel and distemper. 27½ × 19 ins. Signed upper left. *Circa* 1880.

Exhibitions. Centennale de l'Art Français, 1900; *Degas*, Galerie Georges Petit, Paris, 1924, No. 130 (reproduced); *Ecole Impressioniste*, Lucerne, 1929, No. 4; *Degas*, Musée de l'Orangerie, Paris, 1937, No. 105 (reproduced).

Reproduced. Vollard, 98 Reproductions signed by Degas (pub. Bernheim Jeune, 1918), in colour, between Pls. 65 and 66; Paul Lafond, *Degas*, Vol. I (1918), opp. p. 72, in colour; Henri Hertz, *Degas* (1920), Pl. 12; Julius Meier Graefe, *Degas* (1927), Pl. 99; Camille Mauclair, *Degas* (1941), p. 121, in colour; Denis Rouart, *Degas, à la Recherche de sa Technique* (1945), p. 19, and detail, p. 20.

Owned by Mrs Edward Jonas, New York.

Photograph. Knoedler & Co., London.

As dancers appeared in the costumes of butterflies, flowers, etc., in so many ballets, these dresses do not help in the identification of this particular performance.

65. ETUDE DE DANSEUSE ALLONGEE

Her weight is on her right leg as she bends forwards. Study of an arm at top of page.

Charcoal heightened with pastel. 18 × 12 ins. Stamp of the Degas sale lower left. The paper is squared horizontally and diagonally for painting. *Circa* 1877.

Collection. Atelier Degas.

Reproduced. Catalogue vente Degas, III (1919), No. 367*b*.

Owner unknown.

Photograph. Durand Ruel, Paris.

66. DANSEUSE RAJUSTANT SA CHAUSSURE. MELINA DARDE

She is facing a quarter right, and with her left hand pulls the back of the toe-shoe on her raised foot. Behind her is the sketch of a standing figure.

Charcoal heightened with white. 16¼ × 12 ins. Stamp of the Degas sale on the original. A plumb-line runs through the figure which is enclosed in a square. Drawn 1878.

Collection. Atelier Degas.

Reproduced. Catalogue vente Degas, II (1918), No. 350; Paul Lafond, *Degas*, Vol. II (1919), opp. p. 28.

Owner unknown.

The model is obviously Melina Darde (see Pl. 68), of whom Degas did numerous drawings at this time.

67. DANSEUSE ASSISE. MELINA DARDE

She is sitting in a chair facing three-quarter right. Her feet are apart and her right hand is visible on her ankle. Her skirt is lifted up behind her.

Charcoal heightened with white. 17 × 12 ins. Signed lower left. Drawn *circa* 1878.

Collection. Manzi (sold March 1919).

Owner unknown.

Photograph. Sir Robert Witt Library, London.

The sitter is obviously the same as Pls. 66, 68 and 69.

68. MELINA DARDE ASSISE

She is seated facing right with both hands on her ankles as she forces her *pointes*.

Chalk. 12 × 9¾ ins. Stamp of the Degas sale lower left, and inscribed 'Melina Darde, 15 ans, d'aujourdhui à la Gaieté, Dec. '78'. Also inscribed at top with comments on colour, etc.

Collection. Atelier Degas; Paul Mathey.

Exhibitions. Degas, Galerie Georges Petit, Paris, 1924, No. 126; *Degas*, Musée de l'Orangerie, Paris, 1937, No. 95.

Reproduced. Catalogue vente Degas, II (1918), No. 230a.

Owner. M. Paul Mathey, Paris.

Photograph. Durand Ruel, Paris.

The drawing is said to have been exhibited in the Impressionist Exhibition of 1879, No. 2, but there is no such number among Degas' exhibits, neither is there a title which can be identified with this drawing.

For another inscribed drawing of Melina Darde see *Catalogue vente Degas*, III (1919), No. 359a. Pls. 66, 67 and 69 are also of the same sitter. For a similar position see *Catalogue vente Degas*, III (1919), No. 133c.

69. MELINA DARDE A SON 'ADAGE'

She stands facing a quarter left, with arms in second, and only the supporting leg sketched in.

Charcoal heightened with white. 18 × 12 ins. Stamp of the Degas sale lower left. Drawn 1878.

Collection. Atelier Degas.

Reproduced. Catalogue vente Degas, III (1919) No. 357b.

Owner unknown.

Photograph. Durand Ruel, Paris.

See Pls. 66–8 also, for studies of the same model.

70. DANSEUSE SE MASSANT LA CHEVILLE

She sits facing quarter right, the near hand resting on the knee, the other rubbing her ankle.

Pastel. 25 × 20 ins. Signed upper right. Circa 1878.

Collection. G. Caillebotte.

Exhibition. Degas, Musée de l'Orangerie, Paris, 1937, No. 133.

Reproduced. Paul Lafond, *Degas*, Vol. I (1918), p. 95; Julius Meier-Graefe, *Degas* (1927), Pl. 37; Georges Rivière, *Mr Degas (Bourgeois de Paris)* (1935), p. 77; Georges Grappe, *Degas* (1936), title-page.

Owned by the Musée du Louvre (bequeathed Caillebotte 1894; in Musée du Luxembourg until 1929, then transferred to Louvre).

Photograph. Archives photographiques.

See also Pls. 71, 71a.

71. L'ATTENTE

On a bench placed diagonally across the picture, a dancer and her mother sit side by side. The dancer bends forward and massages her ankle; the mother draws patterns on the floor with her umbrella.

Pastel. 19 × 24 ins. Signed upper left. Circa 1879–80.

Collections. Clapison; H. O. Havemeyer.

Exhibition. Degas, Pennsylvania Museum of Art, Philadelphia, 1936, No. 41 (reproduced).

Reproduced. Paul Lafond, *Degas*, Vol. II (1919), between pp. 36 and 37; Paul Jamot, *Degas* (1924), Pl. 58; Georges Rivière, *Mr Degas (Bourgeois de Paris)* (1935), p. 85; Camille Mauclair, *Degas* (1941), p. 117.

Owned by Horace Havemeyer, New York.

Photograph. Durand Ruel, Paris.

For study of the dancer see Pl. 71a; see also Pl. 70.

71a. DANSEUSE ASSISE SE MASSANT LA CHEVILLE DU PIED. ETUDE

She is seated facing a quarter right, bending well forward and rubbing her ankle with her left hand.

Charcoal heightened with pastel. 18¼ × 24 ins. Stamp of the Degas sale on the original. Circa 1879–80.

Collection. Atelier Degas.

Reproduced. Catalogue vente Degas, III (1919), No. 373.

Owner unknown.

The drawing is a study for the dancer in Pl. 71. See also Pl. 70.

72. LA FAMILLE MANTE

The mother is dressing the young dancer for her class while her sister stands by in out-door clothes.

Pastel. 35½ × 19¾ ins. Signed lower right. Painted 1880.

Collections. Viau (sold 1907); Mrs Montgomery Sears.

Exhibitions. Centennale de l'Art Français, 1900, No. 882; *Degas*, Pennsylvania Museum of Art, Philadelphia, 1936, No. 48 (reproduced).

Reproduced. P. A. Lemoisne, *Degas* (1912), Pl. 37; Gustave Coquiot, *Degas* (1924), p. 104; Paul Jamot, *Degas* (1924), Pl. 72; Georges Grappe, *Degas* (1936), p. 34.

Owned by Mr and Mrs John Wintersteen.

Photograph. Georges Wildenstein, New York.

Suzanne Mante is the child being dressed; Blanche Mante is in every-day clothes; Mme Mante is posing with her daughters. See also later version, Pl. 73.

73. LA FAMILLE MANTE

The picture of the mother dressing one of her two daughters for class, is an almost exact replica of the earlier version.

Pastel. Size unknown. Signed lower right. Painted *circa* 1882.

Reproduced. Georges Grappe, *E. Degas* (1909), p. 52; Paul Lafond, *Degas*, Vol. I (1918), p. 65; Julius Meier-Graefe, *Degas* (1927), Pl. 72; Marguerite Rebatet, *Degas* (1944), Pl. 86.

Owner unknown.

See also Pl. 72.

74. JEUNE DANSEUSE A LA BARRE

She stands facing right, both hands on the *barre*, looking down on her left foot which is pointed.

Pastel. $26\frac{1}{4} \times 18\frac{1}{2}$ ins. Signed upper right. *Circa* 1880.

Reproduced. *La Renaissance*, October 1929.

Owned by Mr and Mrs J. Watson Webb, New York.

Photograph. The owners.

For another version of the same subject see Pl. 75.

The young dancer is making the poor effort of a beginner at *pointe tendue*.

75. DANSEUSE EN BLEU A LA BARRE

The position of the young girl standing with both hands on the *barre* and left foot pointed, is almost identical with that of the earlier version.

Pastel. $26\frac{3}{4} \times 18\frac{7}{8}$ ins. Stamp of the Degas sale lower left. *Circa* 1880–2.

Collections. Atelier Degas; René de Gas (sale Nov. 1927, reproduced); Paul Guillaume.

Reproduced. *Catalogue vente Degas*, II (1918), No. 92; Denis Rouart, *Degas, à la Recherche de sa Technique* (1945), p. 27.

Owner unknown.

Photograph. Reid and Lefevre, London.

For an earlier version see Pl. 74.

In this pastel the young dancer is seen trying to force her instep by bending her knee.

76. 'BATTEMENTS SUR LES POINTES A LA BARRE'

The little *rat* is seen back view with her disengaged arm raised.

Charcoal on pink paper. Size unknown. Signed lower left; inscribed with name of step lower right. *Circa* 1883–5.

Reproduced. Paul Lafond, *Degas*, Vol. II (1919) between pp. 36 and 37; Marguerite Rebatet, *Degas* (1944), Pl. 94.

Owner unknown.

The child is attempting an exercise which requires great muscular control, as the working foot should beat the *cou-de-pied* of the supporting leg as rapidly and as evenly as possible.

The model is a child by the name of Dugés, and all Degas' drawings of her show the faults that might be expected of a beginner, especially the *knobbly* knees whose muscles she has not yet learned to draw up, and the *drooping* elbows. See also Pls. 77 and 78.

77. 'BATTEMENTS A LA SECONDE A LA BARRE'

The little Dugés is holding on to the *barre* with her left hand as she executes her *grands battements* with the right leg.

Charcoal and white chalk on pink paper. $12\frac{3}{4} \times 11\frac{1}{2}$ ins. Signed lower right and inscribed with name of exercise. Above the disengaged arm is written the comment *bien arrondir l'os du coude. Circa* 1883–5.

Collection. H. O. Havemeyer.

Owned by the Metropolitan Museum of Art, New York. (H. O. Havemeyer Collection.)

Photograph. Metropolitan Museum of Art.

The girl instead of looking ahead, has turned to watch her working leg. The *barre* is much too high to be of full support to so small a child, it should be about three inches above waist height. For other studies of the same model see Pls. 76 and 78. See also Pl. 87 and note.

78. 'RONDS-DE-JAMBE-A-TERRE A LA BARRE'

The child is holding the *barre* with her left hand; she is drawn facing three-quarters right.

Charcoal on pink paper. $12 \times 9\frac{1}{2}$ ins. Inscribed top right with name of the exercise and *Dessin de Dugés. H. Rouart. Circa* 1883–5.

Collection. H. Rouart (sale 1912).

Owned by Louis Clarke, Esq., Cambridge.

Photograph. The owner.

The child is in the middle of the exercise and is dropping the working heel so as to pass the foot through first and fifth positions without bending the knee. Again she is not able to resist the temptation of watching her leg.

For other pictures of Dugés see Pls. 76 and 77.

79. PENDANT LE REPOS

The dancer is standing on the left of the picture warming herself before a stove and reading a paper.

Pastel. $29\frac{5}{8} \times 21\frac{5}{8}$ ins. Signed lower right and inscribed 'à mon ami Duranty'. *Circa* 1880–2.

Collection. Duranty.

Reproduced. Fifteen Lithographs by G. W. Thornley (1895–1900); Camille Mauclair, *Degas* (1941), p. 124.

Owner unknown.

Photograph. Knoedler & Co., London.

80. JEUNE DANSEUSE EN CINQUIEME POSITION

She is standing facing a quarter right with both arms and feet in fifth position.

Charcoal heightened with white. $17\frac{1}{2} \times 12$ ins. Stamp of the Degas sale on the original. *Circa* 1878–80.

Collection. Atelier Degas.

Reproduced. Catalogue vente Degas, II (1918), No. 312; Paul Lafond, *Degas,* Vol. I (1918), opp. p. 138.

Owner unknown.

See also *Catalogue vente Degas,* III (1919), Nos. 145*a* and 218.

81. DANSEUSE SE DEGOURDISSANT A LA BARRE

She is facing right, holding on with the left hand and, with the other supporting the knee, she forces the leg as high as possible behind her.

Charcoal. 12×9 ins. Stamp of the Degas sale lower left. *Circa* 1880–2.

Collection. Atelier Degas.

Reproduced. Catalogue vente Degas, III (1919), No. 84*a*.

Owner unknown.

Photograph. Durand Ruel, Paris.

Degas has obviously traced this from his drawing reproduced *Catalogue vente Degas,* III (1919), No. 121*a*. For Impressions see *Catalogue vente Degas,* IV (1919), Nos. 340*b* and 345. For another study of the same model see Pl. 80.

82. LA LEÇON DE DANSE

The master holding his stick is seen back-view on the left watching a pupil at work; on the right other dancers are grouped, two of whom are standing on the grand piano.

Pastel. $17 \times 31\frac{1}{2}$ ins. Signed lower right. *Circa* 1876–8.

Collection. Sardnal (1918).

Reproduced. Paul Lafond, *Degas,* Vol. I (1918), p. 67; Paul Jamot, *Degas* (1924), Pl. 37; Julius Meier-Graefe, *Degas* (1927), Pl. 24; Camille Mauclair, *Degas* (1941), p. 128.

Owner unknown.

Photograph. Durand Ruel, Paris.

The movement of the *danseuse* is reminiscent of *L'Etoile* (Pl. 55); the *maître* is probably M. Eugène Coralli. The figure on the extreme right appears again in Pls. 83, 84 and 98.

82a. LE PAS 'BATTU'

It seems that the two dancers in the centre are doing a series of *petits battements sautés,* while the third, on extreme left, kneels on one leg throwing open her arms.

Monotype in black heightened with pastel. $10\frac{1}{2} \times 11\frac{3}{4}$ ins. Signed lower left. *Circa* 1880.

Collections. Alexis Rouart (sold 1919, No. 127 reproduced); Lucien Guiraud.

Exhibition. Degas, Galerie Georges Petit, 1924, No. 118.

Reproduced. Paul Lafond, *Degas,* Vol. II (1919), opp. p. 24; Ambroise Vollard, *Degas* (1924), p. 36; Julius Meier-Graefe, *Degas* (1927), Pl. 63; Denis Rouart, *Degas, à la Recherche de sa Technique* (1945), p. 57.

Owner unknown.

83. GROUPE DE DANSEUSES EN DIVERSES ATTITUDES

Arranged diagonally across the picture with a window in the background, two are standing in fifth position; two others in *arabesque sur la pointe*; while the one on the right rests her leg on a bench as she pulls on her shoe. A figure in out-door dress stands among them.

Oil on canvas. 24 × 19¾ ins. Stamp of the Degas sale lower right. *Circa* 1880–3.
Collections. Atelier Degas; Robert Treat Paine.
Exhibition. Museum of Fine Arts, Boston.
Reproduced. Catalogue vente Degas, I (1918), No. 70.
Owned by Sam. Salz, New York.
Photograph. Jacques Seligmann & Co. Inc., New York.

For another version see Pl. 84, and for pastel, Pl. 183.

84. GROUPE DE DANSEUSES DANS UNE SALLE

They are arranged diagonally across the canvas in various dancing positions; the one nearest the spectator on the right, fastens her shoe while resting her leg on a bench.

Oil on canvas. 29½ × 29½ ins. Stamp of the Degas sale lower right. *Circa* 1880–2.
Collection. Atelier Degas.
Reproduced. Catalogue vente Degas, II (1918), No. 30.
Owned by the Tate Gallery, London.
Photograph. Tate Gallery.

For another version of this picture see Pl. 83 and for pastel, Pl. 183.

85. 'PAS DE TROIS'. UNE REPETITION

The three dancers are standing with *pointe tendue* and arms in fifth *en haut*; in the left foreground a bench with shoes and violin; behind it part of the back of a dancer and the *maître de danse*.

Oil on canvas. 20 × 24 ins. The stamp of the sale is not visible. *Circa* 1880.
Collection. Atelier Degas.
Reproduced. Catalogue vente Degas, I (1918), No. 76.
Owned by Sam. Salz, New York.
Photograph. The owner.

86. DANSEUSES PRATIQUANT DANS UNE SALLE A COLONNES

Six dancers are seen holding on to the pillars and working at various exercises. In the background, long windows.

Oil on canvas. 28½ × 36 ins. Stamp of the Degas sale lower right. *Circa* 1882–3.
Collection. Atelier Degas.
Reproduced. Catalogue vente Degas, I (1918), No. 46.
Owned by Ny Carlsberg Glyptotek, Copenhagen.
Photograph. Rischgitz Studios, London.

The dancer doing *grand battement à la seconde* also appears in Colour Plate VI, in which picture Degas has used the 'trees' on the set, as he has the pillars in the class-room.

For other studies of *grand battement à la seconde*, see Pl. 87 and note.

87. 'GRAND BATTEMENT A LA SECONDE'

She is facing right and working with the right leg.

Pastel and crayon. 12½ × 9½ ins. Stamp of the Degas sale lower left. *Circa* 1880–2.
Collection. Atelier Degas.
Reproduced. Catalogue vente Degas, II (1918), No. 220b.
Owned by Sam. Salz, New York.
Photograph. The owner.

For dancers in the same position see Pls. 48a, 77, 103 and 190; see also *Catalogue vente Degas*, II (1918), Nos. 325 and 352; and III (1919), No. 372.

88. LA REPETITION AVANT LE BALLET

Dancers are seen practising in the wings whilst a performance goes on, on the stage.

Oil on canvas. 22 × 27 ins. Stamp of the Degas sale lower left. *Circa* 1883–5.
Collections. Atelier Degas; Theodore Schempp; James Philip Gray.
Reproduced. Catalogue vente Degas, I (1918), No. 25.
Owned by the Springfield Museum of Fine Arts, Mass. (James Philip Gray Collection.)
Photograph. Springfield Museum of Fine Arts.

88a. DEUX DANSEUSES DANS LA COULISSE

One is seen back view, with long hair, standing behind a flat; on the extreme right, part of another dancer is visible.

Drypoint. 2nd state. 4½ × 4¼ ins. *Circa* 1875–80.
Reproduced. Loys Delteil. *Edgar Degas, Le Peintre-Graveur Illustré*, No. 9 (1919), No. 23.
This state is extremely rare.

89. LA CLASSE DE DANSE. MOMENT DE PAUSE

Two dancers are standing in the middle of the room; two are just visible in the left distance; while there is another group—two sitting and others with their arms raised, around the teacher on the right. Behind are long windows.

Oil on canvas. 22¾ × 33¾ ins. Stamp of the Degas sale lower left. *Circa* 1884.
Collection. Atelier Degas.
Reproduced. Catalogue vente Degas, I (1918), No. 47.
Owner unknown.
Photograph. Georges Wildenstein, New York.

89a. DANSEUSE EN 'QUATRIEME CROISEE'

She is standing with the left foot *pointe tendue.*

Charcoal on pink paper. 12¾ × 8¼ ins. Stamp of the Degas sale lower right. *Circa* 1885.
Collections. Atelier Degas; Viau.
Reproduced. Catalogue vente Degas, IV (1919), No. 271b.
Owned by Jacques Seligmann & Co., New York.
Photograph. The owners.

90. DANSEUSE DEBOUT VUE DE DOS, ET ETUDES DE PIEDS

The dancer is standing on the left of the picture; her left hand is on her shoulder and she forces the *pointe* of her right foot.

> *Pastel.* 19 × 24 ins. Stamp of the Degas sale lower left. *Circa* 1878–80.
> *Collection.* Atelier Degas.
> *Reproduced. Catalogue vente Degas*, II (1918), No. 190.
> *Owner* unknown.
> *Photograph.* Durand Ruel, Paris.

For other studies, with legs in the same position, see Pls. 91–93a; all of which relate to the *Petite Danseuse de Quatorze Ans* (Pls. 96 and 97).

90a. DANSEUSE DEBOUT VUE DE DOS

Her head is turned to the left, only the lower part of it being visible.

> *Pencil.* 13 × 19 ins. Stamp of the Degas sale lower left. Inscribed near the left leg 'petits reflets au bord'. *Circa* 1878–80.
> *Collection.* Atelier Degas.
> *Reproduced. Catalogue vente Degas*, III (1919), No. 81d.
> *Owned* by J. N. Bryson, Esq., Oxford.
> *Photograph.* The owner.

91. TROIS ETUDES DE DANSEUSE 'EN QUATRIEME'

She is seen facing to the left, the right and full-face; her hands are held behind her back and the weight, instead of being evenly distributed as the fourth position requires, tends to be more on the back leg.

> *Charcoal heightened with pastel.* 19 × 24 ins. Signed lower left. *Circa* 1878–80.
> *Reproduced.* Georges Grappe, *Degas* (1936), p. 35; Camille Mauclair, *Degas* (1941), p. 150.
> *Owner* unknown.
> *Photograph.* Durand Ruel, Paris.

Degas obviously did these studies in order to gain information for his *petite Danseuse de Quatorze Ans*, Pls. 96 and 97. See also Pls. 90, 91a and 95, and *Catalogue vente Degas*, III (1919), No. 386.

91a. CINQ ETUDES D'UNE PAIRE DE JAMBES

Various views of legs in fourth position.

> *Charcoal heightened with white.* 19 × 12 ins. Stamp of the Degas sale lower left. *Circa* 1878–80.
> *Collection.* Atelier Degas.
> *Reproduced. Catalogue vente Degas*, III (1919), No. 149a.
> *Owner* unknown.
> *Photograph.* Durand Ruel, Paris.

These drawings are studies for *La Petite Danseuse de Quatorze Ans*, Pls. 96 and 97. See also notes.

92. DEUX ETUDES D'UNE DANSEUSE DEBOUT

She is seen, side and back view, standing in fourth position, her hair over her shoulder.

Pastel and charcoal on green paper. $25\frac{1}{8} \times 19\frac{1}{4}$ ins. Signed lower left. *Circa* 1878–80.

Collection. H. O. Havemeyer.

Owned by the Metropolitan Museum of Art, New York. (H. O. Havemeyer Collection.)

Photograph. The Metropolitan Museum of Art.

The pastel relates to the *La Petite Danseuse de Quatorze Ans*, and it would seem as if Degas were contemplating doing the sculpture with this different angle of the head and placing of the arms.

See also Pls. 90, 91, 91*a*, 93 and 93*a*.

93. TROIS ETUDES DE DANSEUSE DEBOUT

All of them are back views; in two she wears her hair in a plait down her back.

Charcoal and pastel on grey paper. 18 × 24 ins. Signed lower right. *Circa* 1878–80.

Collection. J. Doucet.

Reproduced. Paul Lafond, *Degas*, Vol. II (1919), in colour, between pp. 36 and 37; H. Rivière, *Les Dessins de Degas* (1922–23), p. 95.

Owner unknown.

See also Pls. 90, 91–92*a* and 93*a*.

93*a*. TROIS ETUDES D'UNE JEUNE DANSEUSE NUE

She is standing with one arm across her breast resting the hand on the other arm.

Charcoal heightened with white. 19 × 25 ins. Stamp of the Degas sale on the original. *Circa* 1878–80.

Exhibition. Degas, Cleveland Museum of Art, 1947, No. 69.

Collection. Atelier Degas.

Reproduced. Catalogue vente Degas, III (1919), No. 369.

Owned by Charles E. Roseman, Jr.

These drawings are studies for Pl. 92. See also note.

94. ETUDES DE TETE ET DE BRAS POUR 'LA PETITE DANSEUSE DE QUATORZE ANS'

Charcoal. 19 × 12 ins. Stamp of the Degas sale lower right. *Circa* 1878–80.

Collection. Atelier Degas.

Reproduced. Catalogue vente Degas, III (1919), No. 341*b*; H. Rivière, *Dessins de Degas* (1922–3), Pl. 36.

Owned by the Musée du Louvre.

Photograph. Archives photographiques.

See Pls. 95–7. Also *Catalogue vente Degas*, III (1919), No. 277.

95. ETUDE DE NUE POUR 'LA PETITE DANSEUSE DE QUATORZE ANS'

Bronze, No. 56. Height 28¾ ins. Executed 1879–80.

Exhibitions. Hebrard exhibition, 1921; *Degas—Portraitiste, Sculpteur*, Musée de l'Orangerie, 1931, No. 37.

Reproduced. John Rewald, *The Sculptures of Edgar Degas—a complete catalogue* (1944), No. 20.

Photograph. The Leicester Galleries, London.

See Pls. 96 and 97 and notes. See also *Catalogue vente Degas*, III (1919), No. 386; and IV (1919), No. 287.

96. LA PETITE DANSEUSE DE QUATORZE ANS

She stands in fourth position, her hands clasped behind her back, her hair worn in a plait. The plate shows the figure in profile, facing left.

Bronze with tarlatan skirt and satin hair-ribbon, on wooden base. Height 39½ ins. 1880.

Exhibitions. The original model in wax, now in the Louvre, appears in the catalogue of the Fifth Impressionist Exhibition in 1880, but as it was not ready it was actually shown the following year. This model was also shown in the exhibition organised by Hebrard in 1921 upon the completion of the casting. The bronze was exhibited in *Degas—Portraitiste, Sculpteur* exhibition, Musée de l'Orangerie, Paris, 1931, No. 73; and *Degas*, Cleveland Museum of Art (1947), No. 78.

Reproduced. Paul Jamot, *Degas* (1924), Pl. 52 (wax); Georges Grappe, *Degas* (1936), p. 58 (wax); Marguerite Rebatet, *Degas* (1944), Pl. 102; John Rewald, *The Sculptures of Edgar Degas* (1944), No. 20.

Photograph. From the bronze belonging to Robert Sainsbury, Esq., London.

For a study of the Nude in bronze see Pl. 95; for drawing studies see Pls. 90, 91, 91a and 94. The sculpture is also known as *Grande Danseuse habillée*.

Of the seventy-three sculptures cast in bronze only *La Petite Danseuse de Quatorze Ans* bears no stamped number. Twenty-two copies were cast of each of the seventy-two numbered bronzes; the first twenty, lettered from A to T were destined for sale, and of the other two sets, one was reserved for the founder and the other, marked 'HER' for the artist's heirs.

It does not seem to be known how many copies of *La Petite Danseuse de Quatorze Ans* were cast, apart from the one belonging to Mr Sainsbury, other casts are in the Musée du Louvre, the Virginia Museum of Fine Arts, and the Metropolitan Museum of Art, New York.

97. LA PETITE DANSEUSE DE QUATORZE ANS

Back view of bronze Pl. 96.

For details see Pl. 96.

98. LA REPETITION DANS LA SALLE D'UN 'PAS DE TROIS'

The master, probably Eugène Coralli, is watching the three dancers who are in the left distance. In the foreground a young woman in hat and outdoor clothes lolls on a chair reading a paper; behind her stand other dancers.

Oil on canvas. 32 × 29½ ins. Signed lower left. *Circa* 1880.

Collections. Cassatt; Wilstach.

Exhibitions. Degas, Pennsylvania Museum of Art, Philadelphia, 1936, No. 35 (reproduced);
Degas, Musée de l'Orangerie, Paris, 1937, No. 30 (reproduced).

Reproduced. Marguerite Rebatet, *Degas* (1944), Pl. 85.

Owned by the Pennsylvania Museum of Art, Philadelphia (Wilstach Collection.)

Photograph. The Pennsylvania Museum of Art.

For the same poor position of the *arabesque* see Pls. 82, 83 and 84. See also Pls. 54 and 54*a*, as well as note to Pl. 34*a*.

99. LE REPOS. DEUX DANSEUSES ASSISES

They are seated on benches at right angles to each other, wearing shawls around their necks and looking thoroughly exhausted.

Pastel. 19¾ × 23 ins. Signed lower left. *Circa* 1880–2.

Collections. Tchoukine, Paris; J. H. Whittemore, Connecticut (1900–13); Hannah Mary Edwards and other members of her family.

Reproduced. Georges Grappe, *Degas* (1909), p. 54; Paul Lafond, *Degas*, Vol. II (1919), between pp. 34 and 35; Camille Mauclair, *Degas* (1941), p. 116; Marguerite Rebatet, *Degas* (1944), Pl. 99.

Owned by the Museum of Fine Arts, Boston (Juliana Cheney Edwards Collection).

Photograph. The Museum of Fine Arts, Boston.

For study see Pl. 99*a*; also *Catalogue vente Degas*, III (1919), No. 362.

99*a*. DEUX DANSEUSES ASSISES. ETUDE

They are seated at right angles to each other and are wearing shawls.

Pastel and charcoal. 11⅞ × 18 ins. Signed lower right. *Circa* 1880–2.

Exhibitions. Degas, Pennsylvania Museum of Art, Philadelphia, 1936, No. 83 (reproduced);
Degas, Cleveland Museum of Art, 1947, No. 70 (reproduced).

Owned by Mrs Murray S. Danforth, Providence, R.I.

Photograph. Rhode Island School of Design.

The pastel is a study for Pl. 99.

100. VIOLINISTE JOUANT

He is seated three-quarter length facing left and is so large in scale as to occupy most of the picture.

Pastel and black chalk on green paper. 15½ × 11⅞ ins. Stamp of the Degas sale lower left; the squares for painting are faintly visible. *Circa* 1882–4.

Collection. Atelier Degas.

Reproduced. Catalogue vente Degas, II (1918), No. 171.

Owned by the Metropolitan Museum of Art, New York.

Photograph. Metropolitan Museum.

A study for *Exercices à la Barre au Violon* (Pl. 101); for another see *Catalogue vente Degas*, IV (1919), No. 247*b*.

101. EXERCICES A LA BARRE AU VIOLON

The violinist occupies the right hand corner of the foreground; on the left the young dancer faces him as she does her *grands battements en avant*.

> *Pastel.* 27 × 23½ ins. Signed upper right. *Circa* 1882–4.
> *Collection.* Havemeyer, New York.
> *Reproduced.* Paul Lafond, *Degas*, Vol. II (1919), between pp. 33 and 37; Paul Jamot, *Degas* (1924), Pl. 63; Julius Meier-Graefe, *Degas* (1927), Pl. 47; Georges Rivière, *Mr Degas (Bourgeois de Paris)* (1935), p. 83; Camille Mauclair, *Degas* (1941), p. 130.
> *Owner* unknown.
> *Photograph.* Durand Ruel, Paris.

For a study of the violinist see Pl. 100.

102. AVANT LA CLASSE

Two mothers are giving the final touches to their daughters' toilet before the class begins. The dancer on the extreme right is practising *battement tendu à la seconde*; the one standing behind her is bending forward to pull up her tights; while she does so her mother fluffs out her *tutu*.

> *Pastel.* 24½ × 18½ ins. Signed lower right. *Circa* 1882.
> *Reproduced.* Georges Grappe, *Degas* (1909), p. 43; Paul Lafond, *Degas*, Vol. I (1918), p. 69; Paul Jamot, *Degas* (1924), Pl. 47; Julius Meier-Graefe, *Degas* (1927), Pl. 36; Georges Rivière, *Mr Degas (Bourgeois de Paris)* (1935), p. 99; Camille Mauclair, *Degas* (1941), p. 119; Hans Graber, *Edgar Degas* (1942), opp. p. 172.
> *Owned* by the Denver Art Museum, Colorado.
> *Photograph.* The Denver Art Museum.

The old lady seen full-face seems to be Degas' housekeeper, Sabine Neyt, who also appears in Pl. 60.

103. DEUX DANSEUSES EXECUTANT 'GRANDS BATTEMENTS A LA SECONDE A LA BARRE'

They are facing the right; the one in front being cut by the edge of the picture.

> *Pastel.* 25¼ × 18¾ ins. Signed upper right. *Circa* 1882–4.
> *Owned* by Mr and Mrs J. Watson Webb, New York.
> *Photograph.* The owners.

See also the pastel, Pl. 87, for a dancer doing the same exercise.

As in all the pictures showing this position, it is difficult to know whether the dancer is doing *developpé* or *grand battement*.

104. JEUNE DANSEUSE AUX BRAS ETENDUS

She is seen full face with her head slightly bowed.

> *Pastel.* 25 × 19 ins. Stamp of the Degas sale lower left. *Circa* 1882–5.
> *Collection.* Atelier Degas.
> *Reproduced.* Catalogue vente Degas, III (1919), No. 41.
> *Owner* unknown.
> *Photograph.* Durand Ruel, Paris.

105. 'PORTE DE BRAS'

The child is standing full-face with her right leg behind her in *quatrième croisée, pointe tendue*. Her right arm is raised above her head and her body is bent away from it.

Charcoal. 14 × 9 ins. Stamp of the Degas sale lower left. Inscribed with remarks concerning the position, upper left. *Circa 1880–5*.

Collection. Atelier Degas.

Reproduced. Catalogue vente Degas, III (1919), No. 101*a*.

Owner unknown.

Photograph. Durand Ruel.

Degas has written pertinent remarks regarding the faulty position: 'abandon du corps. . . . Bras droit pas bien allongé.'

106. DANSEUSE AU BOUQUET DERRIERE UNE FEMME A L'EVENTAIL

The woman, whose head is seen on extreme right, holds a fan which makes a large dark shape in the foreground; behind it in the full light of the stage the *sujet* takes her call while all around the stage stand the *corps de ballet*.

Pastel. 16 × 19¾ ins. Signed lower left. *Circa 1878–80*.

Reproduced. Henri Hertz, *Degas* (1920), Pl. 18.

Owned by the Museum of Art, Rhode Island School of Design, Providence.

Photograph. Georges Wildenstein, New York.

The members of the *corps de ballet* are standing in the same casual manner as was noted in *Danseuse, un Bouquet à la Main* (Pl. 56). For other pictures on the same theme see Pls. 107–10; see also Pls. 52 and 53 for the *motif* of the dark double-bass scroll in the foreground.

106*a*. ETUDE DE MAIN GANTEE TENANT DES JUMELLES DE THEATRE

Black chalk. 12 × 7¼ ins. Stamp of the Degas sale on the original. *Circa 1883–5*.

Collection. Atelier Degas.

Reproduced. Catalogue vente Degas, IV (1919), No. 134*b*.

Owner unknown.

Study for Pl. 109; see also *Catalogue vente Degas*, IV (1919), No. 134*a*.

107. LOGE D'AVANT SCENE. FEMME A L'EVENTAIL

Back view of woman with long curls and holding fan, in right foreground; on the stage three dancers with long hair in movement.

Lithograph. 9 × 8 ins. *Circa 1883*.

Reproduced. Loys Delteil, *Edgar Degas; Le Peintre-Graveur Illustré*, No. 9 (1919), No. 56.

This lithograph is very rare.

For other pictures on the same theme see Pls. 106 and 108–10.

NOTES ON THE PLATES

108. LE BALLET VU D'UNE LOGE DE THEATRE

On the left of the picture sits a woman holding a closed fan under her chin and looking to the left; beneath the box, on the stage, dancers in strong light are seen.

Pastel. 27 × 23¼ ins. The stamp of the Degas sale is not visible. *Circa* 1883–5.

Collections. Atelier Degas; Fattorini.

Exhibition. French 19th Century Painters, National Gallery, London, 1942, No. 70.

Reproduced. Catalogue vente Degas, II (1918), No. 85.

Owned by the Matthiesen Gallery, London.

Photograph. The National Gallery, London.

For other pictures on this theme see Pls. 106, 107, 109 and 110.

109. AU BALLET. LA FEMME A L'EVENTAIL

She sits on the right of the picture holding her fan and opera glasses; on the stage the danseuse makes her bow, behind her other dancers are partly visible.

Pastel. 18⅞ × 24½ ins. Signed lower left. *Circa* 1883–5.

Owned by the John G. Johnson Art Collection, Philadelphia.

Photograph. The Pennsylvania Museum of Art, Philadelphia.

For other pictures on the same theme see Pls. 106–8, 110 and frontispiece. Note how also in Pls. 110–12 Degas has further concentrated upon the pattern made by arms and legs.

For a study of the hand holding opera glasses see Pl. 106a; also *Catalogue vente Degas*, IV (1919), No. 134a and for a pastel of the figure, *Catalogue vente Degas*, III (1918), No. 56.

110. AU THEATRE. LE BALLET VU D'UNE LOGE

The foreground is entirely occupied by the head and shoulders of a woman holding a fan; behind her in the strong light of the stage the arms and legs of the dancers make an intricate pattern.

Pastel. 24 × 18 ins. Stamp of the Degas sale lower left. *Circa* 1885.

Collections. Atelier Degas; Mlle Fevre (sale, June 1934, reproduced, No. 94).

Reproduced. Catalogue vente Degas, II (1918), No. 162.

Owned by Mrs Kay, Berkshire.

Photograph. Reid and Lefevre, London.

For other pictures on *La Femme à l'Eventail* theme see Pls. 106–9.

111. DANSEUSES EN SCENE

They are large in scale and closely massed diagonally along the upper part of the picture, great emphasis being laid upon the pattern made by the arms.

Pastel. 25½ × 19½ ins. Signed lower left. *Circa* 1884–6.

Collections. Viau; Wilhelm Hansen.

Exhibition. Degas, Pennsylvania Museum of Art, Philadelphia, 1936, No. 42.

Reproduced. Paul Lafond, *Degas*, Vol. II (1919), opp. p. 26; Paul Jamot, *Degas* (1924), Pl. 62. Knut Hoppe, *Degas* (1922), p. 52.

Owned by Mr and Mrs Frank H. Ginn, Cleveland.

Photograph. National Gallery, Stockholm.

112. DANSEUSES PENDANT LE REPOS

Three of them are seated on a bench in the foreground, one is bending forward massaging her ankle, another pulls up her tights, the third is leaning with both arms on her leg. Behind, the *tutus* and legs of many other dancers are seen.

Pastel. 19 × 25½ ins. Signed lower left. *Circa* 1880–3.

Reproduced. Georges Grappe, *Degas* (1909), p. 144; P. A. Lemoisne, *Degas* (1912), Pl. 36; Paul Jamot, *Degas* (1924), Pl. 51; Julius Meier-Graefe, *Degas* (1927), Pl. 57; Georges Rivière, *Mr Degas (Bourgeois de Paris)* (1935), p. 63; Camille Mauclair, *Degas* (1941), p. 146; Marguerite Rebatet, *Degas* (1944), Pl. 82; John Rewald, *History of Impressionism* (1946), p. 337.

Owner unknown.

Photograph. Durand Ruel, Paris.

For a study of the three dancers see Pl. 113.

112a. ETUDE DE DEUX DANSEUSES

The one on the left holds her face in her hands; the other sits, bending forward with one hand on her knee, the other on her ankle.

Charcoal heightened with white on pink paper. 18¼ × 24 ins. Stamp of the Degas sale lower right. *Circa* 1884–5.

Collection. Atelier Degas.

Reproduced. Catalogue vente Degas, III (1919), No. 223.

Owned by the Matthiesen Gallery, London.

Photograph. The owners.

The drawing is a study for two of the figures in Pl. 114. See also *Catalogue vente Degas*, III (1919), Nos. 88a and 124a,

113. TROIS DANSEUSES ASSISES

The one on the right bends forward and massages her ankle, the dancer next to her chats with the girl on her right as she stretches her tights at the knee.

Pastel and charcoal. 18¼ × 24½ ins. Signed upper right. *Circa* 1880–3.

Owned by Mr and Mrs J. Watson Webb, New York.

Photograph. The owners.

This is a study for *Danseuses pendant le Repos* (Pl. 112).

The pastel seems to have suggested the long *friezes* of dancers which soon followed. See Pls. 114, 115, 116, 116a.

113a. TROIS ETUDES DE LA TETE D'UNE DANSEUSE

The smiling girl, wearing a fringe, is seen in three different positions.

Coloured crayon. 7½ × 22¼ ins. Signed lower right. *Circa* 1886–90.

Collections. Boussod; Isaac de Camondo.

Reproduced. Paul Jamot, *Degas* (1924), Pl. 71; Julius Meier-Graefe, *Degas* (1927), Pl. 53; Georges Grappe, *Degas* (1936), p. 33.

Owned by the Musée du Louvre (bequeathed in 1911 by Camondo).

Photograph. Archives photographiques.

114. LA CLASSE DE DANSE. FRISE

The picture is divided almost in half by a pole; on the left of it, in the distance, four dancers are doing *grand battement à la barre*; on its right, another four are grouped around a bench set diagonally, two of them are sitting.

> *Oil on canvas.* 15 × 34½ ins. Signed lower left. *Circa* 1884–5.
>
> *Exhibitions.* Yale University, 1937; Colorado Springs Fine Art Centre, 1942–4.
>
> *Reproduced.* Paul Lafond, *Degas* (1918), p. 85; Julius Meier-Graefe, *Degas* (1927), Pl. 52a.
>
> *Owned* by the Phillips Memorial Gallery, Washington.
>
> *Photograph.* Phillips Memorial Gallery.

For studies of resting dancers see Pls. 112a and 130a. For other pictures of similar composition see Pls. 116, 116a and 246. See also *Catalogue vente Degas*, II (1918), No. 226; III (1919), No. 248; and IV (1919), Nos. 176 and 191.

114a. QUATRE DANSEUSES DANS LA SALLE DE DANSE

They are standing on the right of the picture; one of them whose back is reflected in the mirror is in *quatrième derrière pointe tendue*.

> *Pastel.* 15¼ × 29 ins. Signed upper left. *Circa* 1884.
>
> *Reproduced.* Georges Grappe, *Degas* (1909), p. 52.
>
> *Owner* unknown.
>
> *Photograph.* Durand Ruel, Paris.

115. QUATRE DANSEUSES ATTACHANT LEURS CHAUSSONS. FRISE

They are seated side by side on chairs, each at a different angle, tying their ribbons.

> *Oil on canvas.* 28 × 80 ins. Signed lower right. *Circa* 1885–90.
>
> *Collections.* Max Liebermann, Berlin; Mme Kurt Riezler.
>
> *Exhibitions. Degas*, Musée de l'Orangerie, 1937, No. 40; *Works by Edgar Degas*, Cleveland Museum of Art, 1947, No. 40 (reproduced).
>
> *Reproduced.* Julius Meier-Graefe, *Degas* (1927), Pl. 62; Georges Grappe, *Degas* (1936), p. 33.
>
> *Owned* by the Cleveland Museum of Art (Gift of the Hanna Fund, 1946).
>
> *Photograph.* Durand Ruel, Paris.

In width, this must be the largest of all Degas' pictures. The attitude of the dancer bending down to tie her shoe is one of which Degas was particularly fond; he explored its possibilities over and over again, e.g. Pls. 115a and 119.

For a nude study of one of the figures see *Catalogue vente Degas*, III (1919), No. 332.

115a. DANSEUSE ATTACHANT SES RUBANS

She is sitting on a chair facing a quarter right; her head is almost touching her ankle as she bends down to tie, with both hands, the shoe ribbon on her right foot.

> *Pastel.* 25 × 19 ins. Signed lower right. *Circa* 1880.
>
> *Collection.* Capt. Victor Cazalet.

Owned by the National Gallery of Victoria, Melbourne (Felton Bequest).

Photograph. National Gallery of Victoria.

This pastel is a study for one of the figures in the oil painting, Pl. 118.

For another pastel of the same position, with the dancer wearing a 'butterfly' sash, see Pl. 119, and *Catalogue vente Degas*, II (1918), No. 191. For Nude study, see *Catalogue vente Degas*, I (1918), No. 324.

116. SEPT DANSEUSES DANS UNE SALLE DE CLASSE. FRISE

Two dancers are sitting on a bench on the extreme right; in the middle stands another with a fan; in left distance, in front of windows, the other four are practising *grand battement à la barre*.

Oil on canvas. $15\frac{1}{2} \times 34\frac{3}{4}$ ins. Signed upper right. *Circa* 1883.

Owner unknown.

Photograph. Knoedler & Co., London.

In this picture the dancer standing with the fan supplies the *upright* provided in Pl. 114 by the pole. For a similar composition see Pls. 116a and 246; and for the dancer with the fan see the pastel, Pl. 117.

116a. SIX DANSEUSES DANS UNE SALLE DE CLASSE. FRISE

In the left distance four dancers are doing *grand battement à la barre*; in the right foreground another two are sitting, one pulling up her tights, the other rubbing her foot.

Oil on canvas. $16 \times 35\frac{1}{2}$ ins. Signed lower left. *Circa* 1884–6.

Collection. Widener.

Reproduced. Paul Lafond, *Degas*, Vol. I (1918), p. 6.

Owned by the National Gallery of Art, Washington. (Widener Collection.)

Photograph. The National Gallery of Art.

See also Pls. 114, 116 and 246. In the first, the two dancers in the right foreground are in almost identical positions.

117. DANSEUSE DEBOUT A L'EVENTAIL

She is standing on the left-hand side facing a quarter right; her left hand is behind her head, in the other she holds an open fan.

Pastel on green paper. $24 \times 16\frac{1}{2}$ ins. Signed upper right. *Circa* 1883.

Collection. H. O. Havemeyer.

Owned by the Metropolitan Museum of Art, New York. (H. O. Havemeyer Collection.)

Photograph. The Metropolitan Museum.

The pastel is a study for a figure in *Sept Danseuses dans une Salle de Classe*; it is another example of how closely Degas adheres to his drawings.

118. DANSEUSES AVEC CONTREBASSE. FRISE

In the left foreground is a double-bass with a dancer bending forward tying her shoe; in the right distance the room opens out and other dancers are seen standing.

Oil on canvas. $15\frac{1}{8} \times 35\frac{1}{4}$ ins. Signed lower left. *Circa* 1880–3.

I

Collections. E. F. Milliken, H. O. Havemeyer.

Owned by the Metropolitan Museum of Art, New York. (H. O. Havemeyer Collection.)

Photograph. The Metropolitan Museum.

See also Pl. 120.

For a study of the dancer tying her shoe see Pl. 115*a*. See also Pl. 119.

118*a*. DEUX DANSEUSES SE REPOSANT

They are seated on a bench along the back of the wall; one bends forward with a hand on each leg just below the knee, the other extends her leg along the bench and clasps her instep.

Pastel. $18\frac{1}{2} \times 26\frac{1}{4}$ ins. Signed upper right. *Circa* 1880–3.

Collection. Viau.

Owned by Mr and Mrs J. Watson Webb, New York.

Photograph. The owners.

See also Pls. 204 and 251.

119. DANSEUSE ATTACHANT SES RUBANS

She is facing a quarter right and is bending right down to adjust the ribbon on her right shoe. Behind her, her skirt is spread and she wears a sash with a huge bow.

Pastel and crayon. $17\frac{1}{4} \times 16$ ins. Signed lower left. *Circa* 1880.

Reproduced. Degas, *Vingt Dessins*, Album Manzi (1896), No. 16.

Owned by Mr and Mrs J. Watson Webb, New York.

Photograph. The owners.

See also Pl. 115*a*, also *Catalogue vente Degas*, II (1918), Nos. 193 and 330.

120. DANSEUSES AVEC CONTREBASSE DANS LA SALLE DE DANSE. FRISE

In the foreground are three dancers, the one on the left has her foot on a double-bass lying on the floor. In the right distance the room widens out and other dancers are seen.

Oil on canvas. $17\frac{1}{2} \times 35\frac{1}{4}$ ins. Stamp of the Degas sale lower right. *Circa* 1880–3.

Collection. Atelier Degas.

Exhibition. Degas, Cleveland Museum of Art, 1947, No. 30 (reproduced)

Reproduced. *Catalogue vente Degas*, I (1918), No. 35.

Owned by the Detroit Institute of Arts, Michigan.

Photograph. The Detroit Museum.

See also Pl. 118.

For a study of the dancer standing arranging her sash see Pl. 121; the same figure appears in Pl. 120*a*; for a study of the dancer with her foot on the double-bass see *Catalogue vente Degas* III (1919), No. 86*c*.

120*a*. DANS LA SALLE DE DANSE. FRISE

In the lower left corner sits a dancer in a shawl; in the centre are two others, one sitting and one standing; in the right distance the room widens and other dancers are visible.

Oil on canvas. $15 \times 35\frac{1}{2}$ ins. Signed lower right. *Circa* 1880–3.

Collections. Keanward, Jr.; Rev. Fiske.

Exhibition. Degas, Musée de l'Orangerie, 1937, No. 39 (reproduced).

Reproduced. Julius Meier-Graefe, *Degas* (1927), Pl. 52c; Camille Mauclair, *Degas* (1941), p. 129, in colour.

Owned by Mrs Esther Fiske Hammond, Santa Barbara, California.

Photograph. Durand Ruel, Paris.

For pictures of similar composition see Pls. 118 and 120; the view of the room is just the reverse from that in Pls. 114, 116 and 116a.

For a study of the standing figure see Pl. 121. See also *Catalogue vente Degas*, III (1919), No. 362a.

121. DANSEUSE DEBOUT ATTACHANT SA CEINTURE

She is facing left, her head lowered as with both hands she fastens her sash at the back. Around her shoulders is a shawl.

Charcoal heightened with white. 19 × 12 ins. Stamp of the Degas sale lower left. Squared for painting. *Circa* 1880–3.

Collection. Atelier Degas.

Reproduced. Catalogue vente Degas, II (1918), No. 351.

Owner unknown.

Photograph. Durand Ruel, Paris.

The drawing is a study for the standing figure in Pls. 120 and 120a. A similar figure is seen in Pl. 118. See also *Catalogue vente Degas*, I (1918), No. 123; and III (1919), No. 204.

122. 'DEVELOPPE EN AVANT, FONDU'

Charcoal heightened with pastel. 12 × 9 ins. Stamp of the Degas sale lower left. Inscribed at the top with the criticisms 'Soutenir le coude droit et allonger la pointe droite. Arrondir le bras gauche'. *Circa* 1885.

Collection. Atelier Degas.

Reproduced. Catalogue vente Degas, II (1918), No. 228b.

Owner unknown.

Photograph. Durand Ruel, Paris.

The dancer's position is a preparatory one, probably for *ballotté en avant.*

123. DANSEUSE EN 'QUATRIEME', VUE DE PROFIL

She is standing facing left with her head turned a quarter left.

Charcoal heightened with pastel. 12 × 9 ins. Signed lower left. *Circa* 1885.

Collection. Atelier Degas.

Reproduced. Catalogue vente Degas, II (1918), No. 214b.

Owner unknown.

Photograph. Durand Ruel, Paris.

124. ETUDE. BALLET DE 'FAUST'

The dancer wears an Eastern costume with hair hanging down her back. She is standing with her right foot in *pointe tendue* behind her, with her body bent forward and her right arm slightly raised.

Charcoal. 12 × 10 ins. Signed on the right and inscribed upper left, 'ballet de Faust, Egyptiennes.' *Circa* 1885.

Owner unknown.

Photograph. Durand Ruel, Paris.

This is one of the few pictures in which Degas has shown a dancer in anything other than a ballet skirt.

Faust was repeatedly performed at the Opéra since its first production in 1869 when Faure sang 'Mephistopheles'. The title does not therefore help in the dating of this drawing.

125. 'DEGAGE EN QUATRIEME OUVERTE'

Charcoal retouched with bistre. 12 × 9 ins. Stamp of the Degas sale lower right. *Circa* 1885.

Collections. Atelier Degas; Koenigs.

Reproduced. Catalogue vente Degas, III (1919), No. 81c.

Owned by the Boymans Museum, Rotterdam.

Photograph. Boymans Museum.

126. 'PORTE DE BRAS'. DANSEUSE VUE DE DOS

She is standing with her legs and arms in fourth position, left foot in front and left arm raised, head turned to right shoulder.

Sanguine. 12 × 10 ins. Stamp of the Degas sale lower left. *Circa* 1885.

Collection. Atelier Degas.

Reproduced. Catalogue vente Degas, III (1919), No. 259 (one of two drawings).

Owner unknown.

Photograph. Durand Ruel, Paris.

127. PREPARATION POUR UNE 'PIROUETTE EN DEHORS'

The dancer is seen from behind standing in a *plié à la seconde*. She is about to turn to the right, on the left leg, swinging the arms across as impetus.

Charcoal. 9 × 12 ins. Stamp of the Degas sale lower left; inscribed with the name of the position on the upper left and with two other remarks of criticism—*bras mauvais* and *trop large*. *Circa* 1885.

Collection. Atelier Degas.

Reproduced. Catalogue vente Degas, III (1919), No. 119b.

Owner unknown.

Photograph. Durand Ruel, Paris.

Degas has rightly remarked that the *plié* is too wide and the right arm bad, the latter because the elbow should be raised so as to be level with the hand, and not beneath it.

See also *Catalogue vente Degas*, III (1919), Nos. 118, 120a and 124c.

127a. DANSEUSE EN 'QUATRIEME DEVANT'

She stands facing left, her arms in opposition and her head turned to the spectator.

Charcoal heightened with white. 11¾ × 9 ins. Inscribed top left, 'coude trop sorti'. Plumb line through the figure. *Circa* 1885.

Owned by Dr Hans Halban, Oxford.

Photograph. The owner.

From the classical ballet point of view, this position is wrong in almost every respect.

128. DEUX ETUDES D'UNE DANSEUSE

On the left she is standing facing right holding a fan; on the right she has the back foot raised on to a bench and is adjusting her shoe with her left hand.

Chalk and pastel. 18 × 24 ins. Signed lower right. *Circa* 1885.

Reproduced. Camille Mauclair, *Degas* (1941), p. 151.

Owner unknown.

Photograph. Durand Ruel, Paris.

For study of the figure on the right see Pl. 128a.

128a. DANSEUSE AJUSTANT SON CHAUSSON. ETUDE

She faces a quarter right, her left foot supported on a chair as she pulls her shoe.

Charcoal. 24 × 18¼ ins. Stamp of the Degas sale on the original. *Circa* 1885.

Collection. Atelier Degas.

Reproduced. *Catalogue vente Degas*, III (1919), No. 233.

Owner unknown.

The drawing is a study for Pl. 128.

129. ETUDE DE DANSEUSE SALUANT

She is seen full-face, standing in fourth position, her hands holding out her skirts as she bows.

Chalk. 12 × 8¾ ins. Unsigned. *Circa* 1885–7.

Collections. René de Gas; G. Pellet; Exsteens.

Owner unknown.

Photograph. Gallery Thannhauser, New York.

130. DANSEUSE ASSISE TIRANT SON MAILLOT

She is seated facing left with her right leg raised as, with both hands, she pulls her tights at the knee.

Charcoal and wash. 9½ × 12½ ins. Stamp of the Degas sale lower left. *Circa* 1883–5.

Collection. Atelier Degas.

Reproduced. *Catalogue vente Degas*, II (1918), No. 218b.

Owned by the Bucholz Gallery, New York.

Photograph. The owners.

This drawing is a study for one of the seated figures in *La Classe de Danse—Frise* (Pl. 114). It was a favourite position of Degas'; see also drawing, Pl. 130a, as well as pictures, Pls. 116 and 116a.

Other drawings of the position are reproduced in *Catalogue vente Degas*, II (1918), No. 217b; III (1919), Nos. 112d, 138d, 371; IV (1919), Nos. 160 and 270b.

NOTES ON THE PLATES

130a. DANSEUSE ASSISE TIRANT SON MAILLOT

She is facing left. Her right leg is raised in the air as, with both hands, she pulls her tights at the knee. Study of an arm below.

Charcoal. $9\frac{1}{4} \times 11\frac{7}{8}$ ins. Stamp of the Degas sale lower right. Squared for painting. *Circa* 1883–5.

Collection. Atelier Degas.

Reproduced. Catalogue vente Degas, III (1919), No. 109d.

Owned by A. S. F. Gow, Esq.

Photograph. The owner.

The drawing is a study for one of the figures in Pl. 114. See also Pl. 130 and note.

131. DANSEUSE ASSISE TIRANT SON MAILLOT

She is seated full face with her skirt spread out behind her, and her right leg extended on the floor as she pulls her tights at the knee.

Charcoal heightened with white. $15\frac{3}{4} \times 10\frac{3}{4}$ ins. Stamp of the Degas sale lower left. *Circa* 1883–5.

Collection. Atelier Degas.

Reproduced. Catalogue vente Degas, III (1919), No. 343.

Owner unknown.

Photograph. Knoedler & Co., London.

For another study of this figure see *Catalogue vente Degas*, III (1919), No. 336b.

132. L'ENTREE DES MASQUES

In the foreground two dancers are standing behind the flat, one is peeping through a hole in it, the other is pulling the ribbon at her neck. Behind them, on the stage, dancers with white hoods and black masks are seen.

Pastel. 20×26 ins. Signed lower left. *Circa* 1884–6.

Collection. Viau.

Exhibitions. Grafton Galleries, London, 1905, No. 67 (reproduced); *Degas*, Galerie Georges Petit, Paris, 1924, No. 131 (reproduced).

Reproduced. Paul Lafond, *Degas*, Vol. II (1919), between pp. 36 and 37; Meier-Graefe, *Degas* (1927), Pl. 56; Camille Mauclair, *Degas* (1941), p. 147.

Engraved by Lauzet for *l'Art Impressioniste* by Georges Lecomte (1892).

Owner unknown.

Photograph. Durand Ruel, Paris.

This is one of the series of dancers wearing corselets (Pls. 133–8), most of whom have a certain expression of mimicry. Degas himself was said to have been an excellent mimic.

132a. 'LA FAMILLE CARDINAL'. DANS LES COULISSES

The mother in bonnet and shawl stands on the right next to a man in a top-hat. On the left the stage.

Monotype in colour. $6\frac{1}{4} \times 8\frac{1}{4}$ ins. *Circa* 1880–3.

Photograph. Bibliothèque Nationale.

One of the illustrations Degas did for Ludovic Halévy's *La Famille Cardinal*. They were engraved by Maurice Potin. See Pls. 167a, 179a; p. 34 and note, also p. 69.

133. DANSEUSE AU CORSELET, SE REPOSANT

She is sitting with her skirt arranged behind her and her limbs spread out, the left foot being raised on a chair and the left elbow resting on the knee. In the lower right corner the skirt of another dancer is visible.

Pastel. 24⅜ × 18½ ins. Signed lower right. *Circa* 1884–6.

Owned by a private collector in France.

Photograph. Reid and Lefevre, London.

134. TROIS DANSEUSES EN LIGNE DIAGONALE SUR LA SCENE

The front two are kneeling on one leg, while the back one seems to be in the position of a *plié* so that she can be seen above the heads of her companions.

Pastel. 24½ × 18½ ins. Signed upper right. *Circa* 1884–6.

Owned by a private collector in Scotland.

Photograph. Reid and Lefevre, London.

135. TROIS DANSEUSES A GENOUX SUR LA SCENE

In the form of a triangle they are kneeling on one leg; one holds a tambourine above her head; behind, other dancers are standing.

Pastel. Size unknown. Signed lower left. *Circa* 1884–6.

Reproduced. *Illustrated London News*, December, 1936.

Owner unknown.

Photograph. Sir Robert Witt Library, London.

For a study of this picture see *Catalogue vente Degas*, IV (1919), No. 137a.

An almost identical pastel was lithographed by Thornley in his series of fifteen lithographs after Degas.

136. DANS LES COULISSES. DEUX DANSEUSES EN ROSE

They are standing in between the flats, one facing, the other with her back to the spectator.

Pastel. 19⅝ × 15¾ ins. Signed lower right. *Circa* 1884–6.

Owner unknown.

Photograph. Reid and Lefevre, London.

137. TROIS DANSEUSES EN CORSELETS, DEBOUT

They are standing side by side in fourth position, one is holding her skirt, the other her wrist, while the third has her hands on her hips.

Pastel. 32 × 20 ins. Signed lower right. *Circa* 1884–6.

Owner unknown.

Photograph. Durand Ruel, Paris.

As time progressed Degas paid less and less attention to the dancers' faces, but this pastel—like others—obviously shows different studies of the same sitter who bears a resemblance to Mlle Salle. See Pls. 173, 173a and 184a.

138. DANSEUSE VERTE VUE DE DOS

She is standing in front of a flat facing three-quarters left.
> *Pastel.* 18 × 12 ins. Signed on right. *Circa* 1884–6.
> *Owner* unknown.
> *Photograph.* Durand Ruel, Paris.

139. EN ATTENDANT L'ENTREE

Four dancers are standing in the wings; with them is a man with a beard behind whom, on the extreme right, part of another dancer is visible.
> *Pastel.* 12¼ × 10 ins. Signed lower left. *Circa* 1884–6.
> *Reproduced.* Paul Lafond, *Degas*, Vol. II (1919), between pp. 36 and 37; Camille Mauclair, *Degas* (1941), p. 152; Marguerite Rebatet, *Degas* (1944), Pl. 84.
> *Owned* by the Corcoran Gallery of Art, Washington. (W. A. Clark Collection.)
> *Photograph.* The Corcoran Gallery of Art.

140. LE COMMENCEMENT DES 'PIROUETTES SUR LA POINTE EN DEDANS'

She is seen on the left, with arms to the left, and foot *pointe tendue* with bent knee, about to turn to the right.
> *Pastel.* 18 × 14 ins. Signed lower left. *Circa* 1880–3.
> *Reproduced.* Camille Mauclair, *Degas* (1941), p. 141.
> *Owner* unknown.
> *Photograph.* Durand Ruel, Paris.

For a study of the picture see *Catalogue vente Degas*, IV (1919), No. 281*b*.

141. DANSEUSE AU BOUQUET

She is seen, having just completed a *jeté*, holding a bouquet of flowers in her right hand; behind stand members of the *corps de ballet*.
> *Pastel worked over with oil paint.* 26 × 14½ ins. Signed lower left. *Circa* 1882–4.
> *Collection.* Isaac de Camondo.
> *Exhibition.* Degas, Musée de l'Orangerie, Paris, 1937, No. 96.
> *Reproduced.* Paul Lafond, *Degas*, Vol. I (1918), p. 55; Gustave Coquiot, *Degas* (1924), opp. p. 208; Julius Meier-Graefe, *Degas* (1927), Pl. 51; Camille Mauclair, *Degas* (1941), p. 140.
> *Owned* by the Musée du Louvre (bequeathed in 1911 by Camondo).
> *Photograph.* Archives photographiques.

For studies see *Catalogue vente Degas*, III (1919), No. 182, 276 and 398; also IV (1919), No. 281*a*. See also Pls. 55, 142–5 and 178 for a similar position without the bouquet.

142. LE PAS SEUL SUR LA SCENE

The dancer is seen on the left in what seems to be an *attitude*, but it may be that she has just completed *chassé, coupé, jeté en tournant*.
> *Pastel.* 14½ × 10½ ins. Signed lower right. *Circa* 1880–3.

Owner unknown.

Photograph. Knoedler & Co., London.

See also Pls. 55, 141, 143–5 and 178.

143. LE BALLET SUR LA SCENE

Three dancers are seen in movement in the right foreground; up stage in the centre, four others are standing in different poses.

Pastel. 22½ × 16 ins. Signed upper left. *Circa* 1883–5.

Owned by the Art Institute of Chicago. (Potter Palmer Collection.)

Photograph. The Art Institute of Chicago.

This picture is reminiscent of the 'Etoile' theme of 1875–6 (Pl. 55); see also Pls. 141, 142, 144, 145 and 178.

144. DANSEUSE BLEUE

The dancer is seen having landed on her right foot, her arms spread out, and her body leaning to the left. On the extreme right is the edge of a ballet skirt of another dancer. Behind is a *décor* of rocks.

Pastel. 28½ × 15¼ ins. Signed lower left. *Circa* 1884.

Collection. Lerolle.

Exhibition. *Degas*, Musée de l'Orangerie, Paris, 1937, No. 114.

Reproduced. Paul Lafond, *Degas*, Vol. I (1918), on cover.

Owned by Jacques Seligmann, New York.

Photograph. The owners.

See also Pls. 55, 141–3, 145 and 178.

145. LE PAS SEUL SUR LA SCENE

The dancer has just landed on her right foot, her arms are spread, and her body inclined to the left.

Pastel. 28½ × 15 ins. Signed lower right. *Circa* 1884–6.

Reproduced. Camille Mauclair, *Degas* (1941), p. 139.

Owned by Mr and Mrs J. Watson Webb, New York.

Photograph. Durand Ruel, Paris.

See also Pls. 55, 141–4 and 178.

146. 'ECHAPPE SUR LES POINTES A LA SECONDE A LA BARRE'

The dancer is facing right, holding the *barre* with her left hand, the other arm raised above her head.

Charcoal. Size unknown. *Circa* 1885. Signed lower left and inscribed 'a M. . . .' Also inscribed with title upper left.

Owner unknown.

Photograph. National Gallery, London.

147. 'PLIE A LA SECONDE A LA BARRE'

She is facing right, holding the *barre* with her left hand and her skirt with her right.

Charcoal heightened with pastel. 12 × 9 ins. Stamp of the Degas sale lower left. Inscribed with name of exercise upper right. *Circa* 1885.

Collection. Atelier Degas.

Reproduced. Catalogue vente Degas, II (1918), No. 214a.

Owner unknown.

Photograph. Durand Ruel, Paris.

There is a tracing of this drawing reproduced *Catalogue vente Degas,* III (1919), No. 84a. See also Pl. 49a as well as *Catalogue vente Degas,* II (1918), Nos. 229a and 358.

In ballet there is a well-known dictum, 'A good *plié* makes a good dancer,' but according to contemporary teaching, this dancer's *plié* is in much too *open* a second position; there should be just the length of the dancer's foot between the heels.

148. DANSEUSE SE DEGOURDISSANT A LA BARRE

She is facing the *barre*, holding it with her right hand, the other is supporting the left knee as she forces that leg as high as possible behind her.

Charcoal heightened with pastel. 12 × 9 ins. Stamp of the Degas sale lower left. Inscribed 'plus croisé le jambe'. *Circa* 1885–90.

Collection. Atelier Degas.

Reproduced. Catalogue vente Degas, II (1918), No. 228a.

Owner unknown.

Photograph. Durand Ruel, Paris.

As Degas has written, the dancer, to receive full benefit from this exercise, must force the leg well behind her instead of to the side.

149. DANSEUSE EXERÇANT A LA BARRE

She is facing left, with her left foot resting on the *barre* behind her and her left hand resting on her waist.

Charcoal heightened with pastel. 12 × 9¼ ins. Stamp of the Degas sale lower left. Inscribed, 'Porter le corps sur la jambe à terre.' *Circa* 1885–90.

Collection. Atelier Degas.

Reproduced. Catalogue vente Degas, III (1919), No. 125d.

Owned by the Cincinnati Museum of Art.

Photograph. Cincinnati Museum.

The inscription is difficult to read, but it seems that Degas has criticised the position by suggesting that the weight of the body should be lifted, instead of sinking on the supporting leg, as the drawing shows.

150. 'RELEVE SUR LA POINTE A LA BARRE'

The dancer is standing on the right *pointe* facing left; her left arm and leg are raised in a manner to suggest that she has just completed the *fouetté* turn.

Charcoal heightened with pastel. 12 × 9 ins. Stamp of the Degas sale lower left; inscribed upper right, 'bras gauche . . . à chercher un autre'. *Circa* 1885.

Collection. Atelier Degas.

Reproduced. *Catalogue vente Degas*, III (1919), No. 125b.

Owner unknown.

Photograph. Durand Ruel, Paris.

151. DANSEUSE PRATIQUANT A LA BARRE

She is standing facing left, her left leg on the *barre* in front of her, her body bent backward and her disengaged arm above her head.

Charcoal heightened with pastel. 12 × 9 ins. Stamp of the Degas sale lower left. Inscribed, 'Mauvais, le corps tourné, jambe gauche moins allongée sur la barre.' *Circa* 1885–90.

Collection. Atelier Degas.

Reproduced. *Catalogue vente Degas*, II (1918), No. 215b.

Owner unknown.

Photograph. Durand Ruel, Paris.

This exercise is for flexibility of the spine. The dancer makes it less effective by turning her body at the waist, and the foot being placed so far away from her on the *barre* pulls the body forward instead of giving it full freedom to stretch backwards. Both Degas' remarks imply these faults.

152. DANSEUSE EN FACE DE LA BARRE

She stands facing the *barre* and holding it with her right hand, while the other holds the right foot behind her back.

Charcoal heightened with pastel. 12 × 9 ins. Stamp of the Degas sale lower left. *Circa* 1885–90.

Collection. Atelier Degas.

Reproduced. *Catalogue vente Degas*, II (1918), No. 215a.

Owner unknown.

Photograph. Durand Ruel, Paris.

This position suggests a curious method of stretching which seems to be unknown in contemporary ballet exercises.

153. DANSEUSE DEGOURDISSANT LES TENDONS DES TALONS

She is facing the *barre* with both hands upon it. Her feet are in first position and bending one knee at a time she transfers her weight first on to one foot and then on to the other.

Charcoal. 12 × 9 ins. Stamp of the Degas sale lower left. *Circa* 1885–90.

Collection. Atelier Degas.

Reproduced. *Catalogue vente Degas*, III (1919), No. 125c.

Owner unknown.

Photograph. Durand Ruel, Paris.

See also *Catalogue vente Degas*, II (1918), No. 233a.

154. DANSE ESPAGNOLE

The dancer stands on the left leg, the right in *pointe tendue* in front of her with the knee bent, and the right arm above her head.

> *Bronze*, No. 45. Height 17 ins. *Circa* 1884.
> *Exhibitions.* Hebrard exhibition, 1921; *Degas—Portraitiste, Sculpteur*, Musée de l'Orangerie, 1931, No. 17.
> *Reproduced.* John Rewald, *Degas. Works in Sculpture—a complete Catalogue* (1944), No. 47.
> *Photograph.* Leicester Galleries, London.

This sculpture may have been suggested, as Pl. 173, by Mérante's *Le Fandango*.
See also John Rewald, *Degas. Works in Sculpture*, No. 66 and drawing studies.

155. DANSEUSE NUE EN GRANDE ARABESQUE

She stands on the right leg, the left well up into the air and the right hand near the ground.

> *Bronze*, No. 40. Height 16 ins. *Circa* 1882–6.
> *Exhibitions.* Hebrard Exhibition, 1921; *Degas—Portraitiste, Sculpteur*, Musée de l'Orangerie, Paris, 1931, No. 8.
> *Reproduced.* John Rewald, *Degas. Works in Sculpture—a complete Catalogue* (1944), No. 40.
> *Photograph.* National Gallery, London.

For another bronze in this position see Rewald, catalogue No. 39. Degas did sculptures of three different positions of the *arabesque* which are curiously called *Grande Arabesque, premier temps*; *Grande Arabesque, deuxième temps*; and *Grande Arabesque, troisième temps*. They should really be distinguished as *Arabesque sur la Terre* (Rewald, catalogue No. 35); *Arabesque*, see Pl. 157; and *Grande Arabesque*, as above.

156. DANS LA SALLE DE DANSE

On the extreme left the corner of the spiral staircase is seen, under it two dancers stand in *arabesque*, and on the right are dancers in various positions.

> *Pastel.* 20 × 25¼ ins. Signed lower right. *Circa* 1880–3.
> *Collection.* S. I. Schukin.
> *Owned* by the Museum of Modern and Western Art, Moscow.
> *Photograph.* S. C. R., London.

See the drawing, Pl. 157*a*, as well as Pls. 34 and 34*a*. See also *Catalogue vente Degas*, I (1918), No. 43; and II (1918), Nos. 299 and 359.

156a. DANSEUSES MONTANT UN ESCALIER. FRISE

On the left three dancers are coming up a staircase in the floor; in the right distance the room widens out and other dancers are standing about.

> *Oil on canvas.* 15½ × 36 ins. Signed lower left. *Circa* 1880–3.
> *Collections.* H. Vever; Isaac de Camondo.
> *Reproduced.* Julius Meier-Graefe, *Degas* (1927), Pl. 52*b*.
> *Owned* by the Musée du Louvre (bequeathed in 1911 by Camondo).
> *Photograph.* Archives photographiques.

For similar compositions see Pls. 118, 120 and 120*a*. For pastel of one of the standing figures, Pl. 191; and dancer on the stairs, Pl. 38*a*.

157. DANSEUSE NUE EN ARABESQUE

She stands on the right leg, the working leg raised at about right angles to it, the left arm extended to the side.

Bronze, No. 36. Height 19 ins. *Circa* 1882–6.

Exhibitions. Hebrard Exhibition, 1921; *Degas—Portraitiste, Sculpteur*, Musée de l'Orangerie, Paris, 1931, No. 6

Reproduced. John Rewald, *Degas. Works in Sculpture—a complete Catalogue* (1944), No. 36.

Photograph. From the bronze belonging to the Rhode Island School of Design.

See Pls. 34, 34*a*, 156 and 157*a* for pictures and drawings of dancers in *arabesque*. See also *Catalogue vente Degas*, II (1918), No. 232*a*.

157a. DEUX DANSEUSES NUES EN ARABESQUE

They are facing right, the line of the spiral staircase sketched in on the left.

Charcoal. 18 × 21¾ ins. Stamp of the Degas sale lower left. *Circa* 1885–90.

Collection. Atelier Degas.

Reproduced. *Catalogue vente Degas*, III (1919), No. 195.

Owner unknown.

Photograph. Durand Ruel, Paris.

See the pastel, Pl. 156; also *Catalogue vente Degas*, III (1919), No. 196.

158. 'DEVELOPPE EN AVANT'

The nude dancer stands on the left leg with arms in opposition.

Bronze, No. 58. Height 23 ins. *Circa* 1882–90.

Exhibitions. Hebrard Exhibition, 1921; *Degas—Portraitiste, Sculpteur*, Musée de l'Orangerie, Paris, 1931, No. 10.

Reproduced. John Rewald, *Degas. Works in Sculpture—a complete Catalogue* (1944), No. 43.

Photograph from the bronze belonging to Mr G. J. F. Knowles, Cambridge.

Degas did two other sculptures in this position, see Pl. 218, and Rewald catalogue, No. 55.

159. DANSEUSE NUE 'EN QUATRIEME DEVANT'

She stands with her weight on the left leg with arms also in fourth position.

Bronze, No. 57. Height 22 ins. *Circa* 1882–90.

Exhibitions. Hebrard Exhibition, 1921; *Degas—Portraitiste, Sculpteur*, Musée de l'Orangerie, Paris, 1931, No. 36.

Reproduced. John Rewald, *Degas. Works in Sculpture—a complete Catalogue* (1944), No. 46.

Photograph. From the bronze belonging to Miss Lillian Browse.

160. DANSEUSE AUX CHEVEUX LONGS SALUANT

She stands facing left, acknowledging her audience with her right hand.

Pastel. 30¼ × 17½ ins. Signed lower right. *Circa* 1884–8.

Reproduced. Vollard, *98 Reproductions signed by Degas* (pub. Bernheim, Jeune 1918), in colour between Pls. 9 and 10; Julius Meier-Graefe, *Degas* (1927), Pl. 46.

Owned by the Museum of Fine Arts, Boston, Mass.

Photograph. Museum of Fine Arts.

For other pastels of this series, for which Mlle van Goeuthen is said to have been the model, see Pls. 161–5.

161. DANSEUSE EN JAUNE SALUANT

She stands facing left in *quatrième croisée sur les demi-pointes* as she acknowledges her audience; behind stand a group of dancers against a *décor* of trees.

Pastel. 28 × 15 ins. Signed lower right. *Circa* 1884–8.

Owned by Mr and Mrs J. Watson Webb, New York.

Photograph. The owners.

For other pastels of the series, *Danseuses aux Cheveux longs* see Pls. 160 and 162–5.

162. DEUX DANSEUSES AUX CHEVEUX LONGS

They are seen back view, with left foot in fourth *pointe tendue* and left arms raised above their heads.

Pastel. 28 × 15½ ins. Signed lower right. *Circa* 1884–8.

Collection. Henri Lerolle, Paris.

Exhibition. Degas, Cleveland Museum of Art, 1947, No. 41 (reproduced).

Reproduced. Paul Lafond, *Degas*, Vol. II (1919), p. 30.

Owned by Leonard C. Hanna, Jr., Cleveland.

Photograph. Jacques Seligmann, New York.

For dancers in the same position see Pl. 163 and others in the series, Pls. 160, 161, 164 and 165.

163. TROIS DANSEUSES VERTES AUX CHEVEUX LONGS

They are standing diagonally one in front of the other, the near one turning towards the audience, the other two away from it. Their left feet are in *quatrième*, *pointe tendue* and they look under their raised left arms.

Pastel. 28½ × 15½ ins. Signed lower left. *Circa* 1884–8.

Exhibition. Grafton Galleries, London, 1905, No. 53 (reproduced).

Reproduced. P. A. Lemoisne, *Degas* (1912), Pl. 33; Paul Lafond, *Degas*, Vol. II (1919), opp. p. 30; Georges Rivière, *Mr Degas (Bourgeois de Paris)* (1935), p. 53.

Owner unknown.

Photograph. Durand Ruel, Paris.

See Pl. 162, also Pls. 160, 161, 164 and 165.

164. DANSEUSE ROSE SALUANT

She stands facing her audience in *quatrième derrière*, *pointe tendue*, her body slightly bending forward, her arms in *demi-seconde*.

Pastel. 28½ × 15¾ ins. Signed lower right. *Circa* 1884–8.

Reproduced. Paul Lafond, *Degas*, Vol. II (1919), between pp. 36 and 37.

Owner unknown.

Photograph. Reid and Lefevre, London.

See also Pls. 160–3 and 165.

165. DANSEUSE ROSE SALUANT

Against a background of women dressed in Eastern costume, she stands in *quatrième croisée*, acknowledging her audience with the right hand.

> *Pastel.* 28 × 15 ins. Signed lower right. *Circa* 1884–8.
> *Exhibition.* Grafton Galleries, London, 1905, No. 54 (reproduced).
> *Reproduced.* Georges Grappe, *E. Degas* (1909), p. 12.
> *Owner* unknown.
> *Photograph.* Durand Ruel, Paris.

See Pls. 160–4, also *Catalogue vente Degas*, II (1918), Nos. 143 and 197.

166. LE BAISSER DU RIDEAU

The curtain is falling on a tableau of dancers, two of whom kneel on one leg, just before the footlights.

> *Pastel.* 22 × 30 ins. Signed upper right. *Circa* 1880–2.
> *Collection.* Joseph Durand Ruel.
> *Exhibitions.* *Degas*, Galerie Georges Petit, Paris, 1924, No. 156; *Degas*, Pennsylvania Museum of Art, Philadelphia, 1936, No. 33 (reproduced); *Degas*, Musée de l'Orangerie, Paris, 1937, No. 104.
> *Reproduced.* Georges Grappe, *Degas* (1909), p. 14; Paul Lafond, *Degas*, Vol. II (1919), between pp. 36 and 37; Paul Jamot, *Degas* (1924), Pl. 51; Marguerite Rebatet, *Degas* (1944), Pl. 87.
> *Owned* by Robert Treat Paine, 2nd, Boston.
> *Photograph.* Sir Robert Witt Library, London.

See Pl. 166a for study of the two dancers.

166a. DEUX DANSEUSES A GENOUX. ETUDE

> *Charcoal.* 18 × 24 ins. Stamp of the Degas sale lower left. *Circa* 1880–2.
> *Collection.* Atelier Degas.
> *Reproduced.* *Catalogue vente Degas*, III (1919), No. 279.
> *Owner* unknown.
> *Photograph.* Durand Ruel, Paris.

The drawing is a study for the pastel, Pl. 166.

167. LES DEUX 'SUJETS' SUR LA SCENE

In front of a line of *corps de ballet*, the two dancers are seen in a position which suggests the end of an *adage*.

> *Pastel.* 14 × 19 ins. Signed lower left. *Circa* 1880–2.
> *Collections.* Von Nemes (sale, Paris, 1913); Prince de Wagram; Gabriel Cognacq.
> *Exhibitions.* Budapest, 1911; Munich, 1911; Dusseldorf, 1912; *Degas*, Galerie Georges Petit, Paris, 1924, No. 163; *Degas*, Musée de l'Orangerie, Paris, 1937, No. 128.
> *Reproduced.* P. A. Lemoisne, *Degas* (1912), Pl. 44; Henri Hertz, *Degas* (1929), Pl. 16; Gustave Coquiot, *Degas* (1924), opp. p. 152.
> *Owned* by Gabriel Cognacq?
> *Photograph.* Sir Robert Witt Library, London.

NOTES ON THE PLATES

167a. 'LA FAMILLE CARDINAL'. LE CORRIDOR DES LOGES

At the top of the staircase a group of men are standing talking to two dancers.

Monotype in colour. 6 × 8 ins. *Circa* 1880–3.
Photograph. Bibliothèque Nationale.

An illustration done by Degas for Ludovic Halévy's *La Famille Cardinal*; engraved by Maurice Potin. See Pls. 132a, 179a; p. 34 and note, also p. 69.

168. SUR LA SCENE. DANSEUSE VERTE

Three dancers form a semi-circle on the left of the picture; only the skirt of the one in the left foreground is seen; the legs and skirt of the next, and the whole figure of the third. Behind stand groups of dancers.

Pastel. 24½ × 14 ins. Signed lower left. *Circa* 1884–6.
Reproduced. Camille Mauclair, *Degas* (1941), p. 138.
Owner unknown.
Photograph. Reid and Lefevre, London.

As in Pls. 110 and 111, strong emphasis is laid upon the pattern made by the arms and legs.

169. ARLEQUINADE

Harlequin is standing, wearing a hat and looking through his mask. In the background are three dancers in *tutus*.

Pastel. 20½ × 25½ ins. Signed lower right. Painted 1886.
Reproduced. Paul Lafond, *Degas*, Vol. II (1919), opp. p. 32; Marguerite Rebatet, *Degas* (1944), Pl. 90.
Owner unknown.
Photograph. Durand Ruel, Paris.

The subject of the pastel is most likely the Harlequinade in the first Act of *Les Jumeaux de Bergame*, with Subra as Coraline, Alice Biot as Harlequin junior, and Sanlaville as Harlequin senior. See p. 58.

See also Pls. 170 and 171.

169a. DANSEUSE SALUANT. ETUDE

She is seen, wearing a corselet, and bowing low to her audience.

Charcoal heightened with pastel. 24 × 18 ins. Signed lower right. *Circa* 1884–6.
Owner unknown.
Photograph. Sir Robert Witt Library, London.

170. LES DEUX ARLEQUINS

One is seated and only partly seen on the left; the other bends over him, one hand on the chair and the other holding a sword.

Pastel. 20 × 15 ins. Signed lower left. Painted 1886.
Collection. Edward Martyn.

392

Owned by the National Gallery of Ireland, Dublin (Edward Martyn bequest).
Photograph. National Gallery of Ireland.
For other pastels on the same theme see Pls. 169 and 171.
It is quite obvious that the standing Harlequin is a woman; see note to Pl. 169.

171. ARLEQUIN MENAÇANT COLOMBINE

'He' stands on the left in *quatrième fondue*, hiding a sword behind 'his' back and holding
Columbine by the arm with the other hand.

Pastel. 16¼ × 16¼ ins. Signed lower left. Painted 1886.
Reproduced. Georges Grappe, *Degas* (1909), opp. p. 6; Paul Lafond, *Degas*, Vol. II (1919),
between pp. 36 and 37; Julius Meier-Graefe, *Degas* (1927), Pl. 78.
Owner unknown.
Photograph. Durand Ruel, Paris.

The dancers are probably Subra as Coraline (Columbine), and Sanlaville as Harlequin senior,
in *Les Jumeaux de Bergame*; see note to Pl. 169.
See also Pls. 169 and 170.

172. DANS LA COULISSE. DEUX DANSEUSES

They are seen back view, standing side by side, one with long dark hair, the other with a big sash.

Lithograph. 9½ × 7 ins. Signed lower left and inscribed 'Auteuil. H et Cie'. *Circa* 1885.
Reproduced. Loys Delteil, *Le Peintre Graveur Illustré—Degas* (1919), No. 59; Paul Lafond,
Degas, Vol. II (1919), between pp. 36 and 37; Georges Grappe, *Degas* (1936), on back
cover.

173. MLLE SALLE EN COSTUME DU 'FANDANGO',
     ET ETUDES DE BRAS ET DE JAMBES

She is standing on the right with a tambourine raised above her head; with her left arm she
holds her skirt while the right foot is in *pointe tendue*. On the left of the page are studies of her
legs and arms.

Pastel. 23 × 27 ins. Signed lower right. Painted 1884.
Collection. Atelier Degas.
Reproduced. *Degas—Vingt Dessins*, Albumn Manzi (1896), No. 15.; *Catalogue vente Degas*,
I (1918), No. 161.
Owned by the Musée du Louvre (formerly in the Musée du Luxembourg).
Photograph. Archives photographiques.

This is a study for the large pastel, *Catalogue vente Degas*, I, No. 191; for another study see
Catalogue vente Degas, III, No. 48.
See also the design for the *Programme de la soirée artistique du 15 juin 1884 chez la Galerie
Ponson; Catalogue vente Degas*, IV, Nos. 257a, 257b, 258a, 258b, 385a, 385b (also 386–90
mentioned but not reproduced).
The second item on the programme was *La Leçon de Danse—Le Fandango*, a ballet by Mérante,
first produced at the Opéra in 1877.
For heads of Mlle Salle see Pls. 173a and 184a.

173a. BUSTE DE MLLE SALLE

Pastel. 25 × 18¼ ins. Stamp of the Degas sale lower left. *Circa* 1888–90.
Collection. Atelier Degas.
Exhibition. Degas—Portraitiste, Sculpteur, Musée de l'Orangerie, Paris, 1931, No. 146.
Reproduced. Catalogue vente Degas, II (1918), No. 168; Georges Rivière, *Mr Degas (Bourgeois de Paris)* (1935), p. 11; Camille Mauclair, *Degas* (1941), p. 50.
Owned by Mme Friedmann.
See also Pls. 173 and 184a.

174. TROIS DANSEUSES DANS LES COULISSES

They are seen on the right of the picture putting the finishing touches to their toilettes; in the left distance the legs of dancers may be seen beneath a back-cloth.

Oil on canvas. 29 × 23¼ ins. Signed lower right. *Circa* 1883–6.
Collection. Mr and Mrs Potter Palmer.
Exhibitions. Art Institute of Chicago, 1933; Metropolitan Museum of Art, New York, 1941; *Degas,* Cleveland Museum of Art, 1947. No. 33 (reproduced).
Lent by the Potter Palmer Estate to the Art Institute of Chicago.
Photograph. The Art Institute of Chicago.

175. DANSEUSE AVEC UN HOMME DANS LES COULISSES

They are standing on the extreme right, she with her arms folded, he wearing a top hat. In the left distance another dancer is seen back view.

Oil on canvas. 24½ × 18½ ins. Signed upper right. *Circa* 1883–6.
Owned by Bignou and Co., New York.
Photograph. Reid and Lefevre, London.
See also *Catalogue vente Degas,* II (1918), No. 29.

176. DANSEUSE EN ARABESQUE SUR LA SCENE

She is on the right of the picture facing left in front of a *décor* of foliage and wearing symbols of an Eastern attire on her *tutu.*

Oil on canvas. 35½ × 46½ ins. Stamp of the Degas sale lower left. *Circa* 1883–6.
Collections. Atelier Degas; Comte Trotti; Herm Heilbuth, Copenhagen.
Exhibition. Degas, Cleveland Museum of Art, 1947, No. 25 (reproduced).
Reproduced. Catalogue vente Degas, I (1918), No. 27.
Owner unknown.
Photograph. The National Gallery, Stockholm.

In the Cleveland catalogue the picture is called *Rosita Mauri* and is said to have been painted in 1875. Mauri did not make her début until 1878, and in the absence of factual evidence it is difficult to know why she is named as being the model.
See also *Catalogue vente Degas,* II (1918), No. 110.

176a. DANSEUSE A L'ADAGE. ETUDE

She is standing on the right leg, facing right, in a position which is apparently meant to be an *arabesque*.

Charcoal. 20¼ × 20¼ ins. Stamp of the Degas sale lower left. *Circa* 1885–90.
Collection. Atelier Degas.
Reproduced. *Catalogue vente Degas*, III (1919), No. 197.
Owner unknown.
Photograph. Durand Ruel, Paris.

See *Catalogue vente Degas*, III (1919), Nos. 138a and 235; also note to Pl. 34a regarding the position.

177. SEPT DANSEUSES DANS LA SALLE DE DANSE

The three on the right are in repose, one is sitting forcing her *pointes*, another ties her shoe-ribbons, and the third is standing. On the left, three dancers are practising; the arms of a fourth are just visible.

Oil on canvas. 21½ × 16 ins. Signed upper right. *Circa* 1883–6.
Reproduced. Marguerite Rebatet, *Degas* (1944), Pl. 72.
Owner unknown.
Photograph. Durand Ruel, Paris.

For a group similar to that on the left see Pl. 98; see also drawing, Pl. 68.

178. PAS SEUL. 'LE GRAND JETE'

The dancer is in the right foreground looking towards the audience. Behind is a *décor* of foliage and two dancers are just visible in the left distance.

Oil on canvas. 24 × 16¾ ins. Signed lower left. *Circa* 1883–6.
Reproduced. Paul Lafond, *Degas*, Vol. I (1918), p. 133.
Owner unknown.
Photograph. Knoedler & Co., London.

For other pictures on this theme see Pls. 55 and 141–5.

179. DANS LES COULISSES. DANSEUSE AU TAMBOURIN

On the right stand three dancers, one holding a tambourine; the stage is seen on the left and on it dancers doing a *pas de deux*.

Oil on canvas. 13 × 16½ ins. Signed upper right. *Circa* 1883–6.
Owner unknown.
Photograph. Durand Ruel, Paris.

For a study of the *Pas de Deux* see *Catalogue vente Degas*, III (1919), No. 123d.

179a. 'LA FAMILLE CARDINAL'. AU FOYER

A group of men are standing talking to two dancers.

Monotype in colour. 6¼ × 5 ins. *Circa* 1880–3.
Photograph. Bibliothèque Nationale.

One of the illustrations done for Ludovic Halévy's *La Famille Cardinal*; engraved by Maurice Potin. See Pls. 132a and 167a; p. 34 and note, also p. 69.

180. DANSEUSES ROSES ET VERTES

They are standing about on the stage; the one on the extreme right rests her head against a flat on the other side of which the dark outline of a man is seen. In the centre a dancer stands with her hands on her waist, behind her another fastens her hair, while others adjust their dresses at the shoulders.

Oil on canvas. 32⅜ × 29¾ ins. Signed lower right. *Circa* 1885–7.
Collection. H. O. Havemeyer.
Owned by the Metropolitan Museum of Art, New York. (H. O. Havemeyer Collection.)
Photograph. The Metropolitan Museum of Art.

181. LES DANSEUSES ROSES AVANT LE BALLET

Five of them are standing in different attitudes, a sixth is visible in the left distance.

Oil on canvas. 15 × 18 ins. Signed upper right. *Circa* 1885–7.
Collections. Duret; Viau; Wilhelm Hansen.
Exhibitions. Art Français, Geneva, 1918; *Degas*, Copenhagen, 1920, No. 9; *Degas*, Musée de l'Orangerie, Paris, 1937, No. 41.
Reproduced. Paul Lafond, *Degas*, Vol. II (1919), p. 24.
Owned by the Glyptotek Ny Carlsberg, Copenhagen.
Photograph. Glyptotek Ny Carlsberg.

182. TROIS DANSEUSES EN ROSE DANS LES COULISSES

They are standing behind a flat, one is holding her skirt as another arranges it for her.

Oil on canvas. 40 × 21¾ ins. Stamp of the Degas sale lower right. *Circa* 1885–7.
Collection. Atelier Degas.
Reproduced. Catalogue vente Degas, I (1918), No. 60.
Owner unknown.
Photograph. Reid and Lefevre, London.

183. GROUPE DE DANSEUSES DANS UNE SALLE DE DANSE

They are arranged diagonally across the page, some in the position of *arabesque*; the one on the extreme right rests her knee on a bench and pulls on her shoe at the heel.

Pastel. 26 × 21 ins. Stamp of the Degas sale lower left. *Circa* 1888–90.
Collection. Atelier Degas.
Reproduced. Catalogue vente Degas, II (1918), No. 153.
Owner unknown.
Photograph. Durand Ruel, Paris.
See Pls. 83 and 84. This pastel seems to have been done from the oil paintings.

184. DEUX DANSEUSES DANS LA LOGE

One is standing with her foot on a chair as she leans on its back; facing her is another fastening her sash. On the extreme right a basin and jug are seen.

Pastel. 17 × 25 ins. Signed upper right. *Circa* 1886–8.

Collection. Edward Martyn.

Owned by the National Gallery of Ireland, Dublin (Edward Martyn bequest).

Photograph. The National Gallery of Ireland.

The dancer standing on the left bears a strong facial resemblance to Mlle Salle, see Pl. 184*a*.

184*a*. MLLE SALLE. TROIS ETUDES DE LA TETE

She is seen full face, in profile, and half profile.

Pastel. 20 × 20 ins. Signed lower left and inscribed top right, 'Mlle Salle, 1886.'

Collection. Hoentschel.

Exhibition. *Degas*, Galerie Georges Petit, Paris, 1924, No. 159 (reproduced).

Reproduced. Paul Lafond, *Degas*, Vol. I (1918), p. 56; Paul Jamot, *Degas* (1924), Pl. 70.

Owned by Mme Lanvin.

See also Pls. 173 and 173*a* for pictures of the same sitter.

185. TROIS DANSEUSES SE PREPARANT A LA CLASSE

Two of them are seated in chairs, the one who is forcing her *pointes* is having her hair done by the third who stands behind her on the extreme right.

Pastel. 21½ × 20½ ins. Signed lower left. *Circa* 1886–8.

Collection. H. O. Havemeyer.

Owned by the Metropolitan Museum of Art, New York. (H. O. Havemeyer Collection.)

Photograph. The Metropolitan Museum of Art.

186. AVANT LA CLASSE. TROIS DANSEUSES

The central figure is standing facing left, one hand on her waist and the other on her right leg which is resting on a chair. In the left distance stand two other dancers.

Pastel. 21 × 20 ins. Signed lower right. *Circa* 1886–8.

Owner unknown.

Photograph. Durand Ruel, Paris.

187. LA PREPARATION A LA CLASSE

Against the light of two windows three dancers are standing; part of one is seen on extreme left holding her skirt; behind her, facing left, another arranges the bow at the back of her dress; on extreme right another is partly seen back view; the arm of a fourth is silhouetted against the window.

Pastel. 25⅝ × 19⅜ ins. Signed lower right. *Circa* 1886–8.

Collection. Martin A. Ryerson.

Owned by the Art Institute of Chicago. (Mr and Mrs Martin A. Ryerson Collection.)

Photograph. The Art Institute of Chicago.

For other pictures with the dancer fastening her bow see Pls. 120, 120*a* and 121.

188. LA REPETITION SUR LA SCENE. CINQ DANSEUSES

Two of them are in *quatrième derrière pointe tendue*; behind them on the right one sits and another kneels on a bench, while a fifth stands with hands on her hips. In the left distance the figure of the *maître* is just visible.

Oil on canvas. 29¼ × 31¾ ins. Stamp of the Degas sale not visible. *Circa 1888–90.*
Collection. Atelier Degas.
Reproduced. Catalogue vente Degas, I (1918), No. 83.
Owner unknown.
Photograph. Reid and Lefevre, London.

For a study of the three figures on the right see Pl. 189, and for a study of the two figures about to dance see *Catalogue vente Degas*, III, No. 394.

189. DANSEUSES A UNE REPETITION. ETUDE

Upon a bench placed diagonally across the picture the dancer on the left sits with her right leg curled in front of her and both hands upon it; she looks to the left; behind her another kneels with one leg on the bench and fastens her shoe ribbons at the heel; part of the figure of a third is visible in the background.

Charcoal heightened with pastel. 24 × 19 ins. Stamp of the Degas sale lower left. *Circa 1888–90.*
Collection. Atelier Degas.
Reproduced. Catalogue vente Degas, II (1918), No. 335.
Owner unknown.
Photograph. Durand Ruel, Paris.

This drawing is a study for Pl. 188; for another see *Catalogue vente Degas*, II, No. 109; and for two Impressions see *Catalogue vente Degas*, III and IV, Nos. 306 and 302 respectively.

190. DANSEUSE VUE DE DOS. 'GRAND BATTEMENT A LA SECONDE'

She is working with her right leg, the right arm also in second position. The left arm is bent as if she were holding on to something rather high.

Charcoal heightened with white and pastel. 12 × 9 ins. Stamp of the Degas sale lower left. Inscribed on the right with notes about the play of light on the working arm and leg, '—reflet très vif, en liséré de la jambe et de la jupe sur le dessus du bras.' *Circa 1885–90.*
Collection. Atelier Degas.
Reproduced. Catalogue vente Degas, II (1918), No. 219*a*.
Owner unknown.
Photograph. Durand Ruel, Paris.

191. DANSEUSE DEBOUT, LES MAINS SUR LE CORSAGE

She is facing a quarter right, her feet in fourth position and her body bent slightly forward.
Charcoal, chalk and pastel. 18⅛ × 12 ins. Signed lower right; plumb line running through figure, and horizontal lines under the feet and through the skirt. *Circa 1885–90.*

Collection. Martin A. Ryerson.

Owned by the Art Institute of Chicago. (Mr and Mrs Martin A. Ryerson Collection.)

Photograph. The Art Institute of Chicago.

See also Pls. 192–5, as well as *Catalogue vente Degas*, I (1918), No. 125; and III (1919), No. 376.

192. DANSEUSE DEBOUT, LES MAINS DANS LES EMMANCHURES

Her hands are holding the arm-holes of her dress and she is looking at her right one. Studies of legs on the lower half of the sheet, and one of the head on the right.

Black chalk heightened with pastel. 12 × 10 ins. Stamp of the Degas sale lower right. Inscribed with remarks 'oreille transparent' and a reference to the position of the leg— 'trop croisé'. *Circa* 1885–90.

Collection. Atelier Degas.

Reproduced. *Catalogue vente Degas*, II (1918), No. 220*a*.

Owner unknown.

Photograph. Durand Ruel, Paris.

See also Pls. 191 and 193–5, as well as *Catalogue vente Degas*, IV (1919), No. 265*b*.

193. DANSEUSE DEBOUT, LES MAINS DANS LES EMMANCHURES

She is standing with her left foot forward and her head inclined to the left. On the right is a study of a leg.

Black chalk heightened with white and pastel. 12 × 10 ins. Stamp of the Degas sale lower left. *Circa* 1885–90.

Collection. Atelier Degas.

Reproduced. *Catalogue vente Degas*, II (1918), No. 218*a*.

Owner unknown.

Photograph. Durand Ruel, Paris.

The drawing, Pl. 192, is almost identical with this one. Degas often traced his drawings and then worked on them and it seems likely that one of these two has been traced from the other. See also Pls. 191, 194 and 195.

194. DANSEUSE DEBOUT, LES MAINS DANS LES EMMANCHURES

She is facing a quarter right, her left leg in front in fourth position. On the right the outline of part of a figure is seen.

Pastel. 18⅝ × 11¾ ins. The stamp of the Degas sale is not visible. *Circa* 1885–90.

Collection. Atelier Degas.

Reproduced. *Catalogue vente Degas*, II (1918), No. 174.

Owned by the Museum of Art, Rhode Island School of Design, Providence.

Photograph. Rhode Island School of Design.

See also Pls. 191–3 and 195, as well as *Catalogue vente Degas*, III (1919), No. 376.

195. DEUX DANSEUSES EN JUPES JAUNES, POSANT SUR LA SCENE

They are standing side by side, one facing, the other with her back to the audience. Both are in fourth position, one has her hands on her hips, the other is holding her bodice at the neck.

Pastel. 24 × 17 ins. Signed lower right. *Circa* 1888–90.

Reproduced. Julius Meier-Graefe, *Degas* (1927), Pl. 95.

Owner unknown.

Photograph. Durand Ruel, Paris.

For various studies of the figure in front see Pls. 191–4, and for the two figures in the nude, Pl. 197. See also *Catalogue vente Degas*, I (1918), No. 178; and IV (1919), No. 265b.

196. DANSEUSE EN 'QUATRIEME', LES MAINS SUR LES REINS

She is in the nude; her head is thrown well back.

Bronze, No. 63. Height 17¼ ins. *Circa* 1882–90.

Exhibitions. Hebrard Exhibition, 1921; *Degas—Portraitiste, Sculpteur*, Musée de l'Orangerie, Paris, 1931, No. 24.

Reproduced. John Rewald, *Degas. Works in Sculpture—a complete Catalogue* (1944), No. 22.

Photograph. The Leicester Galleries, London.

For another nude in the same attitude see Rewald, catalogue No. 23; and for one in a skirt see Rewald catalogue, No. 52. See also Pls. 195 and 197.

197. DEUX DANSEUSES NUES DEBOUT

One is seen front view with her hands above her breasts; the other, back view with her hands on her hips.

Charcoal. 24 × 18½ ins. Stamp of the Degas sale lower left. *Circa* 1900.

Collection. Atelier Degas.

Reproduced. *Catalogue vente Degas*, III (1919), No. 300.

Owner unknown.

Photograph. Durand Ruel, Paris.

See Pl. 195, also bronze Pl. 196 as well as Pl. 252.

198. LE REPOS. QUATRE DANSEUSES

Two are seated on a bench on the right, one of whom holds a fan; another puts her foot on the bench as she ties her shoe, while a fourth stands behind fanning herself.

Pastel. 20 × 29 ins. Signed lower left. *Circa* 1888–90.

Collections. Viau; William McInnes.

Reproduced. Paul Lafond, *Degas*, Vol. II (1919), between pp. 36 and 37; Marguerite Rebatet, *Degas* (1944), Pl. 100.

Owned by the Glasgow Art Gallery. (William McInnes Collection.)

Photograph. Reid and Lefevre, London.

See also Pl. 199 and Colour Plate X, as well as the friezes, Pls. 114, 116 and 116a. For a study of the pastel see Pl. 198a.

198a. QUATRE DANSEUSES NUES EN REPOS

The two on the right are seated on a bench, a third rests her foot on it, while a fourth stands behind with a fan.

Charcoal. 24½ × 30 ins. Stamp of the Degas sale on the original. *Circa* 1888–90.

Collection. Atelier Degas.

Reproduced. Catalogue vente Degas, II (1918), No. 265.
Owner unknown.
The drawing is a study for Pl. 198.

199. LE REPOS. TROIS DANSEUSES

On the right is a bench upon which one dancer sits with her hands upon her legs; another rests her foot upon it as she ties her ribbons, while a third, standing behind, fans herself.

Oil on canvas. 20 × 24½ ins. Unsigned. *Circa* 1888–90.
Collection. Dr Viau.
Reproduced. Georges Rivière, *Mr Degas (Bourgeois de Paris)* (1935), p. 27, in colour.
Owned by H. Rubin, Esq., London.
Photograph. Leicester Gallery, London.

The two standing figures are identical with those in Pl. 198.

200. DANSEUSE ROSE SE DEGOURDISSANT LE COU-DE-PIED

She is seated facing right, her ballet skirt spread behind her as with both hands she stretches the instep of her right foot.

Pastel. 23½ × 17½ ins. Signed lower left. *Circa* 1885–8.
Owned by Sam Salz, New York.
Photograph. The owner.

See also Pls. 201 and 202, as well as *Catalogue vente Degas*, III (1919), Nos. 116a, 143a, 143b, 214a, 251, 298; and IV (1919), Nos. 295, 296 and 310.

201. TROIS DANSEUSES EN TETE A TETE

One sits stretching the instep of her right foot while two others stand behind her and talk.

Pastel. 23 × 16 ins.   Stamp of the Degas sale lower left. *Circa* 1895–1900.
Collection. Atelier Degas.
Reproduced. Catalogue vente Degas, I (1918), No. 150.
Owner unknown.
Photograph. Durand Ruel, Paris.

See also *Catalogue vente Degas*, III (1919), No. 296; and for studies of the dancer stretching her instep see Pls. 200 and 202.

202. LA JUPE VERTE. DANSEUSE SE DEGOURDISSANT LE COUP-DE-PIED

She is seated facing right stretching the instep of her right foot which rests on the other knee.

Pastel. 16 × 13 ins. Signed lower left. Circa 1890–1900.
Collection. Sir William Burrell.
Owned by the Glasgow Art Gallery and Museum. (Sir William Burrell Collection.)
Photograph. The Glasgow Art Gallery.

See Pl. 200 and note; also Pl. 201.

203. DANSEUSE EN JAUNE ASSISE

She is seated in front of a pillar, her right foot resting on the bench, her right hand holding it and the other at her waist. Behind the pillar another dancer can be seen.

Monotype retouched with pastel. 22 × 18 ins. Stamp of the Degas sale lower left. *Circa* 1890–1900.

Collection. Atelier Degas.

Reproduced. Catalogue vente Degas, II (1918), No. 361.

Owner unknown.

Photograph. Gallery Thannhauser, New York.

See *Catalogue vente Degas*, I (1918), No. 257; II (1918), Nos. 90, 99, 177; and III (1919), No. 170.

204. DEUX DANSEUSES SUR UNE BANQUETTE

The one on the left bends down and pulls the ribbons on each of her shoes; the one on the right lifts her left leg on to the bench and holds the instep with her left hand.

Pastel. 31¼ × 43 ins. Stamp of the Degas sale not visible. *Circa* 1890–1900.

Collection. Atelier Degas.

Reproduced. Catalogue vente Degas, I (1918), No. 144.

Owner unknown.

Photograph. Durand Ruel, Paris.

See Pls. 118*a* and 251; for a study of one of the seated figures, Pl. 204*a*. See also *Catalogue vente Degas*, I (1918), Nos. 258 and 262; II (1918), No. 165; and III (1919), No. 299.

204*a*. DANSEUSE ASSISE. ETUDE

She is seated facing right with one leg raised on the bench. In the upper right corner another head is visible.

Charcoal. 25 × 23 ins. Stamp of the Degas sale on the original. *Circa* 1890–1900.

Collection. Atelier Degas.

Reproduced. Catalogue vente Degas, II (1918), No. 294.

Owner unknown.

See Pls. 204 and 205.

205. DEUX DANSEUSES SUR UNE BANQUETTE

One, facing right, sits astride the bench, the other, with the right foot upon it, leans towards her.

Pastel. 34½ × 17½ ins. Stamp of the Degas sale lower left. *Circa* 1890–1900.

Collection. Atelier Degas.

Reproduced. Catalogue vente Degas, I (1918), No. 138.

Owned by the Nordiska Kompaniet, Stockholm.

Photograph. National Gallery, Stockholm.

See also *Catalogue vente Degas*, I (1918), Nos. 269 and 286; II (1918), No. 288; and III (1919), No. 237.

206. DEUX DANSEUSES CAUSANT SUR UNE BANQUETTE

The head of one is seen on the left; the other sits holding one foot on the bench and clasping the left knee with her left hand.

> *Pastel.* $23\frac{1}{4} \times 20$ ins. Signed lower right. *Circa* 1890–1900.
> *Owner* unknown.
> *Photograph.* Wildenstein, New York.

See also Pl. 207 and note; as well as *Catalogue vente Degas*, I (1918), Nos. 130 and 285; II (1918), No. 73; III (1919), Nos. 190, 225 and 410.

207. DEUX DANSEUSES AUX CORSAGES JAUNES, ASSISES

They are both seated on a bench with one leg on the floor; the one on the left holds her long hair, the second has one hand on her knee and holds her instep with the other.

> $33 \times 27\frac{3}{8}$ ins. Stamp of the Degas sale lower left. *Circa* 1890–1900.
> *Collections.* Atelier Degas; Samuel Courtauld, London.
> *Reproduced.* *Catalogue vente Degas*, I (1918), No. 205.
> *Owner* unknown.
> *Photograph.* Wildenstein, New York.

See also Pl. 206 and note; as well as *Catalogue vente Degas*, I (1918), Nos. 200 and 295; II (1918), Nos. 72, 137, 150, 207, and III (1919), No. 206.

208. DANSEUSE A L'EVENTAIL, DANS LES COULISSES

She stands facing left, with her left hand she holds her skirt, with the right she fans herself.

> *Pastel.* $21\frac{7}{8} \times 19\frac{1}{4}$ ins. Signed lower right. *Circa* 1900–5.
> *Collection.* H. O. Havemeyer.
> *Reproduced.* Vollard, *98 Reproductions signed by Degas* (pub. Bernheim Jeune, 1918), Pl. 13.
> *Owned* by the Metropolitan Museum of Art, New York. (H. O. Havemeyer Collection.)
> *Photograph.* The Metropolitan Museum of Art.

See also Pls. 210, 212 and 213, as well as *Catalogue vente Degas*, IV (1919), No. 147 and the Impression No. 344.

209. DANSEUSE DEBOUT S'APPUYANT CONTRE UN PORTANT

She is seen backview, facing right; her head rests upon her arm which is leaning against a flat.

> *Charcoal.* 20×12 ins. Stamp of the Degas sale lower left. *Circa* 1900–5.
> *Collection.* Atelier Degas.
> *Reproduced.* *Catalogue vente Degas*, II (1918), No. 274.
> *Owner* unknown.
> *Photograph.* Durand Ruel, Paris.

See also Pls. 210, 212 and 213, as well *Catalogue vente Degas*, II (1918), No. 384; and IV (1919), No. 298.

210. DEUX DANSEUSES DEBOUT DANS LES COULISSES

They stand side by side on the left of the picture. The one facing right rests against the flat; the other, facing left, fans herself. In the right distance other dancers are just visible.

> *Pastel.* $23\frac{1}{4} \times 18\frac{1}{4}$ ins. Signed lower left. *Circa* 1900–5.

Collections. Horace D. Chapin, Boston (1934); Mrs Robert Osgood, Boston (1937).
Owned by the Museum of Fine Arts, Boston. (Presented by Mrs Osgood, 1938.)
Photograph. The Museum of Fine Arts, Boston.
For studies for this picture see Pls. 208 and 209; the two figures also appear in Pls. 212 and 213. See as well *Catalogue vente Degas*, II (1918), No. 80.

211. DEUX DANSEUSES DEBOUT, DECOR D'ARBRES

They are standing one behind the other, facing left, with their hands on their hips and feet in fourth position.

Pastel. 28 × 21¾ ins. Signed lower right. *Circa* 1900–5.
Collections. Atelier Degas; Robert R. McCormick, Chicago.
Reproduced. *Catalogue vente Degas*, I (1918), No. 129.
Owned by the Art Institute of Chicago. (Amy McCormick Memorial.)
Photograph. The Art Institute of Chicago.
See Colour plate opposite, also *Catalogue vente Degas*, I (1918), Nos. 215 and 284; II (1918), No. 275; III (1919), Nos. 219, 255, 256 and 316.

212. QUATRE DANSEUSES SE REPOSANT DANS LES COULISSES

They are arranged diagonally across the picture; the two front ones on the right are seated, one of them holding a fan; the two distant ones are standing, one fanning herself, the other leaning against a flat.

Pastel. 28 × 26 ins. Signed lower left. *Circa* 1900–5.
Collection. Vollard.
Exhibitions. *Degas*, Pennsylvania Museum of Art, Philadelphia (1936), No. 57 (reproduced); *Degas*, Cleveland Museum of Art (1942), No. 53 (reproduced).
Reproduced. Julius Meier-Graefe, *Degas* (1927), Pl. 102.
Owned by the City Art Museum, St Louis, U.S.A.
Photograph. The City Art Museum, St Louis.
For another version see Pl. 213; for studies of the standing dancers, Pls. 208–10; see also *Catalogue vente Degas*, III (1919), Nos. 62, 260 and 349; and IV (1919), No. 154.

213. QUATRE DANSEUSES SE REPOSANT DANS LES COULISSES

They are arranged diagonally across the picture, two sitting on a bench on the right, and behind them two standing, one fanning herself. One of the seated figures holds a closed fan in one hand, the other hand to her head.

Pastel. 24½ × 27½ ins. Signed lower left. *Circa* 1900–5.
Collections. Max Liebermann, Berlin; Frau Kurt Peitzler, New York.
Owned by the Wadsworth Atheneum, Hartford, Connecticut.
Photograph. The Wadsworth Atheneum.
See also Pl. 212 and notes; as well as *Catalogue vente Degas*, III (1919), No. 297.

214. DEUX DANSEUSES EN CORSAGES VIOLETS AUX BRAS LEVES

They are standing one behind the other facing left, in *quatrième derrière pointe tendue*.

Pastel. $31\frac{1}{2} \times 19\frac{3}{4}$ ins. Stamp of the Degas sale lower left. *Circa* 1900.

Collection. Atelier Degas.

Reproduced. *Catalogue vente Degas*, I (1918), No. 279.

Owner unknown.

Photograph. Reid and Lefevre, London.

For other pictures and studies of the series see Pls. 215–7, as well as *Catalogue vente Degas*, I (1918), Nos. 252 and 288; II (1918), Nos. 78 and 205; and III (1919), No. 208*b*.

215. DANSEUSES ROSES AUX BRAS LEVES

Three of them are standing facing left behind the *décor* of a tree, on the left of it part of another dancer is seen.

Pastel. $33\frac{1}{8} \times 22\frac{7}{8}$ ins. Signed lower left. *Circa* 1900.

Collection. Joseph F. Flanagan, Boston, 1912.

Owned by the Museum of Fine Arts, Boston.

Photograph. The Museum of Fine Arts.

The picture was bought by Durand Ruel from Degas in 1901.

For others of the series see Pls. 214 and 216–7. See also *Catalogue vente Degas*, I (1918), No. 121.

216. ETUDE DE TROIS DANSEUSES AUX BRAS LEVES

They are seen, half length, facing left.

Charcoal heightened with white. $18\frac{1}{2} \times 24$ ins. Stamp of the Degas sale lower left. *Circa* 1900.

Collection. Atelier Degas.

Reproduced. *Catalogue vente Degas*, III (1919), No. 285; Camille Mauclair, *Degas* (1941), p. 133.

Owner unknown.

Photograph. Durand Ruel, Paris.

This is a study for Pl. 217. See also *Catalogue vente Degas*, II (1918), No. 259; and III (1919), No. 273.

216*a*. DEUX DANSEUSES AUX BRAS LEVES. ETUDE

They are seen half-length, facing left.

Charcoal. 17×13 ins. Stamp of the Degas sale lower left. *Circa* 1900.

Collection. Atelier Degas.

Reproduced. *Catalogue vente Degas*, III (1919), No. 149*b*.

Owner unknown.

See Pls. 214–6. See also *Catalogue vente Degas*, I (1918), No. 330.

217. TROIS DANSEUSES EN JUPES VIOLETTES AUX BRAS LEVES

They are standing one behind the other, facing left, with feet in *quatrième derrière pointe tendue.*

Pastel. 28 × 19 ins. Signed lower left. *Circa* 1900.
Reproduced. Camille Mauclair, *Degas* (1941), p. 134.
Owner unknown.
Photograph. Durand Ruel, Paris.

For others of the series see Pls. 214–6. See also *Catalogue vente Degas*, III (1919), No. 379.

218. DANSEUSE NUE. 'DEVELOPPE EN AVANT'

She stands on the left leg with arms in opposition. The view is facing a quarter right.

Bronze, No. 5. Height 22⅜ ins. *Circa* 1882–90.
Exhibitions. Hebrard Exhibition, 1921; *Degas—Portraitiste, Sculpteur*, Musée de l'Orangerie, Paris, 1931, No. 11.
Reproduced. John Rewald, *Degas. Works in Sculpture—a complete Catalogue* (1944), No. 44.
Photograph. The Leicester Galleries, London.

See also Pl. 158 and Rewald catalogue, No. 55.

219. DANSEUSE SE DEGOURDISSANT A LA BARRE, LE BRAS DERRIERE LE DOS

She is facing left with her left leg stretched on the *barre* in front of her. The view is from behind.

Pastel. 44 × 25 ins. Stamp of the Degas sale not visible. *Circa* 1900–5.
Collection. Atelier Degas.
Reproduced. *Catalogue vente Degas*, I (1918), No. 241.
Owner unknown.
Photograph. Durand Ruel, Paris.

See also Pls. 220 and 221, as well as *Catalogue vente Degas*, I (1918), No. 332; and II (1918), No. 221b.

220. DEUX DANSEUSES SE DEGOURDISSANT A LA BARRE

The further dancer is seen back view stretching her leg in front of her on the *barre*; the nearer one is facing it, her right leg upon it and her hand holding the ankle.

Oil on canvas. 51 × 38 ins. Signed lower right. *Circa* 1900–5.
Collections. Atelier Degas; Mrs G. W. Harriman.
Reproduced. *Catalogue vente Degas*, I (1918), No. 93.
Owned by the Phillips Memorial Gallery, Washington.
Photograph. The Phillips Memorial Gallery.

Oil paintings of these last years are rare.

For a pastel, almost identical, see Pl. 221; see also Pl. 219; also *Catalogue vente Degas*, II (1918), Nos. 108, 152 and 262.

221. DEUX DANSEUSES SE DEGOURDISSANT A LA BARRE

One is seen from behind holding the *barre* with her hand behind her back; the other faces it and stretches her leg to the right.

Pastel. $50 \times 43\frac{1}{4}$ ins. Stamp of the Degas sale lower left. *Circa* 1900–5.
Collection. Atelier Degas.
Reproduced. Catalogue vente Degas, I (1918), No. 118.
Owned by the National Gallery of Canada, Ottawa.
Photograph. The National Gallery of Canada.

See also Pls. 219 and 220, and note.

222. DANSEUSE AUX BAS ROUGES

She sits on the right pulling up her working tights with both hands. On the left a study of a dancer with folded arms.

Pastel. $24\frac{1}{4} \times 18\frac{1}{2}$ ins. Signed lower right. *Circa* 1900.
Collections. Chausson (sale 1936); Lord Ivor Spencer Churchill.
Exhibition. Degas, Musée de l'Orangerie, Paris, 1937, No. 134.
Reproduced. Paul Lafond, *Degas*, Vol. II (1919), opp. p. 24, in colour.
Present owner unknown.

223. QUATRE DANSEUSES A MI-CORPS

They are standing behind a pole, one with hands on shoulders, another on waist, the furthest with a hand on the wall.

Charcoal or pastel. $26\frac{3}{8} \times 18\frac{3}{8}$ ins. Signed lower left. *Circa* 1900.
Reproduced. Georges Grappe, *Degas* (1909), p. 57.
Owner unknown.
Photograph. Knoedler & Co., London.

224. QUATRE DANSEUSES DANS LES COULISSES, DECOR DE PAYSAGE

They are grouped on the left of the picture, three of them in different attitudes arranging their dresses at the shoulders, the fourth, just partly visible, rests her arm on the flat.

Oil on canvas. $59\frac{1}{4} \times 71\frac{1}{4}$ ins. Stamp of the Degas sale not visible. *Circa* 1900.
Collections. Atelier Degas; Wilhelm Hansen, Copenhagen.
Reproduced. Catalogue vente Degas, I (1918), No. 10; Paul Lafond, *Degas*, Vol. I (1918), p. 77.
Owned by the Chester Dale Collection, on loan to the National Gallery of Art, Washington.
Photograph. The National Gallery of Art.

For a pastel of dancer in the left corner see Pl. 237; for other pictures on the theme, Pls. 226, 227, 240 and 241. See as well *Catalogue vente Degas*, I (1918), No. 335; II (1918), Nos. 179 and 195; and III (1919), No. 392.

225. QUATRE DANSEUSES SUR LA SCENE

They are standing in a group on the right against a *décor* of foliage. The head of the figure on extreme right is not seen; the dancer in the centre holds her skirt with one hand and with the other arranges her hair.

Oil on canvas. 29 × 37 ins. Stamp of the Degas sale not visible. *Circa 1900–5.*
Collection. Atelier Degas.
Reproduced. Catalogue vente Degas, I (1918), No. 113.
Owner unknown.
Photograph. Durand Ruel, Paris.

226. QUATRE DANSEUSES BLEUES A MI-CORPS

The two on the right arrange their dresses at the shoulders; the one on the left holds on to the flat behind her, while in the left foreground the head and back of another is visible as she bends forward.

Pastel. 25½ × 26 ins. Signed upper left. *Circa 1900–5.*
Collection. S. I. Schukin.
Reproduced. Hans Graber, *Edgar Degas* (1942), opp. p. 228; Denis Rouart, *Degas, à la Recherche de sa Technique* (1945), p. 38.
Owned by the Museum of Modern and Western Art, Moscow.
Photograph. S. C. R., London.

For a similar composition with three figures see Pl. 227. See also *Catalogue vente Degas*, I (1918), No. 177; III (1919), No. 247; and IV (1919), No. 193.

227. TROIS DANSEUSES A MI-CORPS

Two are seen back-view with their hands to their shoulders; the third smilingly looks at them.

Pastel. 24¼ × 26 ins. Unsigned. *Circa 1900–5.*
Collection. Joseph Durand Ruel.
Exhibitions. Grafton Galleries, London, 1905, No. 64 (reproduced); *Degas*, Galerie Georges Petit, Paris, 1924, No. 164; *Degas*, Pennsylvania Museum of Art, Philadelphia, 1936, No. 56 (reproduced); *Degas*, Musée de l'Orangerie, Paris, 1937, No. 178 (reproduced); *Degas*, Cleveland Museum of Art, 1947, No. 50 (reproduced).
Reproduced. Georges Grappe, *Degas* (1909), p. 30; Julius Meier-Graefe, *Degas* (1927), Pl. 98; Camille Mauclair, *Degas* (1941), p. 137; Denis Rouart, *Degas, à la Recherche de sa Technique* (1945), p. 35.
Owned by the Toledo Museum of Art, Toledo.
Photograph. The Toledo Museum of Art.

See also Pl. 226, as well as *Catalogue vente Degas*, I (1918), Nos. 185 and 227; and III (1919), No. 59.

228. DEUX DANSEUSES ROSES, TROIS-QUARTS

The one facing right scratches her head; the other, facing left, touches her ear.

Pastel. 25 × 23 ins. Signed lower right. *Circa 1905–12.*
Collection. Prince de Wagram.

Reproduced. Knut Hoppe, *Degas* (1922); Julius Meier-Graefe, *Degas* (1927), Pl. 97.
Owned by the National Museum, Stockholm.
Photograph. The National Museum.
See also *Catalogue vente Degas*, I (1918), No. 310; and II (1918), Nos. 202 and 375.

229. QUATRE DANSEUSES, JUPES SAUMON

They are standing before a *décor* of mountains, the one in the left foreground adjusting her shoe and holding on to the waist of her neighbour for support.

Pastel. 36 × 26 ins. Stamp of the Degas sale lower left. *Circa* 1900–12.
Collection. Atelier Degas.
Reproduced. *Catalogue vente Degas*, I (1918), No. 229.
Owner unknown.
Photograph. Durand Ruel, Paris.

230. DANSEUSES DANS LES COULISSES OBSERVANT LE SPECTACLE

On the left is a 'tree'; behind, two dancers are looking towards the stage to the right, a third is bending forward with her hand behind her heel.

Pastel. 30 × 24 ins. Stamp of the Degas sale lower left. *Circa* 1905–12.
Collection. Atelier Degas.
Reproduced. *Catalogue vente Degas*, I (1918), No. 139.
Owned by Winkel and Magnussen, Copenhagen.
Photograph. National Gallery, Stockholm.
See charcoal study, Pl. 247; also *Catalogue vente Degas*, I (1918), Nos. 167, 236, 261 and 283; II (1918), No. 151.

231. TROIS DANSEUSES DANS LES COULISSES

Those on the right and left are standing *pointe tendue*, the centre one is seated. All are looking to the right.

Pastel. $37\frac{1}{2}$ × 32 ins. Stamp of the Degas sale not visible. *Circa* 1905–12.
Collection. Atelier Degas.
Reproduced. *Catalogue vente Degas*, I (1918), No. 204; Denis Rouart, *Degas, à la Recherche de sa Technique* (1945), p. 36; John Rewald, *History of Impressionism* (1946), in colour, opp. p. 418.
Owned by the Museum of Modern Art, New York. (Gift of William S. Paley, 1941.)
Photograph. Museum of Modern Art.
See also *Catalogue vente Degas*, I (1918), Nos. 296 and 297.

232. SIX DANSEUSES SUR LA SCENE

Four dancers are standing in a group on the right half of the picture; in the left distance another two are standing back to back, bending forward, sweeping the ground with one of their hands in a circular movement as they do a *port de bras*.

Pastel. 30 × 44 ins. Stamp of the Degas sale lower left. *Circa* 1905–12.
Collection. Atelier Degas.

Reproduced. Catalogue vente Degas, I (1918), No. 210.
Owner unknown.
Photograph. Durand Ruel, Paris.
For another pastel of this subject see Pl. 233.
Port de Bras is a generic term for a group of exercises designed for the perfection of arm movements.
For a study of this subject see Pl. 232a.

232a. 'PORT DE BRAS'

The dancer is standing in *quatrième fondue*, her right arm sweeping the ground as she begins the circular movement of her body and arms.

Charcoal heightened with pastel. $12\frac{1}{4} \times 21\frac{1}{2}$ ins. Stamp of the Degas sale on the original.
Inscribed upper right, 'Beaucoup trop baissé, trop . . . en avant,' *Circa* 1885–90.
Collection. Atelier Degas.
Reproduced. Catalogue vente Degas, II (1918), No. 233b.
Owner unknown.

See Pls. 232 and 233 for similar figure seen in profile. See also *Catalogue vente Degas*, II (1918), No. 213a; III (1919), No. 133b; and IV (1919), No. 339.

233. DANSEUSES DEBOUT SUR LA SCENE

The dancer on the left is practising one of the *port de bras* exercises; the rest are standing in a group on the right.

Pastel. $29\frac{1}{2} \times 22\frac{1}{2}$ ins. **St**amp of the Degas sale lower left. *Circa* 1905–12.
Collection. Atelier Degas.
Reproduced. Catalogue vente Degas, I (1918), No. 209.
Owner unknown.
Photograph. Durand Ruel, Paris.

See Pls. 232a and 233a. See also Pl. 232, as well as *Catalogue vente Degas*, II (1918), No. 81.

233a. DEUX DANSEUSES DEBOUT. ETUDE

Both are standing in *quatrième derrière*; one is seen from the front, the other from behind.

Charcoal. 21 × 23 ins. Stamp of the Degas sale lower left. *Circa* 1905–12.
Collection. Atelier Degas.
Reproduced. Catalogue vente Degas, III (1919), No. 287.
Owner unknown.
Photograph. Durand Ruel, Paris.

See Pls. 232, 233, 254 and 255.

234. DANS LES COULISSES, TROIS DANSEUSES DEBOUT

The two on the right are seen back view; the third, in the left distance, is just about to dance on to the stage.

Pastel. 36 × 34 ins. Signed lower left. *Circa* 1905–12.
Reproduced. Vollard, *98 Reproductions signed by Degas* (pub. Berheim Jeune, 1918), Pl. 26.
Owner unknown.
Photograph. The National Gallery, Stockholm.

235. TROIS ETUDES D'UNE DANSEUSE

The two at the top show her back view and bending to the left; in the lower she faces right and arranges her hair.

> Charcoal heightened with white. 19 × 25 ins. Stamp of the Degas sale lower left. Circa 1900–12.
> Collection. Atelier Degas.
> Reproduced. Catalogue vente Degas, III (1919), No. 375.
> Owner unknown.
> Photograph. Durand Ruel, Paris.

235a. BLANCHISSEUSES ET CHEVAUX

Two women carrying laundry baskets are arranged in a composition with two horses.

> Pastel. 42 × 48½ ins. Stamp of the Degas sale on the original. Circa 1885–1900.
> Collection. Atelier Degas.
> Reproduced. Catalogue vente Degas, I (1918), No. 182.
> Owner unknown.

Although this subject does not come under the title Danseuses, its inclusion has been prompted by the desire to show Degas' innate sense of, and emphasis upon, rhythm through posture, which he stressed even in his arrangement of photograph portrait groups. See Le Salon Chausson, p. 16. Compare the figure of the blanchisseuse on the left with studies Pl. 235.

236. DANSEUSE A MI-CORPS SE COIFFANT

She is seen facing right with both hands raised to her head; on extreme right, part of another dancer's skirt is visible.

> Pastel. 14½ × 11 ins. Signed lower left. Circa 1900–12.
> Owner unknown.
> Photograph. Reid and Lefevre, London.

237. DEUX DANSEUSES A MI-CORPS, DOS-A-DOS

The one in front, arranging her bodice at the shoulder, occupies most of the picture; just behind her, to the right, the head and shoulders of another is seen.

> Pastel. 18 × 14⅛ ins. Signed lower left. Circa 1900–12.
> Collection. Martin A. Ryerson.
> Reproduced. Camille Mauclair, Degas (1941), p. 135.
> Owned by the Art Institute of Chicago. (Mr and Mrs Martin A. Ryerson Collection.)
> Photograph. Art Institute of Chicago.

For studies see Catalogue vente Degas, I (1918), No. 186; II (1918), Nos. 54 and 76; III (1919), No. 185 and IV (1919), Nos. 349 and 368.

238. TROIS DANSEUSES A MI-CORPS, DECOR D'ARBRES

The central figure is seen back view, head turned to the left with one arm over it; the other is scratching her back.

> Pastel. 25¾ × 20 ins. Stamp of the Degas sale not visible. Circa 1900–12.

Collection. Atelier Degas.
Reproduced. *Catalogue vente Degas*, I (1918), No. 306.
Owned by the Detroit Institute of Arts, Detroit, Michigan.
Photograph. The Detroit Institute of Arts.
See also Pl. 239; and *Catalogue vente Degas*, I (1918), Nos. 145, 275 and 276; II (1918), Nos. 136 and 295; and III (1919), No. 281.

239. TROIS DANSEUSES VUES A MI-CORPS

The central figure is seen from behind, her left arm resting on her head, her right hand scratching her back.

Pastel. 26 × 20 ins. Stamp of the Degas sale lower left. *Circa* 1900–12.
Collection. Atelier Degas.
Reproduced. *Catalogue vente Degas*, I (1918), No. 187.
Owner unknown.
Photograph. Durand Ruel, Paris.
See also Pl. 238 and note, as well as *Catalogue vente Degas*, II (1918), Nos. 295 and 298.

240. DANSEUSES A MI-CORPS S'ARRANGEANT LES EPAULETTES

The front two are standing back to back arranging their dresses at the shoulders, as is another in the distance. The dancer on the left stands with one hand on her waist, the other on her head.

Pastel. 24 × 25¼ ins. Unsigned. *Circa* 1900–12.
Reproduced. Gustav Coquiot, *Degas* (1924), opp. p. 176.
Owner unknown.
Photograph. Durand Ruel, Paris.
See also Pls. 224, 226 and 227.

241. QUATRE DANSEUSES VUES A MI-CORPS

Three of them are arranging their bodices at the shoulders, the fourth on the left rests her hand on her head.

Pastel. 29 × 28 ins. Stamp of the Degas sale lower left. *Circa* 1900–12.
Collection. Atelier Degas.
Reproduced. *Catalogue vente Degas*, I (1918), No. 217; Camille Mauclair, *Degas* (1941), p. 132.
Photograph. Durand Ruel, Paris.
See also Pl. 240, as well as *Catalogue vente Degas*, II (1918), No. 142.

242. DANSEUSE RUSSE. LE 'HOPAK' DU BALLET 'LE FESTIN'

The dancer is facing left, standing on her right leg with the other raised in front of her; one hand on her waist, the other behind her head. She is wearing national costume.

Pastel. 24⅜ × 18 ins. Signed lower left. Painted 1909.
Collection. H. O. Havemeyer.

Reproduced. Vollard, *98 Reproductions signed by Degas* (pub. Bernheim Jeune, 1918), Pl. 87; Henri Hertz, *Degas* (1920), Pl. 13; Georges Grappe, *Degas* (1936), p. 42; Marguerite Rebatet, *Degas* (1944), Pl. 103.

Owned by the Metropolitan Museum of Art, New York. (H. O. Havemeyer Collection.)

Photograph. The Metropolitan Museum.

This is a study of one of the figures in Pl. 243. See pp. 63–64. See also *Catalogue vente Degas*, I (1918), No. 192; II (1918), Nos. 122, 184 and 278; and III (1919), No. 307.

243. TROIS DANSEUSES RUSSES. LE 'HOPAK' DU BALLET 'LE FESTIN'

They are arranged diagonally, standing on one leg, with one arm behind the head, the other at the waist.

Pastel. 25 × 27 ins. Signed lower left. Painted 1909.

Reproduced. Knut Hoppe, *Degas* (1922).

Owned by the National Museum, Stockholm.

Photograph. The National Museum.

See also Pl. 242, and *Catalogue vente Degas*, I (1918), Nos. 160, 265, 266 and 270; II (1918), No. 271; and III (1919), Nos. 203 and 286.

244. TROIS DANSEUSES, LES CHEVEUX EN TRESSE

They are standing next to a flat, the middle one bending forward and supporting herself against it with the left hand.

Pastel. 26 × 21 ins. Stamp of the Degas sale lower left. *Circa* 1905–12.

Collection. Atelier Degas.

Reproduced. *Catalogue vente Degas*, I (1918), No. 230.

Owner unknown.

Photograph. Durand Ruel, Paris.

See also Pl. 245, as well as *Catalogue vente Degas*, I (1918), Nos. 149, 216, 254, 301, 302 and 331; III (1919), No. 189; and IV (1919), No. 148.

245. TROIS DANSEUSES DEBOUT DANS LES COULISSES

Two of them are looking to the left while the central figure leans forward with her left hand resting against the flat.

Pastel. 23 × 28 ins. Stamp of the Degas sale lower left. *Circa* 1905–12.

Collection. Atelier Degas.

Reproduced. *Catalogue vente Degas*, I (1918), No. 228.

Owner unknown.

Photograph. Durand Ruel, Paris.

See also Pl. 244, as well as *Catalogue vente Degas*, II (1918), No. 250; and III (1919), No. 272.

246. DANSEUSES DANS LA SALLE DE DANSE. FRISE

Two are seated on a bench on the right, a third ties her shoe, while the three in the left distance are divided by a post.

Pastel. 18 × 34 ins. Stamp of the Degas sale lower left. *Circa* 1905–12.

Collection. Atelier Degas.

Reproduced. *Catalogue vente Degas*, I (1918), No. 274.

Owner unknown.

Photograph. Kunsthistorik Pladearkiv, Copenhagen.

See also Pls. 114, 116 and 116a; as well as *Catalogue vente Degas*, I (1918), Nos. 162 and 220; II (1918), Nos. 11, 39 and 265; and III (1919), Nos. 200, 241, 253, 264 and 274.

246a. TROIS DANSEUSES EN ARABESQUE

They are facing right and standing on the right leg.

Charcoal heightened with pastel. 16 × 26 ins. Stamp of the Degas sale lower left. *Circa* 1905–12.

Collection. Atelier Degas.

Reproduced. *Catalogue vente Degas*, III (1919), No. 198.

Owned by the Ashmolean Museum, Oxford.

Photograph. The Ashmolean Museum.

See Pl. 156 and note; also *Catalogue vente Degas*, I (1918), No. 43; II (1918), No. 299; III (1919), No. 196; and IV (1919), No. 151.

247. TROIS DANSEUSES NUES

Two are seated on a bench, the one on extreme right—whose head is not visible—holds her ankle; the third stands behind the others resting one hand on the wall.

Charcoal. 34½ × 30½ ins. Stamp of the Degas sale lower left. *Circa* 1905–12.

Collection. Atelier Degas.

Reproduced. *Catalogue vente Degas*, I (1918), No. 322.

Owner unknown.

Photograph. Durand Ruel, Paris.

See pastel, Pl. 230; also *Catalogue vente Degas*, II (1918), No. 230b.

248. DEUX DANSEUSES, L'UNE A L'EVENTAIL

The one holding the fan stands facing left; the other, behind her, leans against the wall.

Charcoal. 24 × 15 ins. Stamp of the Degas sale lower left. *Circa* 1905–12.

Collection. Atelier Degas.

Reproduced. *Catalogue vente Degas*, II (1918), No. 283.

Owner unknown.

Photograph. Durand Ruel, Paris.

See Pls. 208–10, 212 and 213.

249. DEUX DANSEUSES NUES, L'UNE A L'EVENTAIL

The one on the right holds a fan and faces the left; the other behind her faces right and leans against the wall.

> *Charcoal.* 22½ × 19 ins. Stamp of the Degas sale lower left. *Circa* 1905–12.
> *Collection.* Atelier Degas.
> *Reproduced. Catalogue vente Degas*, III (1919), No. 239.
> *Owner* unknown.
> *Photograph.* Durand Ruel, Paris.

See also Pl. 248 and note; as well as *Catalogue vente Degas*, III (1919), Nos. 167, 168 and 232.

250. TROIS DANSEUSES EN MAILLOT

The one on the right is seated on a bench with a foot upon it; the other two stand behind her, also facing right and leaning against the wall.

> *Charcoal.* 34½ × 30½ ins. Stamp of the Degas sale lower left. *Circa* 1905–12.
> *Collection.* Atelier Degas.
> *Reproduced. Catalogue vente Degas*, I (1918), No. 318.
> *Owner* unknown.
> *Photograph.* Durand Ruel, Paris.

See also *Catalogue vente Degas*, I (1918), Nos. 319 and 322.

251. DEUX DANSEUSES NUES SUR UNE BANQUETTE

> *Charcoal.* 18½ × 24 ins. Stamp of the Degas sale lower left. *Circa* 1905–12.
> *Collection.* Atelier Degas.
> *Reproduced. Catalogue vente Degas*, III (1919), No. 299.
> *Owner* unknown.
> *Photograph.* Durand Ruel, Paris.

See Pls. 118a and 204.

252. DEUX DANSEUSES NUES DOS-A-DOS

They are standing in fourth position, the front one with hands on her breasts, the back one with hands on her hips.

> *Charcoal heightened with pastel.* 25 × 19 ins. Stamp of the Degas sale lower left. *Circa* 1900–12.
> *Collection.* Atelier Degas.
> *Reproduced. Catalogue vente Degas*, II (1918), No. 277.
> *Owner* unknown.
> *Photograph.* Durand Ruel, Paris.

See Pl. 197; also *Catalogue vente Degas*, II (1918), No. 366; III (1918), Nos. 207, 300 and 301; and IV (1919), No. 149.

253. DEUX DANSEUSES EN MAILLOT

The dancer on the left—seen back view—kneels on one leg and puts her arm around the waist of the other who stands next to her.

> *Charcoal.* 20 × 16 ins. Stamp of the Degas sale lower left. *Circa* 1905–12.

Collection. Atelier Degas.

Reproduced. *Catalogue vente Degas*, II (1918), No. 340; H. Rivière, *Albumn Degas* (1922–3), Pl. 49.

Owner unknown.

Photograph. Durand Ruel, Paris.

See also *Catalogue vente Degas*, II (1918), Nos. 56 and 185; and IV (1919), No. 155.

254. QUATRE DANSEUSES NUES

The one in the right foreground is bending down with both hands at her ankle; the others are standing in a group behind.

Charcoal. $22\frac{1}{2} \times 19$ ins. Stamp of the Degas sale lower left. *Circa* 1905–12.

Collection. Atelier Degas.

Reproduced. *Catalogue vente Degas*, III (1919), No. 242.

Owner unknown.

Photograph. Durand Ruel, Paris.

For a group of the figures behind, in ballet skirts, see Pl. 255. See also *Catalogue vente Degas*, IV (1919), Nos. 170 and 171.

255. GROUPE DE TROIS DANSEUSES DEBOUT

They are standing talking on the right hand side.

Pastel. $23 \times 21\frac{1}{2}$ ins. Stamp of the Degas sale lower left. *Circa* 1905–12.

Collection. Atelier Degas.

Reproduced. *Catalogue vente Degas*, III (1919), No. 60.

Owner unknown.

Photograph. Knoedler & Co., London.

See also Pl. 254, as well as *Catalogue vente Degas*, I (1918), Nos. 51 and 101; and II (1918), No. 344.

256. DEUX DANSEUSES EN 'QUATRIEME DERRIERE POINTE TENDUE'

They are standing facing three-quarter left, their bodies showing clearly through the lightly sketched *tutus*.

Pastel. 25×19 ins. Stamp of the Degas catalogue lower left. *Circa* 1905–12.

Collection. Atelier Degas.

Reproduced. *Catalogue vente Degas*, II (1918), No. 160.

Owner unknown.

Photograph. Durand Ruel, Paris.

See also *Catalogue vente Degas*, II (1918), No. 57; and III (1919), No. 394.

VIGNETTES

DEUX DANSEUSES VUES DE DOS. ETUDE DE JAMBE (*Half Title*)

Pen and ink. $6\frac{1}{4} \times 4\frac{1}{4}$ ins. Stamp of the Degas sale on the original. Inscribed 'M.- Mme.- Mlle.
Astruc'. *Circa* 1876.
Collection. Atelier Degas.
Reproduced. Catalogue vente Degas, IV (1919), No. 207a.
Owner unknown.

TROIS DANSEUSES. ETUDE (*Title Page*)

Sepia with touches of blue ink. Part of a sheet measuring $7\frac{7}{8} \times 9\frac{7}{8}$ ins. Unsigned. *Circa* 1876.
Collections. G. Kalebjian; Paul Sachs.
Exhibition. Degas, Pennsylvania Museum of Art, Philadelphia, 1936, No. 79 (reproduced).
Reproduced. H. Rivière, *Les Dessins de Degas* (1922), No. 25.
Owned by the Fogg Museum of Art, Cambridge, Mass.
Photograph. The Fogg Museum.
This is the lower left hand corner of a sheet of studies of dancers in different positions.

DEUX DANSEUSES. ETUDE (*Page 71*)

Charcoal. 19×21 ins. Stamp of the Degas sale lower left. *Circa* 1876.
Collection. Atelier Degas.
Reproduced. Catalogue vente Degas, IV (1919), No. 282a.
Owner unknown.
Photograph. Sir Robert Witt Library, London.

COVER OF 'LA SCENE' (*Page 422*)

The *décor* of the studio of the artist Dupuis for the comedy *La Cigale* is reproduced on this cover.
Photograph. Bibliothèque de l'Arsénal, Paris.
See p. 26.

DANSEUSE METTANT SON CHAUSSON (*on back of Dust Jacket*)

Etching. $7 \times 4\frac{1}{4}$ ins. *Circa* 1880.
Reproduced. Loys Delteil, *Le Peintre Graveur Illustré—Degas* (1919), No. 36.
Photograph. The Brooklyn Museum, New York.

SCALE CHART OF COMPARATIVE SIZES

Scale: 1 mm. = 1 inch

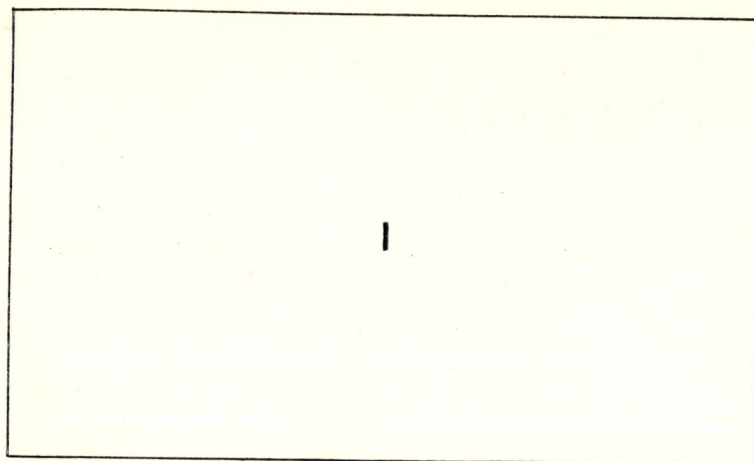

1

59 x 102 ins.

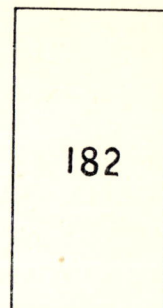

182

40 x 21¾ ins.

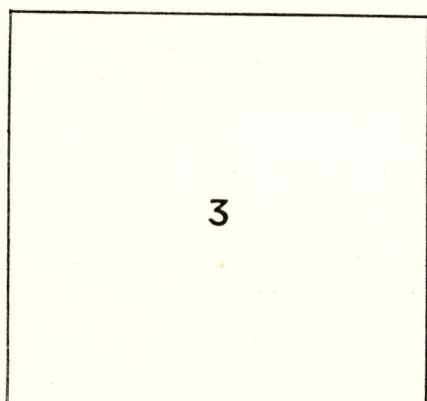

3

52 x 57¾ ins.

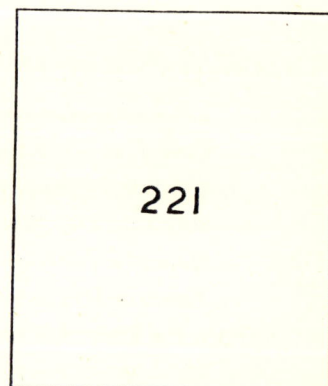

221

50 x 43¼ ins.

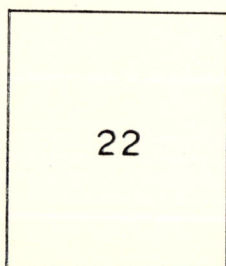

16

13 x 18½ ins.

17

7¾ x 10⅝ ins.

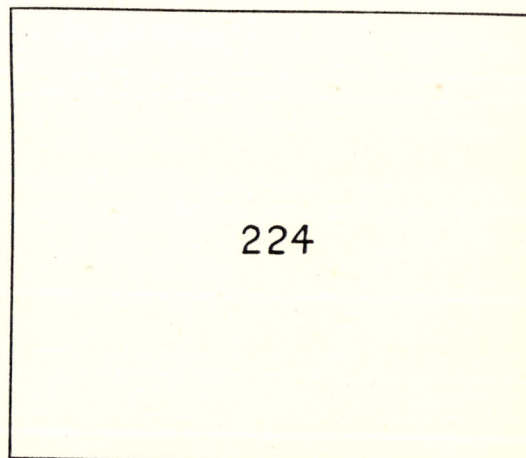

224

59 x 71¼ ins.

22

34 x 30 ins.

48

6¾ x 8¾ ins.

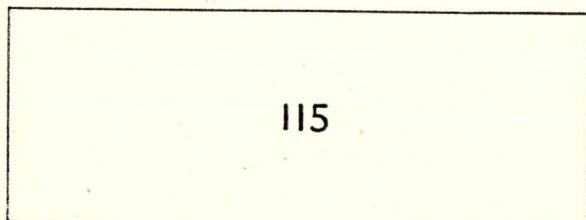

115

28 x 80 ins.

236

14½ x 11 ins.

246

18 x 34 ins

TRANSLATIONS

page

34. The 'grains' are going well, even without you (who should be guiding us instead of leaving us to grope about in the dark).

Printed by Degas.

Delicious examples of engraving.

If Rembrandt had known about lithography, heaven only knows what he might have done with it.

35. The fact is that, at the first stroke, M. Degas has overthrown the traditions of sculpture as long ago he shook off the conventions of painting . . . this statuette is the only truly modern attempt that I know in sculpture.

36. It's very tempting . . . with that money I could buy a Delacroix that I have coveted for a long time; but in this picture there is decidedly something that I do not like.

37. On Wednesday morning I left everything to study for a long time, in the light of day and with a magnifying glass, the magnificent Gavarnis that you gave me. . . . Don't deprive me of the little Ingres copy; it would be such an affront and such a grief. I really need it. . . . I have thought about it all night.

38. If I were not as I am with people, I would no longer have a minute to myself for working.

The role of butterfly must be very tiring. . . . I prefer the one of bull, eh?

39. One should marry. You do not know what solitude in old age is like.

While laid up with my cold I have been thinking about celibacy, and for the most part my thoughts have been sad ones.

Keep your eye on Barnes, look after him and see that he is happy.

41. One evening, towards six o'clock, the latter arrived enveloped in his Macfarlan, he carefully examined everything humming the while, made a tour of the gallery without saying a word and started down the stairs. Then turning, with part of his bust emerging from the narrow staircase like a snail from its shell, M. Degas said to the timid and anxious Lautrec, 'So, Lautrec, it is clear that you are one of us.' I can still see Lautrec glowing with deep contentment at this carelessly uttered approbation.

43. I am a colourist in line.

44. If I was the fool who conceived this journey, Bartholomé is the sage who will end by carrying it out.

Impossible to be away from my studio and not to work.

45. What Parisian has not met and looked at, and, having once seen, has forgotten this singular figure, this old man with a white beard, covered by a heavy Macfarlan, indifferent to the rain, walking with rapid steps, bending slightly forwards and tapping the edge of the pavement with the end of his stick? His walks lasted for hours and often continued into the night. Neither Homer with his vacant eyes, nor the haggard Lear on the edge of the cliff, presented a grandeur more tragic than the aged Degas wandering in our Paris streets. The last exhibition at which we saw him was the one which preceded the sale of the collection of his great friend, Henri Rouart; Degas leaned towards the dear pictures, his life's companions—the Daumiers, the Prudhons, the Delacroix and the Corots, he touched them as if to recognise them, to seize in his hands their colouration, their line, their pictorial beauty for which he was still eager. He returned each day; a group of collectors, friends, and young men replacing each other at his side so as not to leave him alone in his grief.

TRANSLATIONS

If, Forain, you make one, you will simply say, 'He loved drawing very much, so do I,' and you will return home.

48. *Note 4.* Although the *entrechats-quatre* beaten by la Camargo in 1730, that is thirty years after Mlle Lamy had already beaten *entrechats-six*, have been spoken of as marvellous.

51. The sparkling brilliance of Mlle Beaugrand, a little dancer with the head and feet of a bird, is always applauded.

Wearing a cap in the shape of a mitre, tightly laced in her bodice (d'icoglan), her legs floating in trousers of gauze picked out in gold, she dances, holding in her arms a long guitar with a slim neck. It is an almost exact reproduction of a painting often seen on Persian boxes.

Note 6. Last night at the Opéra, during the performance of the ballet, a rider who took part in the procession was unable to prevent his mount quenching its thirst in the stream. . . . Everything went off wonderfully. Even the horses, usually so troublesome in the Third Act, behaved this evening without reproach. . . . This distribution indicates that *La Source* according to the ballet is represented by Mlle Sangalli; *la Source* after Ingres, as well as real plasticity, by Mlle Eugénie Fiocre.

55. He fills the dancers with terror, and physically the man is made to do so. . . . His physiognomy breathes pedantry, cowardice and hardness of heart—cringing before his superiors, arrogant with his inferiors. Coarse and impolite, this man never replies to a 'good-day' or to a greeting. . . .

58. Could you possibly get me, from the Opéra, a pass for the day of the ballet examinations, which should be Thursday, according to what I have been told. I have done so many of these dancing examinations without ever having seen them, that I am a little ashamed. . . . I thought of slipping into the Opéra, in the midst of the mothers, with a little paper, and you wish to take me before Mr. Vaucorbeil. . . .

Each year there shall be one or two examinations, as much to check up upon the state of the classes, as to promote the advancement of students and fill up the vacancies occasioned thereby. The director will fix the day.

59. How cold it all was.

61. The new professor of childrens' classes will always remain one of the two little girls in *La Famille Mante* . . . now that our Theo has gone, it is through Degas that the link between two phases of theatrical dancing will be retained; in a painting in London, the artist has perpetuated on canvas all the ghostly eeriness of the sepulchral ballet of Nuns in *Robert le Diable*, the prototype of Romantic choreography.

Without doubt Mlle Sangalli will remain for the winter. I shall therefore be able to enjoy her performances on my return.

She willingly devotes herself to travesty roles. Besides, masculine attire suits her somewhat impetuous temperament; dancing is not enough for her, she is very keen on cycling, fencing and other sports.

You must know what a dancer is like when she wants you to put in a word for her. She returns twice a day to find out whether you have seen anybody or whether you have written. Are you better? If you have the courage and strength write a word to Vaucorbeil or to Mérante, not about her salary, which would be wrong, but about her dancing, her past and her future. I have never known anybody so worked up. She wants everything done immediately. She would wrap you up and carry you to the Opéra if she could.

62. The roguish Mlle Salle, the mime Salandri, and the frisky Mlle Hirsch, dancers that the painter has placed with obvious pleasure in the centre of his canvases.

A model for painters. She frequented the Brasserie des Martyrs, the Café de la Nouvelle-Athènes, and the Estaminet du Rat-Mort.

64. This masterpiece has returned to the artist's studio. Let us hope that the author's great disdain for his time will not induce him either to destroy his work or allow it to get lost.

It is VERY PROBABLE that your theory is correct and that this picture was suggested by the impression made upon the master by one of the 'numbers' in the *divertissement*, *le Festin*, which was danced to the music of Moussorgski's *Hopak*, with Mme Fedorova in the leading role . . . since he has put the action into the 'open air' of the Steppes, and even the colours of the costumes do not seem to me to be identical with those which were used in our performance.

BIBLIOGRAPHY

DEGAS

Les Carnets de Degas (au Cabinet des Estampes, Paris)

Catalogues: *Exhibitions 'Impressionistes'*, Paris, 1874, 1876, 1877, 1879, 1880, 1881, 1882 and 1886

Edmond Duranty, *La Nouvelle Peinture*, Paris, 1876

J. K. Huysmans, *L'Art Moderne*, Paris, 1883

George Moore, *Impressions and Opinions*, London, 1891

Georges Grappe, *Degas*, Paris, 1909

P. A. Lemoisne, *Degas*, Paris, 1912

Catalogues: *Atelier vente Degas*, 4 vols, Paris, 1918 and 1919

Paul Lafond, *Degas*, 2 vols, Paris, 1918 and 1919

Loys Delteil, *Le Peintre Graveur Illustré, vol. 9, Degas*, Paris, 1919

Henri Hertz, *Degas*, Paris, 1920

Julius Meier-Graefe, *Degas*, Munich, 1920

Knut Ragnar Hoppe, *Degas och hans arbeten i Nordisk ägo*, Stockholm, 1922

Marcel Guérin, Catalogue, *Exposition Degas*, Galerie Georges Petit, Paris, 1924

Gustav Coquiot, *Degas*, Paris, 1924

Paul Jamot, *Degas*, Paris, 1924

Ambroise Vollard, *Degas*, Paris, 1924

J. B. Manson, *The Life and Work of Edgar Degas*, London, 1927

Jamot and Vitry, Catalogue, *Exposition Degas—Sculpteur et Portraitiste*, Musée de l'Orangerie, Paris, 1931

Lettres de Degas recueillies et annotées par Marcel Guérin, Paris, 1931 and 1945

Sir William Rothenstein, *Men and Memories*, London, 1934

Georges Rivière, *Mr Degas (Bourgeois de Paris)*, Paris, 1935

Georges Grappe, *Degas*, Paris, 1936

H. P. McIlhenny, Catalogue, *Degas Exhibition*, Philadelphia, 1936

J. Emile Blanche, *Portraits of a Lifetime*, vol. 1, London, 1937

J. Bouchot-Saupique and M. Delaroche-Vernet, Catalogue, *Exposition Degas*, Musée de l'Orangerie, Paris, 1937

Camille Mauclair, *Degas*, London, 1937

Paul Valéry, *Degas, Danse, Dessin*, Paris, 1938

Ambroise Vollard, *En écoutant Cézanne, Degas, Renoir*, Paris, 1938

Robert Emmons, *The Life and Opinions of Walter Richard Sickert*, London, 1939

Lionello Venturi, *Les Archives de l'Impressionisme*, 2 vols, Paris, New York, 1939

W. Vanbeselaere, *Edgar Degas*, Brussels, 1941

Hans Graber, *Edgar Degas: Nach eigenen und fremden Zeugnissen*, Basel, 1942

John Rewald, *Camille Pissarro, Letters to his Son*, New York, 1943

Marguerite Rebatet, *Degas*, Paris, 1944

BIBLIOGRAPHY

DEGAS

John Rewald, *Degas, Works in Sculpture. A Complete Catalogue*, New York, 1944

R. H. Wilenski, *Modern French Painters*, London, 1944 and 1945

Jean Nepveu Degas, *Huit Sonnets d'Edgar Degas*, Paris, 1945

Denis Rouart, *Degas: A la Recherche de sa Technique*, Paris, 1945

John Rewald, *History of Impressionism*, New York, 1946

Catalogue, *Exhibition Degas*, Cleveland Museum of Art, 1947

BALLET AND THE PARIS OPERA

Charles de Boigne, *Petits Memoires de l'Opéra*, Paris, 1857

Sutherland Edwards, *History of the Opera*, 2 vols, London, 1862

La Chronique des Arts et de la Curiosité, Paris, 1877

Théodore de Lajarte, *Bibliothèque Musicale du Théâtre de l'Opéra—Catalogue historique, chronologique, anecdotique*, Paris, 1878

Octave Fouque, *Histoire du Théâtre Ventadour*, Paris, 1881

Jane Hugard (d'après Prod'homme), *Ces Demoiselles de l'Opéra*, Paris, 1883

Gabrielle Randon, *Mystères des Coulisses de l'Opéra*, Paris, 1885

Berthe Bernay, *La Danse au Théâtre*, Paris, 1890

Clement and Larousse, *Dictionnaire des Opéras*, Paris, 1897

Gaston Vuillier, *La Danse*, Paris, 1898

Charles Bouvet, *L'Opéra*, Paris, 1925

Cyril W. Beaumont, *The Romantic Ballet as seen by Théophile Gautier*, London, 1932 and 1947.

Cyril W. Beaumont, *A Miscellany for Dancers*, London, 1934

Cyril W. Beaumont, *Three French Dancers of the 19th Century*, London, 1935

Cyril W. Beaumont, *A Complete Book of Ballets*, London, 1937

Alexandre Benois, *Reminiscences of the Russian Ballet*, Paris, 1941

Cyril W. Beaumont, *A Short History of the Ballet*, London, 1944

Pierre Tugal, *Initiation à la Danse*, Paris, 1947

Deryck Lynham, *Ballet Then and Now*, London, 1947

. . . . . .

Many other books have been consulted as well as catalogues, articles in periodicals, and contemporary press cuttings. Personal interviews, as well as research at the Bibliothèque de l'Opéra and the Bibliothèque de l'Arsénal, have yielded invaluable information.

INDEX

M

INDEX

INDEX

INDEX

INDEX

INDEX

INDEX